Teaching History with Museums

Teaching History with Museums provides an introduction and overview of the rich pedagogical power of museums. In this comprehensive textbook, the authors show how museums offer a sophisticated understanding of the past and develop habits of mind in ways that are not easily duplicated in the classroom. Using engaging cases to illustrate accomplished history teaching through museum visits, this text provides pre- and in-service teachers, teacher educators, and museum educators with ideas for successful visits to artifact and display-based museums, historic forts, living history museums, memorials, monuments, and other heritage sites. Each case is constructed to be adapted and tailored in ways that will be applicable to any classroom and encourage students to think deeply about museums as historical accounts and interpretations to be examined, questioned, and discussed.

Key features of the chapters include:

- An introduction to the type of museum presented in the chapter, key pedagogical issues for this type of museum, and specific connections to developing students' historical understanding at this type of museum.
- Specific pre-visit, during visit, and post-visit activities for students at each museum.
- A reflection on the case, analyzing and discussing both pitfalls and possibilities that can be applied more broadly to similar museums.
- A listing of resources specific to the museum and history content for each chapter.

Teaching History with Museums is a valuable textbook promoting instruction in support of rigorous inquiry into the past and the goals of democratic values of tolerance and citizenship in the present.

Alan S. Marcus is an Associate Professor in the Department of Curriculum & Instruction at the Neag School of Education, University of Connecticut.

Jeremy D. Stoddard is a former middle-school teacher and curriculum and technology professional development specialist. He is currently an Associate Professor in the School of Education at The College of William & Mary.

Walter W. Woodward is an Associate Professor in the Department of History, University of Connecticut and is the Connecticut State Historian.

Teaching History with Museums
Strategies for K-12 Social Studies

Alan S. Marcus

Jeremy D. Stoddard

Walter W. Woodward

Routledge
Taylor & Francis Group

NEW YORK AND LONDON

First published 2012
by Routledge
711 Third Avenue, New York, NY 10017

Simultaneously published in the UK
by Routledge
2 Park Square, Milton Park, Abingdon, Oxon OX14 4RN

Routledge is an imprint of the Taylor & Francis Group, an informa business

Library of Congress Cataloging in Publication Data
Marcus, Alan S.
  Teaching history with museums: strategies for K-12 social studies/
  by Alan S. Marcus, Jeremy D. Stoddard and Walter W. Woodward.
  p. cm.
  Includes bibliographical references and index.
  1. Museums—Educational aspects—United States. 2. Museums—
  Educational aspects—United States—Case studies. 3. History—Study
  and teaching (Elementary)—United States. 4. History—Study and
  teaching (Secondary)—United States. I. Stoddard, Jeremy D.
  II. Woodward, Walter William. III. Title.
  AM7. M364 2012
  907.5—dc23   2011029797

ISBN: 978-0-415-89164-6 (hbk)
ISBN: 978-0-415-89165-3 (pbk)
ISBN: 978-0-203-13641-6 (ebk)

Typeset in Aldine 401 and Helvetica Neue by
Florence Production Ltd, Stoodleigh, Devon
Printed and bound in the United States of America by Edwards Brothers Malloy

To my mom, Ann Marcus, for all of her support and love the past forty-two years (especially the teenage years), and to my sister, who is a wonderful sister, daughter, aunt, mother, and wife. And in memory of my grandfather, Abraham Merer. I see your ninety-nine years of life experiences in many of the museums I visit and it always makes me smile.—Alan

To my museum-exploring wife Kim, my furry writing companions Stuart and Evelyn, and all the dedicated history teachers and museum educators who go above and beyond to challenge students to explore, question, and construct their own understandings of the past.—Jeremy

To Beatrix Lucinda, Abigail Grace, and Zoe Jay: The Future. —Walter

Contents

Acknowledgments

Thank you to all of the wonderful and dedicated museum staff who spoke with us, provided resources, pushed our thinking, and toured us around their facilities. They include Peter Fredlake, Peter Black, Sara Weisman, Carly Gjolaj and other staff from the United States Holocaust Memorial Museum, Wendy Jones and the Minnesota History Center staff, Megan McCollum from the Johnson County Historical Society, Craig Hotchkiss from the the Mark Twain House and Museum, Tom Patton from Preservation Virginia, Richard Strum from Fort Ticonderoga, Wendalyn Baker from the Fort at No. 4, and Jae Ann White and Menzie Overton from Colonial Williamsburg. We remain quite grateful to them and are very impressed with their professionalism and expertise.

We are also indebted to Tom Levine, Rochelle Marcus, Elysa Engelman, Julie Bray, Adam Nemeroff, Catherine Mason Hammer, Carolyn Larson, and Mary Rinaldo-Ducat, who read various chapters of the manuscript and offered valuable feedback and advice. Our work is greatly impacted by Anne Raymond and the teachers participating in the Capitol Region Education Council's Teaching American History Grant. Their support of our scholarship and insights during visits to museums enhanced the rigor of our effort.

We appreciate the support and expertise provided by our editors at Routledge, Catherine and Allison. It was a pleasure to work with them. Thank you to the College of William and Mary and the University of Connecticut for supporting our scholarship in numerous ways. Finally, a hearty shout-out to all of the teachers we work with and observe whose energy and ideas fueled this book.

PART I

Introduction and Framework for Using Museums to Teach History

CHAPTER 1

Introduction

Figure 1.1 Visitors board a recreated stage coach in front of the Bullard Tavern at Old Sturbridge Village, Sturbridge, MA.

Museums offer some of the most promising opportunities for students to actively engage in studying the past. For example, at Old Sturbridge Village in Sturbridge, Massachusetts, students can experience the sights, sounds, and activities of an 1830s New England town. The town includes a working saw mill, tin shop, blacksmith shop, farm, and much more. Visitors are transported back in time through their experiences in this recreated village, and can dip candles, dye yarn, travel in a stage coach, cook over an open fire, play nineteenth-century games, and strut with the roosters and chickens. Old Sturbridge Village recreates the past in a powerful way.

Just outside of St. Louis, in Collinsville, Illinois, the Cahokia Mounds provide the opportunity to explore what is believed to be the remains of the largest prehistoric native civilization north of Mexico. The Cahokia Mounds, a National Historic Landmark and UNESCO World Heritage Site, is 2,200 acres of the archaeological remains of the main component of the ancient settlement. Students can stand on the ground where over 120 mounds were constructed and where in AD 1250 a city larger than London during the same period once stood. Here students can experience the power of walking on the grounds of a historic site.

Meanwhile, in Miami, Florida, students can study their favorite topic—themselves. An exhibit opening in 2012 at History Miami, formerly the Historical Museum of Southern Florida, presents a study of teen culture in Miami from the 1930s to today. The life of a teenager can be studied within the context of historical events and periods such as the Great Depression, World War II (WWII), the Cold War, the 1960s, and more. The goal of the exhibit is: "to address the neglect of teen voices and experiences in national and local history museum exhibitions, collections and archives" (History Miami, 2011). At History Miami students can make a personal connection with the past.

Further west, Colorado's memorial to acknowledge Civil War volunteers and the Sand Creek Massacre is located in Denver. Here students can consider the way the Civil War is remembered in the West and analyze how the monument represents the time period in which it was created (1909). Plaques and chiseled stone on the statue list the names of soldiers from Colorado killed in the Civil War, proclaim that Colorado had the highest rate of volunteers of any state in the Union, discuss the discovery of gold, and explore the controversy surrounding an attack by Union soldiers in 1864 on a village of Cheyenne and Arapaho Indians, known as the Sand Creek Massacre. Students can learn from engaging with and critically analyzing the history presented by the memorial, as well as from learning about the history of the memorial's creation.

In Los Angeles, California, the Autry National Center uses artifacts as the mechanism to create a narrative about life in the West in the late 1880s. The exhibit tells a multicultural story about the development of the West through the artifacts of various racial, ethnic, and religious groups. This narrative offers the potential for students to develop historical empathy by understanding the perspectives of many groups that contributed to the development of the West. In addition, the narratives told and artifacts displayed allow students to more broadly evaluate the authoritative, yet subjective, role of museums in interpreting the past.

Finally, among the numerous opportunities to study the past at museums in Washington, D.C., the National Museum of African American History and Culture's exhibit, "For All the World to See," explores the role of visual images from television, film, magazines, and newspapers during the Civil Rights Movement. The exhibit, on display through 2012 at the museum's temporary space (the permanent museum opens on the National Mall in 2015), helps students to make sense of this pivotal time in United States history through the power and persuasion of visual images. Engagement with these images promotes students' abilities to bolster their skills at analyzing visual historical evidence and encourages students to consider the significance of the Civil Rights Movement for the African American community, as well as within the larger context of U.S. history.

The examples above are only a small sample of the rich possibilities that museums offer for history education. The resources and context of museums are a tremendous resource for K-12 teachers to utilize in promoting a sophisticated understanding of the past and the development of habits of mind in ways that are not easily duplicated in the classroom. Their physical space, artifacts, professional staff, special programs, online resources, and other features create opportunities for students to deepen understanding of specific content, and to develop historical thinking and critical literacy skills. These museum resources and the experiences provided at museums complement the school curriculum (Lenoir & Laforest, 1986) and make studying history more vivid, engaging, and relevant. Leaving the school to visit a museum can allow students to engage with an amalgamation of artifacts, ambience, narratives, and other recreations of the past as well as the geography of historic sites (Nespor, 2000). This combination of experiences during a visit to a museum may be particularly powerful for developing historical empathy. In addition, students may be more inspired to try critical thinking about primary sources or larger interpretations of history when they are confronted by both in museums. Museums also create the potential to interrogate historical interpretations by looking critically at how individual museums choose to present and interpret the past—what narratives they construct about our past and tell us about the present. However, the potential contribution of museums to the history education of students is largely dependent on the practices of teachers and museum staff.

The objective of this book is to provide educators—including teachers, teacher educators, museum educators, and parents of home-schooled students—with both a conceptual model linking museum visits to learning about the past, and a collection of practical strategies illustrated through cases focused on different "types" of museum. (We use the term "museums" to include artifact- and display-based museums, state history museums, historic forts, house museums, living history museums, memorials, monuments, and other heritage sites.) The cases provide detailed models of using museums and museum resources to develop students' understanding of the past. They are designed to complement the excellent activities already enacted by many educators by augmenting a repertoire of skills for implementing effective lessons for before, during, and after museum visits. The cases are also created to address the benefits and hurdles involved in using museums to teach history. We hope one result will be to provide the tools to more critically examine museums as sources of historical knowledge and as teaching resources. Each case is constructed to be adapted and tailored to specific contexts in ways that will make students think deeply about museums, not just as authoritative, or as a day off from real learning, but as providing historical accounts and interpretations to be examined, questioned, and discussed.

The authors are former K-12 classroom teachers and museum educators who now work as educational researchers, teacher educators, and historians. Our own teaching and our experiences working with K-12 teachers brings to mind two key questions. (1) How can museum visits enhance students' understanding of the past? And (2) what do teachers and museum educators need to know and be able to do to effectively incorporate museum visits into their curriculum? The examples described in the chapters that follow will explore these issues in depth. The following sections of this chapter provide background behind these important questions, develop a rationale for the use of museums as part of history education, and preview the cases.

MUSEUMS AND HISTORY EDUCATION

History museums are located in every state, every major city, and in many small towns. From urban centers to rural towns, these museums cover a wide range of events, people, groups, and themes in United States and world history. Even for students without easy physical access to a large comprehensive museum, there are widely available local museums, historic homes, historic forts, monuments, and memorials that offer meaningful learning experiences. More recently, museum resources and experiences have beccome available online to various degrees. These online resources—digital extensions of the museums' offerings—tender potential learning experiences different from other forms of digital content precisely because of their museum connection. Few other disciplines have such a readily available and rich set of resources designed to support student learning and also the staff to collaborate with teachers to formulate these learning experiences.

More specifically, there are three types of resources available at most history museums: physical resources, human resources, and online resources. The physical resources include buildings and other physical structures, artifacts, and exhibitions. The human resources are museum employees who are trained authorities in artifact collection, exhibit creation, history, and education. The virtual resources include archives, online exhibits, databases, simulations, lesson plans, field trip planning information, and more (Leftwich, 2006).

The physical resources of museums provide opportunities not available in the classroom to see, touch, feel, and experience the past. The human resources can support teachers in creating exciting and meaningful learning experiences at the museum and in the classroom. The online and other outreach resources are easily accessible for use as pre- and post-trip resources as well as when a field trip is not feasible. They offer potentially valuable connections between museums and history classrooms (Sheppard, 2007), but because online resources are a relatively recent development all of their advantages and shortcomings are not completely known. The cases in this book will examine all three types of resources for museums.

The goal is that the cases in this book will motivate teachers to design more effective museum visits and provide teachers and museum educators with the skills to create successful learning experiences for students. The limited data available suggest that history teachers plan a limited number of field trips. Marcus, Grenier, and Levine (2009) found that secondary history teachers believed that history museums should be an important part of the history curriculum, but many were unable to overcome the logistical and pedagogical barriers they faced to actually take students to museums—and many were dissatisfied with the number of trips they took each year. The lack of school visits to history museums is particularly glaring at the secondary level. Marcus, Grenier, and Levine report that museum educators are particularly distressed with the number of secondary visitors. Museum staff said the overwhelming majority of their school visitors are elementary students—in some cases as much as 95 percent of all school visitors.

There are many practical concerns and other issues that hinder museum visits. Teachers must overcome logistical hurdles such as district paperwork, bus transportation, parent permission, and coordinating scheduling at school and with the museum. Financial considerations are a huge concern for teachers, districts, and parents. Many teachers experience a lack of administrative support for field trips, particularly to history museums, since history is not formally assessed by the No Child Left Behind education law. Teachers are limited by geographical constraints, strengths and weaknesses of museum staff, and what is currently on display at a museum. Another curricular issue is timing and being able to align a field trip with the curriculum; this is often a very difficult task, especially in places where winter field trips are infrequent. Finally, some teachers may not be confident in their ability to meaningfully connect the curriculum with a visit to a history museum. Unfortunately, few teachers report receiving any formal training in museum education during their pre-service program or through in-service professional development (Marcus, Grenier, & Levine, 2009). While most teachers are pedagogical experts and many possess an excellent background in history content, their knowledge of how to successfully incorporate museum visits into their instruction is more limited. Kisiel (2003) says we should consider teachers "well intentioned novices" when it comes to planning museum visits, because their approaches to museum visits are comparable to inexperienced teachers in the classroom. We will explore these barriers to museum visits more extensively in Chapter 2 and elsewhere in the book.

WHY USE MUSEUMS?

Museums should be an integral part of K-12 history education because: (1) they provide unique learning experiences that can enhance students' historical knowledge and skills; (2) they are sites of history learning throughout students' adult lives; (3) they are often uncontested as authoritative arbiters of historical knowledge; and (4) they serve a function as public historical sites that both influence, and are influenced by, society. The end result of effective museum visits is that students can become more knowledgeable and engaged citizens.

First, museums afford the chance to learn about history in ways not available elsewhere. They break the cycle of textbook- and lecture-oriented instruction that focuses on memorization of facts, and instead create access to deeper historical understanding. History educators and historians emphasize the importance of developing historical understanding including students' ability: (1) to analyze, synthesize, and evaluate historical evidence (Wineburg, 2001); (2) to increase historical empathy—particularly to recognize the perspectives of others (Barton & Levstik, 2004); (3) to examine and interrogate historical narratives (Barton & Levstik, 2004); (4) to know, practice, and advance other historical thinking skills such as asking questions, understanding cause and effect, and determining historical agency (Seixas, 1996); (5) to make connections between the past and today (Seixas, 1996); (6) to recognize and account for presentism (viewing and judging the past through contemporary values and beliefs) (Wineburg, 2001); and (7) to be able to participate in dialogue and decisions about controversial issues (Hess, 2009). Museums support these facets of historical understanding through the physical space they design, the artifacts they preserve and present, the expertise of professional staff, and the special programs and online resources they offer. For example, the Mark Twain House in Hartford, Connecticut, promotes the discussion of the controversies over slavery and the social inequalities of the Gilded Age, while the United States Holocaust Memorial Museum in Washington, D.C., provides incredible opportunities for the development of historical empathy through powerful images and artifacts of the Holocaust. Chapter 2 more fully addresses the relationship between museums and the enrichment of historical understanding.

Second, most students will not take history classes or participate in formal history instruction beyond their K-12 experience. Loewen (1999) suggests that only one in six Americans ever take a course in U.S. history after graduating from high school. However, they are much more likely to visit history museums as adults. Thus, these students will experience historical narratives and learning about the past in a multitude of museum venues as adults (Boyd, 1999). As reported by Falk & Dierking (1997), between four and six of every ten people visit a museum at least once per year, making museum visits a very popular leisure activity outside of the home. In addition, Rosenzweig (2000) reported that 57 percent of Americans in a national survey visited a museum within the past twelve months and that Americans' level of connectedness to museums was higher than that reported for celebrating a holiday, reading a book about the past, or studying history in school. And, in 2006, almost 150 million American adults visited at least one museum (out of all types of museums) and another eight million visited at least one museum online (Griffiths & King, 2008). The same study calculates there were a total of 701 million physical visits to museums in the United States by adults in 2006 (Griffiths & King, 2008). Therefore, if students participate in field trips to museums that incorporate meaningful learning experiences, there is a greater potential for museums to meaningfully influence their lifelong learning of history and the continued development of historical thinking skills.

Third, museums are perceived by students, teachers and the general public as reliable, authoritative, and authentic. Falk and Dierking (2000) report that museums are identified by many people as "reliable, authentic, and comprehensible" (p. 2). Museums are also perceived as very trustworthy sources of historic information—more trustworthy sources than college history professors, high school teachers, and nonfiction books (Rosenzweig, 2000). And, Marstine (2006) reports that United States museums are perceived as the most objective and trustworthy of any educational institution—87 percent of respondents rated museums as trustworthy (67 percent said books are trustworthy, 50 percent said television news is trustworthy). Marcus, Grenier, and Levine (2009) found that teachers hold similar views about museums. The teachers report high levels of trust for the way history museums present the past—a trust that may influence how they develop programs for museum visits and a trust they may pass along to their students.

This trust in museums emerges in part from the fact that many museums are the repositories of authentic objects, images, and documents from the past. The power of the "real" in instilling simultaneously a sense of awe about, and a connection to, the past cannot be underestimated. At the same time, it challenges teachers to help students distinguish between the "truth" of artifacts, and the more contingent interpretations drawn from those artifacts.

The trust of museums extends to their online resources. A study by the Institute for Museum and Library Services (Griffiths & King, 2008) found that libraries and museums are the most trusted sources of online information among adults regardless of age, education level, race, or ethnicity, and are more trustworthy than online information from the government, commercial websites, and private websites. Thus, the beliefs about the trustworthiness of museums and museum artifacts and narratives transfers to all aspects of museum resources because of the way young people and the public view museums as institutions.

However, museums are like any source of historical knowledge. The story of the past on which they focus is influenced by many factors, including subjective decisions by museum staff, financial considerations, and outside social and political pressures, among others. For example, in today's economy, museums often need to combine entertaining elements with traditional museum exhibits, thus exporting history and culture for consumers (Kirshenblatt-Gimblett, 1998). Handler and Gable (1997) have documented this clash between the history and entertainment functions at Colonial Williamsburg, where the entertainment elements (e.g. amusement park, hotels, restaurants) help to finance the history components (historic village, interpreters, visitor education programs), but also influence how the story of the past is told. Museums "are not neutral spaces that speak with one institutional, authoritative voice. Museums are about individuals making subjective choices" (Marstine, 2006, p. 2). Museums select the narratives they desire to tell, often limit the perspectives revealed within a narrative, and can reflect the society within which they exist, sometimes more than the time period within which a narrative exists. The demystification of museums does not make them less accurate or less useful to visit, but instead bestows a wonderful opportunity for students to explore how museums present a subjective and selective past and how history is "made." Students can learn that all history is an interpretation of past events and people, and is laced with subjectivity, interpretation, hypotheses, and particular narratives (Hooper-Greenhill, 2000). Even more problematic is that museums often present history without the supporting documents and research conventions (e.g. footnotes, bibliography) of more traditional history sources, creating problems similar to the textbooks and films so often used in classrooms. Thus, museums are themselves historical sources that need to be critically analyzed and evaluated (Trofanenko, 2006). We can encourage students to see the value in learning from museums while also challenging students to confront museums' objective and all-knowing aura.

Monuments and memorials present the same dilemmas and the same opportunities as more traditional museums. However, they are by nature less comprehensive and more likely focused on a single event and/or person. Monuments function most often to memorialize, commemorate, and celebrate, not necessarily to present an extensive or multifaceted view of the past. Their purposes tend to favor positive narratives and omit controversial or negative stories about the past—they "don't just tell stories about the past; they also tell visitors what to think about the stories they tell" (Loewen, 1999, p. 22). Markers, monuments and preserved historic sites are often locally initiated projects that provide a favorable story about the local community and often use some public funds (Loewen, 1999). Monuments tell the stories of two eras—the one they commemorate and the one in which they were created (Loewen, 1999). One example of the dilemmas of memorials has played out over the past ten years as memorials and monuments are built to remember the events of September 11, 2001. These include numerous local memorials in towns throughout the New York area, in Pennsylvania, and in the Washington, D.C., area, as well as for the national museum and memorial being built at the site of the destroyed Twin Towers. Conflicts continue between various stakeholders, including the families of those who worked in the towers, the families of police and firefighters, the City of New York, the State of New York, the Federal Government, the organizations that raised funds to pay for the project, and others (Marcus, 2007). These groups debate the purposes the museum and memorial should serve as well as the museum and memorial's aesthetic qualities. Teaching with memorials is the focus of Chapter 8.

Figure 1.2 The FDR (Franklin D. Roosevelt) Memorial in Washington, D.C.

Fourth, museums are public spaces of historical narratives that are shaped by society while also influencing society. Museums help students develop ideas, beliefs, and attitudes about public spaces (Nespor, 2000), and also about their own right and ability to enter into civic engagement. We are highly conscious that museums, often the first large institutions students encounter outside the classroom, play a powerful role in shaping students' conceptions of their possibilities as civic actors and help frame students' views of the role cultural institutions can play in their own lives. As such, the formal and informal educational experiences students receive at museums serve two roles: first as occasions of learning; second as invitations to active citizenship.

Incorporation of museums into the K–12 curriculum can demystify the history presented at museums and enhance students' historical thinking skills, thus supporting future adults' inclinations to participate in society as engaged citizens. For over a hundred years, promoting citizenship has been a fundamental goal of K–12 social studies classrooms and of education more generally (Ross, 1997). Promoting citizenship is still a principal rationale for the social studies classroom (Barton & Levstik, 2004). Museum visits and the use of other museum resources can significantly contribute to the goals of preparing citizens for life in a democracy. Barton and Levstik (2004) propose three goals for preparing citizens through history education: promoting reasoned judgment, promoting an expanded view of humanity, and deliberating over the common good. Museum resources can support these three goals. Promoting reasoned judgment requires students to "reach their own conclusions about the causes of historical events, their consequences, and their significance" (Barton & Levstik, 2004, p. 37). By having students analyze and interpret museum artifacts as well as museums' historical narratives they can help students to develop reasoned judgment. Advancing an expanded view of humanity includes "taking us beyond the narrow confines of our present circumstances and confronting us with the cares, concerns, and ways of thinking of people different than ourselves" (Barton & Levstik 2004, p. 37). Students are presented with multiple perspectives within and across museums, and museums offer potentially powerful ways to develop historical empathy, thus expanding students' understanding of the concerns and ways of thinking about people in the past. Finally, asking students to discuss or deliberate issues that "promote consideration of the common good" (p. 39), as Barton and Levstik suggest, could focus around issues of justice in the past and today. The content covered by many museums and memorials focuses on issues of social justice (e.g. slavery, the Holocaust). However, museums may often avoid tackling controversial issues. By having students understand and critique these omissions they will be better able to consider the common good. Directly addressing and deliberating controversial issues is a constructive way to develop critical democratic citizens (Hess, 2009).

HOW CAN MUSEUMS BE USED?

The overall premise of this book is to promote visits to museums as a mechanism to increase students' specific content knowledge about the past in conjunction with developing their historical thinking skills, and to do so in a way that inspires and motivates students. As discussed earlier, we focus on issues of historical empathy, interrogation of historical evidence, evaluating historical narratives, connecting the past to today, and other aspects of historical thinking. While there is not a one-size-fits-all approach to effective museum visits, there are several important issues to take into account, including pre- and post-trip activities, unique pedagogical features of museums, teacher–museum staff collaboration, and the nature of museums as human-created, and thus subjective, organizations.

First, pre- and post-visit activities are an important component of successful museum visits. Though these activities exacerbate the time pressures that already plague K-12 history education, they are crucial for student learning. Pre-visit activities can preview content, prepare students for the museum's context, and set up on-site activities. Pre-visit activities help to focus students and establish learning objectives. Post-visit activities allow students to process their experiences at the museum, allow teachers to assess student learning, and connect the museum visit to the course curriculum.

There are also unique pedagogical considerations for museum visits. Museum visits should complement—not supplement—classroom resources. They are a different type of learning experience that is not a substitute, but an enhancement. Museums are often designed to be less formal centers for learning than classrooms. The interaction between students, teachers, and historical materials presents unique opportunities and challenges. In many cases there is more free choice (Falk, 2001) for students and less control of content and messages by the teacher. Free choice for students can often be valuable and support meaningful learning objectives, while traditional classroom "seat work" such as filling out worksheets can have the effect of dampening motivation (Griffin, 2004). One of the challenges for teachers is how to keep students focused while allowing students some free choice to choose and shape learning experiences. Assessing student learning as part of a field trip to a museum can also pose a challenge. Should field trip experiences be graded? How do you hold students accountable for their learning during a museum visit?

Another critical issue is teacher–museum staff collaboration. This collaboration is a key characteristic of successful museum visits for students (Marcus, 2008). Traditionally, museums were viewed as the "teachers", and the visitors were the learners (Skramstad, 1999). However, both school teachers and museum staff are important stakeholders who can learn from each other and support each other's work. Teachers can rely on the expertise of museum staff for content issues, but also in terms of how museums function and how a particular museum might meet a teacher's learning objectives. Museum staff can do outreach with teachers to understand the context from which students are coming and to connect museum resources and activities directly to a school's curriculum. Unfortunately, many museum visits are only loosely linked to school-based curriculum (Griffin and Symington, 1997). At times there exists a divide between teachers and museum staff—a boundary that needs to be "crossed from both sides" (Griffin, 2004, p. 65).

Finally, museums are unique organizations. They are not neutral spaces, but tell subjective stories created by individuals (Marstine, 2006). Museums should be approached with the same respect, but also the same critical eye, as we would approach any historical source with. Educators have long been critical of textbooks (e.g. Loewen, 1999) and of films (e.g. Marcus, Metzger, Paxton, & Stoddard, 2010) used in history education, but have not taken the same attitude to museums (Trofanenko, 2006). If we continue to view museums as completely authoritative and museum objects as "unmediated anchors to the past" (Marstine, 2006, p. 2), we fail to account for the subjective nature of museums and fail to take advantage of the opportunities museums provide to enliven the study of history. This means we need to reposition museum visits from being viewed by students as a day off to being seen as a rigorous scholarly activity.

WHAT'S TO COME IN THIS BOOK

This book presents and discusses strategies for incorporating museums—artifact and display museums, state history museums, living history museums, historic forts, historic homes, and monuments—into K-12 lessons in order to enhance students' historical knowledge and skills. The strategies are organized into cases that focus on a particular type of museum (e.g. historic house, living history museum, etc.). Each case explores important issues related to the educational potential and difficulties of using each type of museum, and then presents specific strategies for student visits and other uses of museum resources. The book is divided into two parts. Part I (Chapters 1 and 2) provides an overview of key issues inherent in using museums within the K-12 social studies curriculum. A framework for the book is established, museums are scrutinized as interpreters of historical knowledge, and practical considerations are addressed. Part II contains seven case chapters, each of which focuses on a different type of museum or historic site, and there are three appendices with overall suggestions for teaching with museums and lists of resources.

This is a curriculum book designed for working teachers, teachers-in-training, teacher educators, and museum educators. Our goal is to provide compelling and comprehensive strategies for the successful incorporation of museums into the K-12 history curriculum. We created each case to be stimulating, informative, and replicable. The cases presented are not perfect and will require adaptation to specific contexts, but we hope that they make the work of teachers using museums easier and more productive.

Part I: Introduction and Framework for Using Museums to Teach History

In this introductory chapter we provide a rationale for why museums are important resources for social studies teachers, and explore ideas for ways museums can be incorporated effectively to teach history and, specifically, to develop students' historical understanding.

Chapter 2 establishes a theoretical framework for the use of museums as part of the social studies curriculum, with explicit practical implications, and it explores the dilemmas raised by museum education. Chapter 2 addresses the history of the role of museums in society and of shifting missions and methods. The chapter then grounds our cases in the work of history educators and historians by exploring how museums provide opportunities for students to develop historical empathy, practice historical analytic and interpretive skills, make connections between the past and the present, and explore issues of historical significance, historical narrative, and historical agency.

Part II: Case Studies of Museums for Teaching History

Part II presents seven cases of effective learning strategies and activities for various types of museums, as well as concluding appendices with overall suggestions for teaching with museums, a list of museums in this book, and a list of resources.

Artifact and Display Museums

Artifact and display museums provide wonderful resources for teachers to help students develop historical thinking skills. Students can evaluate which artifacts museums use, how they use the artifacts to tell a selective story about the past, and how representations of culture and collective memory or post-memory are constructed through exhibits that include media interactive exhibits and experiences. They can also compare the stories and historical narratives from museums with those found in their textbooks or other historical sources. In addition, these museums often present opportunities for students to develop historical empathy, examine issues of historical agency, and assess questions of historical significance.

The case in Chapter 3 examines the United States Holocaust Memorial Museum (USHMM) in Washington, D.C. The USHMM opened in 1993 as a museum and memorial honoring victims of the Holocaust during World War II. In addition, its goals include "to confront hatred, promote human dignity, and prevent genocide" (USHMM, 2011). The museum provides an excellent case for exploring the use of artifacts to develop historical narratives and for developing historical empathy. As the museum is designed to evoke powerful emotions and raise powerful questions about the Holocaust, it provides rich opportunities for examining the various perspectives, including victims, perpetrators, and liberators.

State History Museums

State history museums have many of the same design characteristics as the artifact and display museums, but also provide a number of other attributes and resources. State history museums often have close connections to state historical societies and archives, provide a strong state-level educational program, and present a broad array of topics through their exhibits. These topics often include the social and cultural history of the indigenous peoples of the state, as well as those who immigrated, the economic and political history of the state, and lesser-known histories of groups or individuals who were involved in significant issues or events.

The subject of Chapter 4 is the Minnesota History Center (MHC) in St. Paul, Minnesota. Although housed in a traditional brick and mortar structure, the MHC was designed to be interactive, and engage visitors in experiencing the social and cultural history of Minnesota. The exhibits focus primarily on the twentieth century, and are built around powerful oral histories and the experiences of Minnesotans in events ranging from a paratrooper's involvement in the Normandy invasion during World War II to a family's narrow escape from a destructive tornado. The museum's interactive exhibits are the focus of this case as we explore how museums use oral histories and the histories of historic buildings and houses to reconstruct perspectives from the past.

Historic Forts

Historic forts recreate the feel of the past and help students to develop historical empathy, take into account the role of geography in history, explore issues of conflict and communication, and evaluate and critique historical narratives. Historic forts can provide a uniquely authentic experience that can rarely be replicated in the classroom.

Chapter 5 presents strategies for supporting student learning at historic forts. This case explores two forts—the Fort at No. 4 in New Hampshire and Fort Ticonderoga in upstate New York. Both forts played important roles in the French and Indian War, and Fort Ticonderoga also was a major site of conflict during the American Revolution. Both forts are excellent examples of historic sites where students can study the importance of geography, the nature of conflict and surrounding issues, and examine competing historical narratives. As a reconstruction, the Fort at No. 4 offers students wide-open access to all areas of the site, as well as a broad range of experiential activities. Fort Ticonderoga uses student role-playing, image analysis, and first-person interpretation by re-enactors to help students understand the complex history of the site, and to gain empathy for the men and women who served and fought at Fort Ticonderoga in the eighteenth century.

House Museums

House museums and related small-scale, single-focus historic properties offer insight into specific time periods as well as change over time. Often focused on specific people, historic homes allow students to physically step back in time, examining how people lived, worked, and played, thus drawing important comparisons between the past and today, examining evidence of social history and daily life, developing historical empathy, and evaluating the use of artifacts. For the case in Chapter 6 we explore the Mark Twain House in Hartford, Connecticut, and the Johnson County Historical Society properties in Coralville, Iowa.

The Mark Twain House was home to Samuel Clemens (author of *The Adventures of Tom Sawyer* and *The Adventures of Huckleberry Finn*) and his family for seventeen years in the late 1800s. The restored Victorian home allows visitors to learn about the author and his family, as well as to experience life for the well-to-do in Hartford, Connecticut, in the late nineteenth century. It also allows visitors to consider the lives and employment conditions of the African Americans and immigrant servants employed in the Twain house. The Johnson County Historical Society maintains three historic house sites: the

1876 Coralville schoolhouse; Plum Grove, the 1844 residence of Iowa territorial governor Robert Lucas and his wife Friendly; and the 1855 Johnson County Poor Farm/Asylum. Visitors learn about Iowa history, particularly in the context of national narratives of westward expansion and immigration during the nineteenth century.

This case will discuss how the historic homes at these two sites provide a gateway into understanding the time period they represent as experienced by a variety of people of differing perspectives. In particular, the Twain home contrasts the different experiences of the members of the extended Twain household to explore issues of class, immigration, status and racism during the Gilded Age. The Johnson County Historical Society properties aspire to help visitors understand how early Iowa settlers lived, how their lifestyles reflected broader national transformations, and how their lifestyles differed from that of contemporary Iowans.

Living History Museums

Living history museums attempt to recreate an account of the past through rebuilt or renovated historic buildings and role-playing staff recreating historic activities. Living history museums are particularly effective for developing historical empathy, thinking about change over time, connecting the past and the present, analyzing historical evidence, and evaluating how heritage sites create historical narratives. Chapter 7 details effective strategies for studying the past at living history museums. The focus of this case is three living history museums from early America: Colonial Williamsburg, the Jamestown Settlement, and Yorktown, all located in the Historic Triangle of Virginia. All three are home to hands-on living history museums that provide opportunities to explore the lives and experiences of the ordinary and famous people who resided there during early colonial America and the American Revolution. Each of these museums provides a form of the recreated and interpreted past mixed with historic buildings, sites, and archaeological and historical artifacts. In addition to providing young students with the opportunities to experience life in the colonies and a glimpse into what famous events may have looked like, these sites also offer opportunities for older students to examine how history is reconstructed and interpreted using the methods of historians, historical interpreters, and archaeologists.

Monuments and Memorials

Through careful examination of monuments and memorials students can study the perspectives included and left out of the story told about the past and how a monument or memorial supports or contradicts national historical narratives. In addition, monuments and memorials can tell us as much about the time period during which they were designed and built as they do about the events and people they commemorate. Chapter 8 considers how memorials and monuments provide excellent resources for students to scrutinize narratives about the past. The case study for this chapter will concentrate on 9/11 memorials in Connecticut, home to 153 victims of the 9/11 attacks.

Since the terrorist attack on September 11, 2001, numerous monuments and memorials have been planned and erected in New York City and the surrounding area, as well as around the nation. The case examines how these monuments and memorials remember the past, as well as discussing the unique features of studying monuments and memorials for such a recent event.

Bringing the Museum to the Classroom: Outreach Programs, Museum Kits, and Virtual Resources

In addition to physical buildings, materials, and museum staff, museums offer extensive opportunities for staff visits to schools, traveling exhibits, online resources, and virtual field trips. Chapter 9 explores each of these programs and resources with outstanding examples of each.

There are numerous museum outreach programs that are valuable resources for teachers, such as museum staff visits to schools and traveling exhibits/artifacts. These programs are available to enhance pre- and post-visit experiences or as a substitution when a visit is not possible. This chapter describes the staff visitation programs for Plimoth Plantation and the Minnesota History Center, and the traveling kits from the Tennessee State Museum and the Autry National Center in Los Angeles, California.

Plimoth Plantation has a nationally renowned outreach program that gives students highly memorable in-class exposure to the life of seventeenth-century English colonists in Massachusetts and the Wampanoag people among whom they settled. Plimoth's approaches to teaching students about the English colonial period, on the one hand, and life for the Wampanoag nation, on the other, are quite different. English colonial life is taught by highly trained character interpreters who come into classes acting in every way as an actual English resident of Plimoth colony in 1627. The power of the experience they provide is based largely on the role-players' extensive training and the fidelity with which they are able to represent people of another time. The Wampanoag education program, on the other hand, is led by twenty-first-century Wampanoag educators who speak with authority about their people's lives in both the seventeenth and twenty-first centuries. Exploring the differences between these two programs gives insight into the rich and richly varied opportunities provided by museum educators during in-school visits.

The Minnesota History Center provides a similar service to Plimoth through their "History Players" program. The history players provide first-person character interpretation of individuals from Minnesota's past that help to provide insights into the social history of the state. These characters include early African American entrepreneurs and the first public school teacher in St. Paul, Minnesota. The History Center is also expanding their programming using two-way streaming video to reach classrooms that may be in locations where it is difficult to appear in person.

Museum kits or "museums in a box" can provide a different type of museum experience. Unlike the more human element in the programs above, the museum kits are focused on artifacts (usually reproduction) from the past. The Tennessee State Museum's traveling trunk program provides a comprehensive set of museum-generated supplemental materials for use in teaching Tennessee history. The traveling trunks filled with reproduction artifacts, costumes, maps, primary sources, CDs, DVDs, books, and lesson plans cover every period in the state's history, and can be used in many ways. Teachers can either follow the lesson plans included with the trunks, or incorporate elements of the kits into their own curriculum. Though not as effective as outreach visits by museum educators, or field trips, traveling trunks are important supplemental educational materials, and Chapter 9 discusses some of the best ways to use them.

The Autry National Center, which houses the Museum of the American West and the Southwest Museum of the American Indian, also hosts the Institute for the Study of the American West. In addition to their on-site materials and activities, the center offers

"Communities' Stories Outreach Kits" that are available for teachers to use in their classrooms. These kits focus on the history of individuals who represent the different immigrant groups who have migrated to California (e.g. African American, Chinese, Tejano). Chapter 9 investigates how the programs from these museums can be used to develop students' historical analytic skills, bring the past alive, and promote historical empathy.

In addition to staff visits and traveling resources, museums have online resources and virtual field trips that can support preparation for a museum visit and/or provide follow-up activities. They also provide access to artifacts and museum-based experiences for students who are unable to visit a museum, particularly through a museum's location in another part of the country or world. Chapter 9 examines how online resources and virtual field trips can be used in conjunction with a museum visit or as a stand-alone activity to increase students' understanding of the past. Two museum websites are examined in particular: The Pocumtuck Valley Memorial Association (PVMA)/Memorial Hall Museum's website about the 1704 raid on Deerfield, Massachusetts, and the California State Railroad Museum's website.

The PVMA/Memorial Hall Museum's website provides multiple historical perspectives about the French and Indian raid on the English settlement of Deerfield, Massachusetts, in 1704, and its aftermath. This highly interactive website provides a model that can be used in preparation for a field trip, or in place of a field trip. The California State Railroad Museum is located in Old Sacramento, California, and maintains a somewhat dated but rich website that can be used to explore artifacts related to the gold rush, westward expansion, and technologies of the nineteenth century. Both sites are explored to consider understanding multiple historical perspectives and evaluating historical evidence when a visit to the actual museum is not possible.

The Appendices

Appendix A provides a list of ten keys for successful teaching with museums, and guiding questions for teachers, teacher educators, and museum educators to consider when developing activities for museum visits by K-12 students. This section presents the key ideas from each of the cases. Appendix B provides a complete list of every museum mentioned in the book, organized alphabetically by type of museum. Finally, Appendix C provides a list of online and print resources.

Contents of Case Chapters

Each case chapter in the book includes several features designed to critically examine the specific museums and to support the transfer of the cases to similar types of museums used by teachers and students. These features are:

- An introduction to the type of museum presented in the chapter, key pedagogical issues for this type of museum, and specific connections to developing students' historical understanding at this type of museum.
- A description of the specific museum for the case study.
- Specific pre-visit, during-visit, and post-visit activities for students at each museum.

- A reflection on the case, analyzing and discussing the key lessons of the case that can be applied more broadly to similar museums.
- A listing of resources specific to the museum and history content for each chapter.

COMMENTS ON THE MAKING OF THIS BOOK

In writing this book we chose cases and strategies that we hope inspire teachers and museum educators, and present models that can be applied to other museums. The cases we illustrate—not formal research case studies but cases about learning at different types of museums—cover a variety of time periods, purposes, and geographic locations. They range from a focus on colonial America to westward expansion, to WWII, to the events of 9/11. The museums are located in states in New England, the Mid-Atlantic, the South, the Midwest, and on the West Coast. However, there are significant gaps in the time periods and geographic locations we cover. We did not intentionally leave out a specific event/time period or region of the country; hundreds of other museums could work equally as well to explore the curricular and pedagogical issues discussed in the book. Ultimately we had to limit our cases.

The criteria we used for choosing museums included museums that work well within our conceptual framework, that are likely to be visited regionally by school groups and/or adults, that the authors were familiar with and had access to interview museum staff, and that represented a variety of time periods and geographic locations. In addition we provide strategies that can be used with elementary and secondary students, but not all cases equally address both of these student populations. Most of the museum cases support the study of U.S. history, though several focus on world history or incorporate foreign policy content and other connections to international topics. For those few and fortunate teachers who travel abroad with students, the conceptual frameworks and practical strategies discussed in the book can easily be transferred to museums around the world. While we hope teachers can use the specific strategies and museums discussed, they are meant to illustrate an example of good practice with each type of museum, and are intended to be adapted based on school and district requirements, students' learning needs and interests, curricular mandates, individual teacher goals, time and geographic logistics, and teachers' objectives and context. The cases provide one approach, but should not be considered as *the* way to support student learning with each type of museum.

The pre-, during-, and post-museum visit activities presented for each case use fictitious names, but represent teachers and museum educators with whom we work or have observed. The activities themselves, and related comments, are an amalgamation of authentic lessons we observed by master teachers, have adapted from museum education programs, and/or are our own pedagogical creations. We have also worked hard to best represent the museums and sites in the case chapters, often visiting sites multiple times and interviewing museum staff, but recognize that our interpretations of the museums and their educational potential may differ from views held by others.

CONCLUSION

Museums are one of the most valuable resources available for teaching K-12 students. Visits to museums and the use of museum resources can support a sophisticated understanding of our past that develops skills to interpret and evaluate sources, promotes historical empathy, and connects the past to today, among others. However, effective lessons to support museum visits and the use of museum resources are as varied as the museums themselves.

We hope this book fills a void in the education and museum studies literature, providing teachers, pre-service teachers, museum educators, and other scholars with a valuable resource that includes practical strategies to use with K-12 students, as well as provoking a dialogue about museums' purposes, value, contributions, and flaws—all within the context of promoting instruction in support of rigorous inquiry into the past, and the goals of democratic values of tolerance and citizenship in the present.

CHAPTER 2

Teaching History with Museums

Figure 2.1 Civil War battlefield marker, Manassas, VA.

INTRODUCTION

Museums have a rich heritage as part of American society. They are the places where our national treasures are held and displayed, they help to tell the stories of the United States and its peoples for all who visit, and they help to preserve artifacts from its past. Until recent decades, the stories being told in most museums were often those of the dominant groups in society, and were nationalistic in tone. Museums often favored Western, Anglo, and male points of view, and did not incorporate the stories and artifacts of other groups, individuals, and perspectives that have a role in the American past.

Or, if other groups' artifacts were included, they were often viewed as archaeological, ethnographic, or exotic, and not part of the shared culture of the United States. This lack of representation for marginalized groups has changed in many museums over the past several decades, and in many ways parallels the multicultural movement in education. Whole museums are now dedicated to the history of African Americans (e.g. Smithsonian National Museum of African American History and Culture; Charles H. Wright Museum of African American History), southern and eastern European immigrants (e.g. New York City Tenement Museum; Ellis Island), and American Indians (e.g. Smithsonian National Museum of the American Indian).

In addition to museums dedicated to the history of specific groups, general history museums and state historical museums have also worked to incorporate representative perspectives into their exhibits and collections. Given the constraints of room and finances, and the need to construct a story that will engage and not confuse visitors, this shift to a more inclusive narrative and the introduction of multiple or even competing perspectives is daunting. As a result, these newly added perspectives are not easily incorporated into the larger story of our nation in national museums such as the Smithsonian's National Museum of American History (Trofanenko, 2006), and are sometimes placed in supplementary roles or in ancillary galleries.

Similarly, most art museums still predominantly favor European and American works as mainstream, but also have expanding collections of indigenous, Asian, and other non-Western forms that are displayed separately from European art from the same period. For history museums, special exhibits will emphasize the contributions of non-white, non-male, or non-Christian groups, but this is often done akin to the breakout boxes in a history textbook. This does not mean that museums have not improved over time in their inclusion of different perspectives or that they do not hold educational value. It is important to recognize that many factors influence the development of a museum and collections, including finances, politics, the need to attract visitors, and the availability of artifacts or special collections.

In this chapter we examine the parallels between museums and schools as sites for learning history, and outline a framework for the pedagogical value and role of museums as part of the history and social studies curriculum. We do this through a theoretical lens that employs theories from history education, history, critical literacy, and museum studies. This chapter provides the groundwork for the cases that follow and will explore how museums have the potential to provide opportunities for students to develop historical empathy, practice historical analytic and interpretive skills, and make connections between the past and the present.

THE HISTORY OF MUSEUMS AS PUBLIC EDUCATION

Museums have long been viewed as sites for educating the masses, both American citizens and foreign visitors. Public museums emerged alongside public education during the nineteenth century to attempt to educate and acculturate adults as well as children to aspire to primarily white and middle-class values. The histories of museums and schools include many similarities and work toward many of the same national, regional, and educational goals.

Museums emerged in great number during the industrial era and in particular in Victorian England. Previously, museum galleries were not accessible to large portions of the population. In England, museums were used as a form of public education that helped both to provide access to high culture for the upward-moving working- and middle-class British, and to maintain class order and establish a national historical narrative during a time of great expansion of the empire. Hooper-Greenhill (2000) explains, "The arts could be open to all classes of society, and in their enjoyment the lower classes would become both more like their betters and more easily governable" (p. 26). Although art museums, such as the National Portrait Gallery in London that Hooper-Greenhill uses as an example, help to establish and reproduce the dominant narrative in society, it is the history museums that shape the history of a nation, state, or historical event and how it will likely be remembered. The roots of the public museum in the Western world were therefore those of public education and engagement, and a way to maintain cultural reproduction and social order as nations industrialized and diversified in population and economy. They were a way of helping the nation to prosper and modernize while also maintaining the status quo and to help assimilate new immigrants.

In the United States, there was also a growth of public museums opened during the 1800s, including the Smithsonian Institution, which was endowed by James Smithson for the "increase and diffusion of knowledge among men" (Smithsonian Institution, 2011). The Smithsonian Institution has played the role that national museums in the United Kingdom such as the British Museum and National Portrait Gallery have played. It has served as a site of public education, as well as a site of collective and national memory that instills particular stories about the history of the United States and its people. During the 1900s there was again an explosion of new museums in the United States, with one museum being opened on an average of every 5 days during the 1950s and every 3.3 days from 1960 to 1963 (American Association of Museums, 1965). Historical monuments, history museums and restored historical sites open during times of heightened nationalism and also often during times of conservative political dominance. It is during this time that the United States also funded memorials in Europe and other theaters of World War II to commemorate men killed in that conflict, although many had a strong Cold War message in their construction and memorialization.

Although museums often started out as sites of public education, the state of museums in this role has shifted over time. National and state funding has diminished even while new museums have been opened as part of urban redevelopment projects or as the result of foundation or special interest group funding. Many museums today, pressed to find adequate funding from multiple sources, represent private–public partnerships, where private donations and sales of merchandise or money made from private events held at museums supplement federal or state funding. For example, five-eighths of the budget for the United States Holocaust Memorial Museum comes from the federal government and three-eighths from private funding (USHMM, 2011).

Many museums started today are established as private museums or public–private partnerships that are either non-profit or even for-profit. Regardless of incorporation, these museums rely on funds from visitors, grants, endowments or foundations, and fundraising instead of having budgets supported fully by federal or state governments. Often, non-profit museums are founded with an endowment or foundation to help support their operations. For example, the Colonial Williamsburg Foundation was started in 1926 with generous gifts from the Rockefeller family and continues to be supported by individual donors and large donors such as the Mars family (of candy bar fame). Similarly, the popular Newseum in Washington, D.C. is supported by the Freedom Forum, a foundation that focuses on free speech and free press issues. Both the Newseum and Colonial Williamsburg ask for substantial admission charges from their visitors, but both also firmly support education and have heavily subsidized educational programs. Other museums like the International Spy Museum in Washington, D.C. are for-profit museums, although for-profit museums are a small segment of the museum world.

One major shift that has occurred with the move from largely private or government-supported public museums to museums that rely heavily on funds from visitors and donors is that museums need to structure their exhibits to attract visitors and therefore appeal to a wide group of potential visitors. The museum gift shop is no longer the only consumer-driven enterprise in the museum. With all of the cultural and entertainment options available today, museums need to find a way to continue to attract visitors and therefore justify their funding and existence. Museum directors seek out private funding for particular special exhibits that often require the sponsor to be promoted as part of the exhibit. Part of the mission to expand or maintain a museum's visitor attendance includes an appeal to educators through their museum education programs. Most museums identify education as part of the organizational mission, and it is often required to be eligible for certain types of funding. However, these market forces and the need to attract visitors have also meant a re-imagining of how museums are structured.

Museums have attempted to become more engaging and interactive, and, as a result, have become more heavily mediated for visitors. This layer of interaction and packaging of culture and history, however, has the potential to further instantiate the narrative that is being structured (Kirshenblatt-Gimblett, 1998). For example, with the advent of audio tours, visual effects, and even holograms or 3-D representations, visitors are asked to do less work in interpreting the meaning or purpose of artifacts they encounter. The increase in some forms of engagement and interaction has not necessarily led to museums where visitors are more fully engaged in their own interpretation of the artifacts, exhibits, or narrative being structured at the museum. Instead, some of these technologies oversimplify and narrow the interpretation of artifacts. Essentially, the mediation may take away the moments of interpretation and contemplation that museums generally provide and instead further instill the story the museum wants to tell. For teachers, it is important to recognize that the narrative or narratives being told through the museum's construction of exhibits and mediating tools will provide intentionally mediated interpretations of the past. It is valuable to engage students actively not only in listening and engaging with the existing interpretations, but also in analyzing the artifacts and stories being told and by asking their own questions about what they encounter.

MUSEUMS AS SITES FOR AUTHENTIC HISTORY PEDAGOGY

Museums offer the potential to support the authentic history pedagogy and more critical and place-based pedagogies that are now at the forefront of history education—a distinct change from past practices in history classrooms. Over the past three decades, there has been a movement in history and social studies education to help students develop historical inquiry skills and the ability to engage with different types of historical evidence. This movement came in part from the evolution of constructivist teaching practices of the 1960s and 1970s, but also from the push for more authentic forms of pedagogy that emulate disciplinary forms of thinking. It is the same movement that has pushed science classrooms to incorporate more lab experiments and the use of the "scientific method" with students as a way to learn. Authentic learning, according to Shaffer and Resnick (1999), entails learning (1) that is personally meaningful, (2) that "relates to the real world outside of school," and (3) "that provides an opportunity to think in the modes of a particular discipline" (p. 195). Museums provide opportunities to meet all of these characteristics through engaging students in real-world explorations of the past from the perspectives of historians, archaeologists, anthropologists, curators, and other staff. For example, the New York City Tenement Museum provides the opportunity for visitors to explore the history of urban immigration through the rooms of an actual tenement building. The tours provide insights into the historical and archive processes that led to the discovery of the building, the stories of the immigrant families that lived there, and the process of selecting and presenting the artifacts in the exhibit rooms.

Scholars in history education have explored the possibilities of engaging students in emulating the work of historians through teaching students skills in historiography and historical inquiry, as well as developing procedural knowledge and skills related to historical narratives, empathy, cause and effect, and historical significance (Seixas, 1996). Though there has been considerable disagreement as to what the overall goals of this "historical thinking" or "historical understanding" should be (e.g. Wineburg, 2001; Barton & Levstik, 2004), this disciplinary way of teaching history and social studies has become instantiated in history standards nationwide, if not necessarily in the nation's history classrooms.

There are a number of significant barriers to the implementation of more authentic historical inquiry in K-12 history and social studies classrooms. Teachers need to be trained and supported in conducting this type of pedagogy for it to be successful. Current issues of accountability and standardized testing may also inhibit the incorporation of historical inquiry. In states where history is not tested, its role in the curriculum is often diminished and there is not enough time to engage students in developing the necessary skills and content knowledge to conduct inquiry. In states where testing in the social studies does occur, this testing often emphasizes rote knowledge on selected response exams instead of assessment items that also measure students' abilities to interpret and analyze historical evidence and accounts (with a few possible exceptions). Despite these barriers, the movement toward an inquiry-based approach to history education has impacted state and national standards, textbooks and curricula, and the pedagogy of many teachers who see it as valuable and rewarding for them and their students.

Museums provide a canvas for this kind of authentic history pedagogy, and also more critical and place-based pedagogies. Museums are rich in visual and physical evidence, often provide rich narratives about the past, and attempt to draw visitors into the subjects they present. They may also be geographically linked to the event and provide a context in which students can begin to better understand the larger context and how much history is connected to it. In our heavily visual and mediated world, museums also provide opportunities for teaching skills in visual and critical literacy that can be applied in and out of the museum.

MUSEUMS AND HISTORY EDUCATION

Museums are constructed with artifacts, objects, reconstructed structures, and other materials that are interpreted and organized in particular ways and in particular contexts. Students need to be engaged in identifying and analyzing these artifacts, objects, etc. They should also be exposed, when possible, to the work of museum curators, historians, or archaeologists. Some museums make this work more transparent than others. For example, the Archaearium Museum at Historic Jamestowne, which is discussed in Chapter 7, is located on the site of an early English settlement and displays archaeological artifacts discovered at the site. It also provides some insights into their process for uncovering and interpreting the artifacts. This model provides a disciplinary viewpoint for students in how museum staff do their work and construct stories through the exhibits they develop. Most museums, however, are not as transparent in their interpretation, providing no "footnotes" such as are found in a scholarly written historical account. Therefore, in order to structure authentic learning, teachers need to involve students in activities during the visit that engage them in recognizing the stories and perspectives that exist in the museum, while also encouraging them to ask questions about the interpretation of these objects and stories. Teachers may enlist the help of museum staff or use preparation activities that provide insights into the disciplinary work of museum staff and historians prior to their visit. Museums provide a perfect site for students not only to develop historical thinking skills that ask them to analyze and reflect upon issues of purpose, interpretation, significance, authenticity, but also to hone skills in visual and critical literacy.

Here we identify three specific ways in which museums enhance K-12 students' understanding of, and engagement with, the past, including: (1) developing historical empathy; (2) promoting a critical and reflective stance toward the past; and (3) connecting the past and the present.

Museums Can Develop Historical Empathy

Given the visual- and narrative-rich exhibits of many museums, and the powerful stories they tell, students can be engaged in affective and more analytical forms of historical empathy. A useful way to think about historical empathy, which some confuse with sympathy or forgiveness for historical wrongs, is Barton and Levstik's (2004) framing of empathy "for perspective recognition," meaning the process of trying to understand the decision-making and experiences of those in the past, and "for caring," which entails a more affective process of recognizing the experiences of others emotionally and physically while also recognizing that it is impossible for students to truly understand what those experiences would have been like. This framework provides students with the tools to empathize without thinking that they fully understand those in the past or that they need to forgive historical actors for past wrongs or simply feel sorry for them.

For example, imagine students working with experts in the Decision Center at the Truman Presidential Library, being engaged in trying to understand Truman's decision-making during the Berlin blockade, the invasion of South Korea by North Korea, or the dropping of the atomic bombs on Japan. The mock-up of the White House's West Wing during Truman's presidency allows students to take on various advisory roles while deliberating these authentic and significant historical issues. This setting and real world application provides students with the opportunity to work with evidence, deliberate, and also develop empathy for Truman and better understand his decisions. This activity could be done anywhere, but the added environment and presence of Truman experts and resources in his library adds to the authenticity of the activity.

Presidential libraries make great models for developing historical empathy, albeit from a very strong and biased perspective. They present the often favorable, but sometimes reflective or even critical, perspectives of the decision-making of powerful historical figures. The Truman example above even places students in the roles of working through types of decision-making similar to those of Truman's cabinet, using the same evidence that was available. Similarly, the National Civil Rights Museum in Memphis, Tennessee, attempts to provide the perspectives of civil rights leaders and evidence for their decision-making and the philosophies that underpin their actions.

In addition to these examples of perspective recognition, the museums of groups or individuals who have suffered historical wrongs at the hands of dominant groups can be powerfully affective examples of developing empathy for caring, though these museums also potentially construct narratives that are heavily weighted toward a narrow interpretation of evidence. The United States Holocaust Memorial Museum in Washington, D.C., discussed in Chapter 3, presents a powerful emotional experience for visitors that attempts to reveal insights to those who suffered during the genocide. The New York City Tenement Museum, discussed above, provides an insider's view of life in the tenements for new immigrants, literally walking you into tenement apartments that were condemned early in the twentieth century to gain a sense of what it would have been like to live in those conditions. It is important to remind students that, despite these powerful affective experiences, it is impossible to fully understand the experiences of others in different historical contexts. While difficult to attain, the ability to empathize with historical actors and groups is believed to help develop more humanistic attitudes and behaviors in students, leading to the traits Barton and Levstik (2004) and Seixas (2000) believe may help develop capable democratic citizens. This is especially the case when students are asked to both identify perspectives and make moral judgments about the decisions made by historical actors, based on either the values of the time or present-day values (Barton & Levstik, 2004).

Museums Can Promote a Critical and Reflective Stance Toward the Past

Museums, historical sites, and monuments are prominent as sites to engage students in the critical, reflective, and important work of critiquing historical accounts and constructing understanding of the past. They are rich in artifacts, objects, and recreated structures that reflect not only the evidence they house but also the values, perspectives and ideologies of the time they were constructed. This is particularly true with monuments, as they are often constructed at a specific point in time and usually are not updated, unlike museums, which update their exhibits to reflect contemporary views more frequently. Thus, these types of museums lend themselves to both critique and re-interpretation.

The initial challenge is to engage students and teachers in re-framing how they view history. In order to participate in meaningful inquiry, they must first conceive of history as a constructed account of the past from a particular value-laden and period-specific perspective. History is a story that is constructed from past events using evidence and told via particular narrative frameworks and points of view.

Once a view of history as being socially constructed and interpreted is achieved, students can be more thoughtfully engaged in investigating museums as well as interpreting their own historical accounts from evidence in the sites. This is what Barton and Levstik (2004) refer to as an analytical stance toward history. Doing historical inquiry engages students in analyzing, interpreting and synthesizing historical artifacts in order to construct a warranted historical account or to critique a particular historical perspective that has been represented. This often includes doing some sort of "source work" (VanSledright, 2002), usually through applying some heuristic to primary documents and artifacts in order to identify the source of the evidence and particular perspective it represents. Students could be engaged in the analysis of individual artifacts or galleries from particular perspectives—to analyze the evidence for themselves or to critique the perspectives of the interpretation done by the museum. Regardless, students are engaged in actively deciphering the epistemology of a text, artifact, or historic site (Wineburg, 2001; Seixas, 1996), and then situating it within the larger context while also attempting to recognize how their own present-day views influence their interpretation (Barton & Levstik, 2004).

Many museums provide opportunities to examine artifacts more closely through their education programs. These programs can help students to also analyze artifacts within context and through corroboration with other pieces of evidence and secondary historical accounts (Wineburg, 2001). At Fort Ticonderoga, as discussed in Chapter 5, the fort's historic cannons become crucial artifacts in some teachers' student education programs. Combining mathematical exercises to determine their weight and shell trajectory with documents describing the necessity and difficulty of transporting the captive cannons to Boston to help end the British occupation of that city, students are led to an artifact-centered understanding of the strategic importance of Fort Ticonderoga and its cannons in the early days of the American Revolution. Artifacts, or reproduction artifacts, are also key components of the Ohio Historical Society's traveling trunk, focused on the prehistoric occupation of Ohio by indigenous peoples. The reproduction artifacts, including scrapers, arrow heads of different shapes and sizes, pottery samples, soapstone effigies, and carved pipe bowls, give students a tangible understanding of the complexity and aesthetic sophistication of American Indian cultures not easily obtainable through text or images.

In addition to looking at historical artifacts, sites, or media as part of historical inquiry, students may also be engaged in attempting to identify the themes or narrative that the overall museum constructs and how it reflects the time of its production and who produced it. Memorials and monuments in particular, as they are frozen in time to some degree, tend to heavily represent the political and social views of the day, region, and often the financial supporter of the site (Loewen, 1999). For example, the Ku Klux Klan often supported the building of Confederate memorials during their rise in the 1920s and 1930s, and again in the 1960s, as they did in Williamsburg, Virginia, during the period of school desegregation and massive resistance to the Supreme Court's order to integrate schools.

Museums and historic sites also combine artifacts through exhibits and the use of mediation, be they the traditional placard, audio tours, or interactive multimedia exhibits, to construct a particular historical story or narrative. As mentioned above, until the last several decades, these narratives generally reflected the dominant story of the United States from a male, middle-class, Christian, and white perspective. As Hooper-Greenhill (2000) points out, art museums such as the National Portrait Gallery in London also construct narratives visually through the way that they place paintings in prominent places, how they light the paintings, and whose images are given the prime locations, and thus look more powerful. A teacher could ask students to identify major themes that they see or even take images showing what they found (if allowed by the museum, of course). Students could be challenged to come up with explanations for why the artifacts of some cultures, such as early European and Mediterranean civilizations, are included as history, while those of other groups are included as natural history or anthropology, even when they were produced during the same period.

Students could also be challenged to compare the way museums tell history compared with other historical sources and media. They could examine how the perspectives of historically marginalized groups are included in a museum and whether they are included in the main story or relegated to a separate exhibit, similar to how the images and histories of marginalized groups are often included in breakout boxes in textbooks and not as part of the main narrative of the text (Ladson-Billings, 2003). Finally, for museums that present non-dominant narratives, students could be asked to look at the perspectives included and compare them with the ones they had commonly heard or learned, and how evidence (e.g. artifacts, mediation) is used by different museums to support the overall "story" they tell. For example, they could analyze how the representation of American Indians differs in the National Museum of the American Indian versus the Museum of Natural History or the National Museum of American History, or how these museums compare with the textbook or popular folklore version they may have encountered.

Museums Can Connect the Past and the Present

Many museums do an excellent job at helping students connect the past and the present. Three features of many museums promote past–present connections. First, numerous museums cover long periods of time. For example, the Jewish History Museum in Philadelphia, Pennsylvania, presents a 350-year narrative of Jewish life in the United States, promoting connections between multiple time periods and leading to life today. And the Mashantucket Pequot Museum and Research Center in Mashantucket, Connecticut, tells the story of the Mashantucket Pequot tribe over thousands of years through modern times.

Second, many museums present exhibits about contemporary issues that are specifically linked to historical issues, in some cases historical content examined in other exhibits within the museum. For instance, the USHMM discussed in Chapter 3 contains a permanent exhibit on modern genocide (e.g. Sudan) with explicit links to the Holocaust. These past–present connections are not just about attracting visitors but, as is the case at the USHMM, often speak to the core mission of the museum.

Third, some museums, particularly living history museums and historic houses, present the past in a way that is recognizable today. They often focus on typical lifestyle issues such as growing and preparing food, leisure and entertainment, education, occupations, relationships, and environmental/human threats. Students today bring a different lens to these issues, but easily recognize their relevance to today. For example, at Pioneer Farms, a living history museum in Austin, Texas that explores life in Texas during the 1800s, students can explore what life was like in central Texas. Pioneer Farm provides information and experiences that delve into how meals were prepared, where children slept, how clothing was made, the chores done by children, and common occupations like carpentry and farming.

CONCLUSION

Museums, once considered supplemental elements in social studies and history education, are increasingly being seen as laboratories for helping students acquire the skills associated with historical thinking. More than just the sites where things happened, or the place where "real" historical objects are preserved and venerated, or memorials to great events in the past, museums are ideal places for engaging students in thinking about how our ideas about the past are generated, mediated, and presented, and how the exhibits that tell us "where we came from" are often as carefully constructed as the institutions that house them. The chapters that follow provide theoretical, pedagogical, and logistical considerations to support teachers, teacher educators, museum educators, and others in their work to create effective experiences for K-12 students at museums.

Case Studies of Using Museums to Teach History

CHAPTER 3

Artifact and Display Museums
The United States Holocaust Memorial Museum

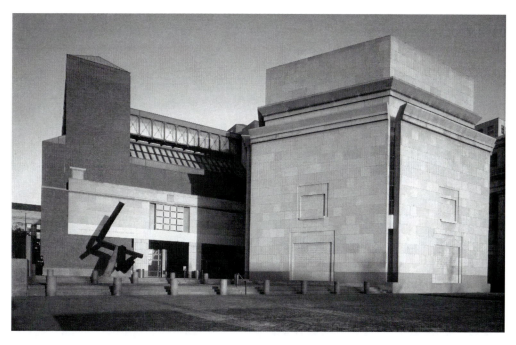

Figure 3.1 The 15th Street/Eisenhower Plaza entrance to the U.S. Holocaust Memorial Museum.

Source: Max Reid, USHMM Photo Archives.

INTRODUCTION

A group of pre-service history teachers recently visited the Louvre Museum in Paris, France, as part of a larger European tour of history museums and historic sites. Among the many treasures that propelled their excitement was the famous *Mona Lisa* painting.

They were sorely disappointed when they discovered that not only were they barred from gathering too close to the *Mona Lisa*, but that it was behind a glass casing. These young college students have grown up expecting more visitor-friendly experiences at artifact and display museums. Their vision of museums includes multimedia presentations and interactive exhibits. To them, the Mona Lisa display represented antiquated museum displays relegated to folklore or films. The Louvre's primary goal is protecting their artifacts and paintings. In the case of the *Mona Lisa* they are cognizant of environmental and human threats to the painting. The *Mona Lisa* aside, artifact and display museums continue to evolve, modifying the way they employ their collections of artifacts and objects. The motivating factors driving renovations in many museums are the needs to increase visitation, to appeal to a broader audience, and to provide more educational programming. The result is museums constructed around more engaging and compelling narratives and exhibits that provide powerful history learning experiences for K-12 students.

The case in this chapter examines how visits to artifact and display museums can promote students' abilities to evaluate the use of historical evidence, analyze and create historical narratives, and develop historical empathy. These museums often provide learning experiences not available in the classroom. The focus of the case is a class visit to the United States Holocaust Memorial Museum (USHMM) in Washington, D.C. After an overview of key issues to consider with artifact and display museums, the chapter provides background on the USHMM, presents a case of activities to use in conjunction with a visit to the USHMM, and finally reflects on the activities and the museum within the broader context of visits to artifact and display museums.

IMPORTANT CHARACTERISTICS OF ARTIFACT AND DISPLAY BASED MUSEUMS

For the purposes of this book we use the term "artifact and display museums" to mean those that rely heavily on their own collections of artifacts, documents, and other objects, and on borrowed items, to create narratives about the past. While there is certainly overlap between types of museums (e.g. living history museums that have formal display components), artifact and display museums' primary means for communicating ideas about the past is through objects.

There are several characteristics of artifact and display museums that are important to consider because they can impact student learning. These include the human element involved in using objects to create displays, the numerous opportunities artifact and display museums create for student learning, the potential of artifact and display museums to overwhelm students, the degree to which artifact and display museums use narratives, and the large number of education staff at many artifact and display museums.

Artifact and Display Museums' Staff Make Informed but Subjective Decisions

The first—and most important— characteristic of artifact and display museums is to recognize that professional museum staff make informed, but subjective, decisions about which objects to display and what to say (or not say) about these objects. Museum historians, curators, exhibit designers, educators, and others use a variety of criteria to make their decisions, including historical accuracy, intended audience, funding, space and other physical constraints, the availability of objects owned or able to be borrowed, objectives for an exhibit, and local, regional, and national politics. As a result of these influences on decision-making, the resulting exhibits are often attractive and engaging, and also reflect the values, perspectives, and ideologies of the museum staff and of society at the time of their creation. Recognizing the socially constructed and interpreted context of exhibits at museums provides students with a more nuanced and sophisticated understanding of the content presented, while also strengthening their ability to analyze the role of museums in presenting the past more broadly. Both students and teachers generally view museums as authoritative (Falk & Dierking, 2000; Marstine, 2006; Rosenzweig, 2000). Artifact and display museums present the opportunity to reinforce the importance of using museums to understand the past while problematizing and evaluating museums' subjectivities. Museums can be viewed as legitimate and relevant, yet operating within a subjective and constructed set of perspectives.

While all types of museums are impacted by subjective decisions, artifact and display museums frequently have multiple staff members making decisions, and often recreate the past through narratives told via artifacts and objects, thus adding complexity in understanding these subjectivities. For example, in 2009–2010 the Smithsonian's American Art Museum in Washington, D.C. created and housed a display titled "1934: A New Deal For Artists", which celebrated Great Depression-era art. It is hard to separate the decision for this exhibit from the economic downturn in 2008–2009 in the United States. However, that is only part of the story. According to the exhibit's curator, they needed to create an exhibit quickly, and the art ultimately used is all owned by the museum. Thus, access to the art was a key issue for the museum staff to consider. The economic condition of the country was an added benefit that enhanced the profile of the exhibit. The staff also had limited space and chose only a small percentage of their overall collection to use in the exhibit. Decisions were made based on a combination of factors, such as whether the works were by well-known artists, whether the works might be perceived as being attractive to visitors, and whether the works would be overly controversial, among other criteria. Therefore, while students could visit the exhibit as a way to study the Great Depression through art, the museum staff subjectively selected which art to include, and many of the decisions were not made based on historical "accuracy" or with history students in mind. This example is illustrative of the larger issue that professional museum staff make informed, but subjective, decisions about displays.

Artifact and Display Museums Present Numerous Opportunities for Student Learning

A second, and related, characteristic of artifact and display museums is that they often present numerous opportunities for students to analyze, interpret, and evaluate artifacts. Traditionally, secondary history classroom instruction revolves around a secondary source textbook, lectures, and multiple-choice exams. Yet the work historians and archaeologists do—and this is what makes history exciting, fun, and relevant—provides the opportunities to examine primary sources, to ask questions, and, with guidance and evidence, to provide one's own interpretation of the past. Visits to museums allow students the opportunity to interact with primary sources, particularly artifacts and other objects, in a way not available in the classroom. And although the traditional image of an artifact and display museum for many is one of stoically and passively viewing objects through glass, more recently many museums have incorporated interactive exhibits and activities that allow students to touch, feel, and experience the past, supported by various objects. Multimedia technology has been particularly important in changing the nature of how we experience museums.

The Chicago History Museum in Chicago, Illinois is a good example of the opportunities available with artifact and display museums. It possess 22 million artifacts, including 40,000 decorative and industrial arts artifacts, 3,400 works of art, 1.5 million photographs, and a 50,000-piece costume collection (Chicago History Museum, 2011). Some of these artifacts are displayed in an exhibit called "Facing Freedom," which is "based on the central idea that the history of the United States has been shaped by conflicts over what it means to be free" (Chicago History Museum, 2011). The exhibit includes provocative images, artifacts, and interactivity to explore topics such as women's suffrage, unions, and Japanese internment. It seeks not just to tell a story of the past, but also asks visitors to interpret the artifacts, construct knowledge, and reach their own conclusions about questions such as, "What does freedom mean?", "To whom should freedom be extended?", and "How are denied rights gained?" The exhibit provides multiple opportunities to analyze and evaluate many types of artifacts in the exhibit while also engaging students in a way not possible in the classroom. For example, visitors can use a touch-screen to answer the same questions given to those entering Japanese internment camps. The screens also play interviews with Japanese American internees. Visitors thus "test their loyalty" and potentially develop empathy for Japanese American internees. Artifact and display museums continue to evolve and become more sophisticated in the opportunities for students to analyze, interpret, and evaluate artifacts.

Artifact and Display Museums Are Potentially Overwhelming for Students

A third important characteristic of artifact and display museums emanates from the size and complexity of many museums. The physical structures, plethora of artifacts and exhibits, and depth of content covered can be intimidating for students. While not all artifact and display museums are equal to the size and complexity of the USHMM or, for example, the Smithsonian's National Museum of American History, many have multiple exhibits, and within each exhibit contain hundreds or even thousands of artifacts, objects, and accompanying written/audio/visual materials. The sheer volume and complexity of exhibits, as well as the length of time periods they cover, can prove overwhelming for students. For example, even a specialized museum like the National Museum of American Jewish History in Philadelphia, Pennsylvania has five floors of exhibits with over 25,000 square feet of space. The exhibits make extensive use of artifacts, written materials, visuals, and interactive media.

Artifact and Display Museums Rely Heavily on Historical Narratives.

A fourth characteristic of artifact and display museums that plays a role in student learning is the narratives they create. While living history museums, memorials, historic homes, historic sites, and other types of museums also tell narratives to some degree, artifact and display museums explicitly work to use evidence, space, and perspectives to tell stories about past events and people. Living history museums have recreated structures and activities to engage visitors; historic sites draw visitors to see or experience where/how something happened. But artifact and display museums rely almost exclusively on their narratives, many of which are created visually, to communicate a message and engage visitors with the past. For example, the Shoah Museum in Paris, France conveys three intertwining narratives about the Holocaust. One is the broader context of WWII, one is an overview of the Holocaust, and the third is a collection of personal stories that bring the first two narratives to life. These narratives are the result of artifacts, particularly images and video, deliberately sequenced and supported by accompanying text.

Artifact and Display Museums Often Have Active and Full-time Education Staff

Finally, a fifth characteristic of many artifact and display museums that is important in planning for visits is that they often have active and full-time education staff. These education professionals can help teachers prepare for a visit, provide programming during a visit, conduct outreach to schools, and develop lessons that are often posted on a museum's website. Many living history museums also have dedicated full-time education staff, but many historic homes, historic sites, and monuments lack the same education resources that artifact and display museums possess. As we will discuss later, the most effective museum visits involve active collaboration between teachers and museum staff, not the teacher turning over the students to the museum staff once the museum threshold is crossed.

THE UNITED STATES HOLOCAUST MEMORIAL MUSEUM[1]

The USHMM traces its roots to the establishment of the President's Commission on the Holocaust by President Jimmy Carter in 1978. Between 1978 and 1993, when the museum opened, the United States Congress and multiple presidents helped to make the museum a reality. The USHMM opened on the national mall in Washington, D.C. in 1993 as a museum and memorial honoring victims of the Holocaust during World War II. The museum is a public–private partnership that receives federal financial

Figure 3.2 Ghetto segment of the special exhibition "Remember the Children: Daniel's Story" at the U.S. Holocaust Memorial Museum.

Source: United States Holocaust Memorial Museum.

support balanced by significant private contributions. The museum employs almost 400 professional staff members and also relies on the dedication of close to 400 volunteers. Over 30 million people have visited the museum since it opened.

The primary mission of the museum is "to confront hatred, promote human dignity, and prevent genocide" (USHMM, 2011) through inspiring citizens and leaders alike. The museum balances remembering the horrific events during WWII with a call to action to prevent genocide today. The USHMM maintains two permanent exhibits: "The Holocaust" and "Remember the Children: Daniel's Story." "Daniel's Story" is an exhibit created for elementary and middle-school students to support an age-appropriate understanding of the Holocaust.

"The Holocaust," the focus of the case in this chapter, is an exhibit that spans three floors and uses over 900 artifacts to tell a chronological story of the Holocaust with three main sections: "Nazi Assault, 1933–1939," "Final Solution, 1940–1945," and "Last Chapter." The exhibit designers aim to do more than just convey information about the Holocaust. The exhibit is intended to impact a visitor emotionally as well as intellectually. Every aspect of the museum's design, from the architecture of the building to the purposely cool interior climate of the museum, are the result of a painstaking design process and conscious choices to shape the visitor's experience. To enter the exhibit

Figure 3.3 Front view of the railcar on display at the U.S. Holocaust Memorial Museum.

Source: Edward Owen, courtesy USHMM Photo Archives.

visitors take a large elevator that "transports" them upstairs and back in time. The exhibit space's walls and ceiling are mostly dark, with all light focused on the artifacts. During peak visitation months the space can be physically crowded, though the tone is hushed and serious. To support the development of historical empathy all visitors receive an ID card when they enter the exhibit. Each card presents the biography of a person living in Europe during the Holocaust and describes their life experiences from 1933 to 1939. The cards then go on to follow the person's biography during the war and, finally, to examine their fate. There are close to 600 ID cards, half of which describe Holocaust survivors and half of which represent those who perished.

As visitors move through the three floors of the main exhibit they observe the systematic dehumanization of Jews during the 1930s, then the process of ghettoization, and finally the genocide and liberation of survivors. The artifacts range from children's pictures to video taken of the liberation of the camps, some of it in color film that adds to the surreal feeling that what you are seeing is in many ways unbelievable. This exhibit leaves you with a better understanding of the events leading up to and during the Holocaust as well as some insights into the rationales, decisions, and experiences of people involved in the genocide from various perspectives, including victims, perpetrators, bystanders, and liberators.

In addition to the two main exhibits, there are temporary special exhibitions. Past examples of temporary exhibits include: "Nazi Olympics Berlin 1936" (1996–1997; 2008); "Nazi Persecution of Homosexuals 1933–1945" (2002–2003); "Anne Frank: The Writer" (2003); "Life in Shadows: Hidden Children and the Holocaust" (2003–2004); and "State of Deception: The Power of Nazi Propaganda" (2009–). Finally, the USHMM has two memorial areas: the Hall of Remembrance and the Children's Tile Wall.

In addition to the exhibits and memorial areas, the museum possesses an extensive library and archive with artifacts, photos, film, documents, etc. The USHMM also sponsors numerous outreach activities and traveling exhibits. For example, the museum operates the Center for Advanced Holocaust Studies, the Committee on Conscience, and the Academy for Genocide Prevention.

The five characteristics of artifact and display museums mentioned earlier—subjective decisions by the staff, opportunities for students to evaluate evidence, potentially overwhelming to students, a focus on narratives, and often full-time staff—are all relevant for the USHMM. Decisions by staff at the USHMM greatly influence the experience of visitors. Some of the issues that the staff grapple with include how to balance the dual role of the museum as a memorial and museum (honoring and remembering victims, resisters, and rescuers, while presenting information about the past), how to cope with the loss of Holocaust survivors and the reality that there will soon be no more first-hand witnesses, and how to balance a study of the past with an exploration of today's related human rights issues and a mission of preventing future genocide. These issues impact what stories the museum chooses to tell and how they choose to tell them.

The USHMM also presents numerous opportunities to analyze artifacts and evaluate narratives. The main "Holocaust" exhibit contains over 900 artifacts, seventy video monitors, and four theaters spanning three floors. The opportunity created by the expanse of the exhibit can also be overwhelming, not only for the scope (the average first-time visitor spends two to three hours exploring the exhibit), but also emotionally overpowering given the nature of the content. And all of this is without visiting the other exhibits.

Finally, as described earlier, the USHMM explicitly describes its main "Holocaust" exhibit as a narrative and tells a chronological story from "Nazi Assault" to "Final Solution" to "Last Chapter." The museum's exhibits are developed and maintained by a staff of over 400 including a large and active education staff.

Activities for a Visit to the USHMM

Overview

This case study chronicles the visit of Mr. Jurel's sophomore world history class to the USHMM. Mr. Jurel is a veteran teacher who is known by colleagues, parents, and students for his cutting-edge pedagogy. He was named "teacher of the year" at his school three times. This is a "B" level class, in-between remedial and college prep, with twenty-four students. About half of the students will go on to a two- or four-year college. The school is located in a blue-collar neighborhood and many of the students' parents work at local industrial centers. Mr. Jurel takes his students to the USHMM each year because he believes it offers a powerful experience to learn about the Holocaust, to connect to present-day human rights dilemmas, and to examine the way a museum presents the past.

The activities presented here focus on Mr. Jurel's pre-, during-, and post-visit activities to the USHMM with students, but do not include activities for his entire WWII unit.

Objectives

The visit is built around four primary objectives that target both Holocaust content and broader historical thinking skills. They are:

- Students will develop a chronological understanding of the events of the Holocaust.
- Students will explore the human experience of civilians and soldiers, and the features that shape human activities during war.
- Students will be able to identify and explain multiple perspectives from the Holocaust, including those of perpetrators, collaborators, rescuers, victims, resisters, bystanders, liberators, and survivors.
- Students will evaluate the evidence and narratives of the USHMM in presenting the Holocaust and in the development of their understanding of WWII.

Pre-Visit Activities

Due to the vast and complicated content of WWII and the Holocaust, the substantial exhibits at the USHMM, and the emotionally powerful nature of studying the Holocaust, Mr. Jurel's pre-visit activities focus on developing adequate background knowledge, understanding important contextual information, and establishing expectations for visit norms. The pre-visit activities take place over several days and assume the students retained basic background knowledge of WWII from earlier components of the unit.

First Mr. Jurel leads an interactive lecture/discussion that provides background on the Holocaust. Although most of the students studied the Holocaust in eighth grade when reading *The Diary of Anne Frank*, he says that most students "know a lot of people were killed and that the Nazis were bad, but beyond that they remember few specifics." He covers six main topics including the rise of Hitler and the Nazi Party; Nazi ideology, particularly around issues of race; tactics of the Nazis to sway public opinion, maintain power, and enact their vision; an outline of key laws passed; background on the Nazis' Final Solution; and a historical background of Jewish life in Europe. Mr. Jurel brings these topics to life through the use of visuals and the stories of individual people. For example, to illustrate Nazi tactics to sway public opinion Mr. Jurel shows Nazi propaganda posters, excerpts from textbooks for young children, and photos from the large Nazi rallies. The use of visuals is particularly effective and generates lots of questions from students about what is "real" and whether students their age really believed the propaganda. Among the many narratives he uses is one of a German Jewish boy who hid his identity during the war to survive, going so far as to serve in the German military and attend a Hitler Youth school.

According to Mr. Jurel, he grapples with the tension between ensuring that students have adequate background knowledge to understand the USHMM exhibits and overwhelming them with facts, dates, and people. In his words, it took me three or four visits to the USHMM before I figured out what was "essential" for my students to know. Without proper background much of what is at the museum goes over their heads and the value of the trip is lost. But if I try to cram everything into their already distracted teenage brains they get turned off and disengage from the topic.

For the next step in pre-visit preparation Mr. Jurel asks students to complete a time-line activity. Students are provided with a list of twenty key events/people/ideas from the history of WWII (e.g. the German invasion of Poland, D-Day, Blitzkrieg, the Battle of Britain) and another list of twenty key events/people/ideas from the history of the Holocaust (e.g. Nuremburg Laws, Kristallnacht, the Final Solution, Himmler). Each of the forty items has a short description. Working in groups of three, students create two parallel timelines by choosing what they believe are the six most important events/people/ideas from WWII and the six most important from the Holocaust. Each group conducts online research and consults with written sources to learn about the events/people/ideas provided and to collect data useful for making their decisions.

At first, students struggle to narrow down twenty items to six items for each timeline. They find it particularly difficult to categorize items like "the Final Solution" that do not have a specific date or person, but instead span a large period of the war. The students often debate items vigorously within the group, but Mr. Jurel finds that the arguments are often emotional and that students only sporadically utilize evidence to buttress their positions. He rotates from group to group, reminding them to think about the criteria they are using to make decisions and to justify their choices with evidence.

Once complete, the timelines are posted around the classroom and Mr. Jurel leads the students in a discussion of what is included and why. Over the course of the discussion Mr. Jurel makes sure each of the forty items provided for the timelines is covered, thus reinforcing key background knowledge. He also asks students to explain why they included some items but not others, encouraging students to justify their choices. In the most recent year's class, one group reported that their key criterion was the number of people impacted—positively or negatively—by an event or person. Another group said they made decisions based on "the importance of a person or event in the war . . . was the event the beginning of something like the invasion of Poland or the end of something like the liberation of concentration camps?" (What Mr. Jurel calls a "turning point" rationale.) A third group admitted that they tended to choose items that they knew the most about (several other students nodded their heads in agreement), while a fourth group commented that while they did not realize it at the time, "in retrospect, we picked the people or events that were about the Americans or the viewpoint of the Allies or showed us in a positive way."

Mr. Jurel also helps students draw explicit connections between decisions about what to include on a timeline and the choices museum staff make about what to include or leave out of an exhibit. As the timeline group work and subsequent discussion progress, he almost always detects an evolution in students' historical thinking. Students begin to consider how all sources of information about the past (e.g. textbooks, films, teachers, museums) make decisions about what to include and what to omit. For Mr. Jurel, this is the payoff of the activity. Students start to ask questions such as "How are these decisions made [about what to include]?" and "What criteria do historians or textbook publishers or museum staff or film directors use . . . and what are the 'correct' criteria to use?" At this point the students see the human element in history, a developing maturity in their approach to history, but are still seeking the "correct" way to make these decisions. From here Mr. Jurel narrows the focus to the history at museums. "I want them [the students] to realize that museums participate in a similar process [to the students in creating the timelines]," Mr. Jurel says.

> Museums take a large segment of history and narrow it down to what the staff— historians, archivists, curators, educators—believe is essential. They use objects and artifacts to support their historic interpretation. The timeline activity helps students to understand this, and I find students are more likely to walk into a museum and immediately ask, "Which people or events did they decide not to include?" Students are not only thinking about the process of presenting history in a museum, but then are curious to learn more about the topic beyond the scope of a museum visit.

The next day students move back into their groups of three. Each group is assigned to one of eight stations (one station each for perpetrators, liberators, survivors, rescuers, bystanders, resisters, collaborators, and victims). Each of the eight stations has three personal stories, one for each person in the student group to read. The personal stories are a combination of first-person accounts and secondary source excerpts that describe the experience of an individual during the war. After individually reading the personal narratives, within the small groups each person briefly presents their story. Each group then rotates to a new station where the process is repeated. This continues until each group has visited all eight stations. The goal is for students to learn some background for each of the eight groupings. For each station, students answer the following questions after reading the personal accounts:

- Who was in the group?
- What was their role in the Holocaust? Why did they assume this role? What factors influenced their decisions?
- What actions did they take to perpetrate or stop any aspect of the Holocaust?

Using personal stories to think about each of the eight groups/roles from the Holocaust hooks students into the content. According to Mr. Jurel, "It makes the impact of the Holocaust 'real'." In addition, the stories begin a journey of developing historical empathy through considering different perspectives and enhance the complexity of the Holocaust. They discover that the Holocaust is not just about evil Nazis and victims. Students consider German bystanders who felt helpless to resist the Nazis, Polish collaborators who enabled the Nazi killing machine, and French resisters who worked behind enemy lines to disrupt the German military, among others. There is no wrap-up discussion at this point in the lesson. Mr. Jurel expects, and desires, the students to be slightly unsure and bewildered about the complexity of the Holocaust. He believes this is the perfect lead-in to the visit. Last year at the end of this activity in class, a student said, "I'm so confused . . . there are so many people doing so many things . . . this is really complicated." To which Mr. Jurel responded, "Good! You should be confused at this point. That means you have lots of questions that you can explore at the USHMM. Write down all of the things you are confused about and have questions about, and bring them to the museum!"

As the final preparation activity, Mr. Jurel presents the history and background on the USHMM, including how the museum was founded, the nature of its public–private partnership, and the museum's mission and goals. In addition, he provides students with an overview of what to expect at the museum, including which exhibits will be visited, what those exhibits contain, the assignments students will complete at the museum and expectations for those assignments, norms for behavior at a museum generally (but also specifically at a museum about the Holocaust), and logistics such as the required security checks at the USHMM. He reminds students, "This trip is not a day off from school. My expectations are that you thoroughly complete all assignments."

During-Visit Activities

Despite bringing students to the USHMM many times, Mr. Jurel reflects that he still gets just as motivated as the first time. "The students are invigorated and I feed off of that energy." He says:

> Each time I go I learn new things and find different artifacts. There is so much there that it never gets old. At times I'm concerned that if I'm still discovering original ideas and artifacts, how can one visit by students be sufficient? But obviously that is all I can do.

The activities for students while visiting the USHMM balance student choice of what to focus on and how quickly to move through the exhibit with a structured focus and specific task. Students are only required to visit the main "Holocaust" exhibit. There is no formal visit to the other exhibits, though students can view them if they have extra time. One of the keys to the success of the during-visit activities is that Mr. Jurel had visited the museum and the museum's website prior to bringing students. The first time he took students, Mr. Jurel debated whether he really needed to visit himself first, but ultimately he chose to do so. His reaction after going was,

> Oh, my goodness, I can't believe I almost didn't go. There is no way I could understand what students would experience if I had not been there—the artifacts, the emotions—my guiding activities would have been a complete failure without that pre-visit.

Meanwhile, the website provided ideas for guiding questions, content background that augmented his other research, and primary sources he could use in the classroom.

To begin the visit, students meet with educational staff at the USHMM. For this particular visit the students meet with Dara, a retired middle-school teacher who works three days a week with student groups visiting the museum. Dara comes across with great authority and seriousness as she reinforces expectations for behavior. "It is very important to be respectful of other visitors," she tells the students. "You could be standing next to a Holocaust survivor, or their child, or someone who is very distraught about what they are seeing . . . this is a great opportunity for you to demonstrate that you are young adults." Dara provides information about the layout of the museum and "Holocaust" exhibit, and concludes with answering questions. One student asked if it is okay to talk in the exhibit since they are working in groups (Dara: "Yes, but softly"), and another student asked if there are certain highlights or parts of the exhibit they should be sure to see (Dara: "no, each individual decides what is important to them"). Mr. Jurel finds students appear a bit anxious about the emotional stress of the upcoming "Holocaust" exhibit, and thus they do not ask many questions.

Next, Dara leads the students to the elevators and they enter the exhibit. Students tour the "Holocaust" exhibit for 100 minutes in groups of three. Each group is assigned to focus on one of four specific perspective pairs (multiple groups will have each perspective). These are (1) perpetrators and liberators; (2) survivors and rescuers; (3) bystanders and resisters; (4) collaborators and victims.

Within each group of three, Mr. Jurel assigns students the following three tasks (students are provided with written instructions as well as a journal to record notes):

1. Choose four personal stories from your assigned perspectives (e.g. perpetrators and liberators) that are told throughout the exhibit and that you find interesting or exciting or disappointing or horrific or wonderful or puzzling—stories about individuals involved in the Holocaust in some way. Take notes on the story so that you are able to retell them to your classmates. You will be asked to explain why you chose these stories and what they represent in the Holocaust.

2. Choose six artifacts displayed throughout the exhibit—three that represent your assigned perspectives and any other three—that you find interesting or exciting or disappointing or horrific or wonderful or puzzling. Take notes on the artifacts so that you are able to explain what they are, describe their physical appearance, explain what they represent in the Holocaust, tell us why you chose to include them as part of your perspective, and tell us why you think the museum staff decided to include them.

3. Answer the following question: overall, how did the museum make you feel about the Holocaust and the groups that you were assigned? What was your reaction as you stepped off the elevator and into the main exhibit? How did your reaction vary as you progressed through the exhibit?

While students tour the exhibit, Mr. Jurel checks in with each group multiple times to assess their learning, answer questions, and monitor behavior norms. Other chaperones are also available to assist. Mr. Jurel finds that the combination of working in small groups with a focused assignment and the freedom of a self-guided tour maximizes student learning. While the perspectives assignment for narratives and artifacts requires students to focus on specific areas of the exhibit, the assignment to find three other artifacts and answer a broader question allows them to explore based on their interests. Mr. Jurel requires students to work in groups of three because he finds, "they push each other intellectually, keep each other on task, and support each other emotionally in what can be an emotionally draining experience."

Mr. Jurel says that year after year students consistently report that the graphic photographs are the most emotionally wrenching component of the exhibit. The incredible display of images includes dehumanizing treatment of people in concentration camps, squalid living conditions in the ghettos, slave labor in work camps and factories, and killing squads in eastern Europe. However, of the six artifacts they choose, most groups only have one or two images. Instead, they select objects. According to Mr. Jurel, while the images are shocking, students are drawn to the objects. More than half the groups each year choose a railroad car that transported Jews to their deaths. Other objects

frequently chosen include a Nazi uniform, personal items taken from victims at a concentration camp, a yellow Star of David required to be worn by Jews, forged identity papers used by resisters, and various Nazi paper documents that provide evidence for the Holocaust. When discussing why they chose various objects many students provided answers such as this, articulated by one student:

> The things we chose made the Holocaust seem real to us. It was not just some random person writing about it or a teacher telling us about it, but it was the actual shoes worn by someone killed or the actual outfit worn by a prisoner. It made you stop and just say "wow." It really hit home.

After touring the exhibit Mr. Jurel arranges a space for the students to meet within their small tour groups to discuss the exhibit and discuss the stories and artifacts chosen and the questions. He believes that,

> An immediate debrief while everything is fresh in their mind is crucial. I've done it at the museum and the next day in class and there is no comparison, debrief at the museum is far superior to meeting my goals. Some might argue that students could be upset about the content of the exhibit—but that is precisely what I want to tap into—their unfiltered, gut reactions. In other museums I might wait to debrief in class, but for the USHMM I've found it more powerful to do it right away, and besides, they don't allow photos, so while at some other museums I ask students to take photos that we can use to recall the exhibit, that is not an option here.

Finally, in years when staff are available, students meet with a historian and an exhibit designer from the USHMM (staff are not always available for this option). The museum staff lead a discussion about features of the exhibit's creation (who was involved, who provided the funding, how decisions were made, what changes have been made), and students are given an opportunity to ask questions. The most common questions Mr. Jurel's students have asked are, "How did you get all of the stuff [artifacts] in the exhibit?" and, "Is it hard to work here and think about the Holocaust all day every day?"

Mr. Jurel does not blindly turn his students over to museum staff. He deliberately collaborates with the USHMM staff for this segment and for the overall visit. As part of this collaboration Mr. Jurel shares his objectives for the visit, explains the pre- and post-visit activities, provides information on the students' abilities and any specific learning needs (e.g. English language learners), and asks the museum staff for input on the planned activities, resources, and insight into the exhibit. The museum staff regularly comment to him that this type of collaboration is rare, and they are thrilled to work so closely with a teacher. The staff see the relationship as mutually beneficial because it provides a better trip for Mr. Jurel's students while also enhancing their ability to work with other school groups.

Figure 3.4 (opposite) Tower of Faces: this three-story tower displays photographs from the Yaffa Eliach Shtetl Collection. Taken between 1890 and 1941 in Eishishok, a small town in what is now Lithuania, they describe a vibrant Jewish community that existed for 900 years. In 1941, an SS mobile killing squad entered the village and within two days massacred the Jewish population.
Source: United States Holocaust Memorial Museum.

Post-Visit Activities

Mr. Jurel designed the post-visit activities to assess students' progress in understanding the Holocaust and in evaluating the role of museums in presenting the past. Specifically, the activities measure students' comprehension of various perspectives of those involved in the Holocaust and students' ability to evaluate the evidence and narratives presented at the museum.

First, Mr. Jurel hangs eight large pieces of poster paper around the room. On each piece of paper is a heading and two questions. The headings are the eight perspectives (perpetrators, survivors, liberators, bystanders, resisters, rescuers, collaborators, victims). The questions are: "What did you learn about this perspective at the USHMM?" and, "What questions do you have about this perspective?" Students walk around the room and write an answer to each of the questions based on their experiences at the museum. Although the students focused on two of the perspectives, Mr. Jurel finds they still have something to say about each perspective, especially since the pre-visit activity covered the eight perspectives. Mr. Jurel then moderates a whole class discussion about the perspectives/questions. Mr. Jurel's biggest challenge is that he feels unable to answer about a third of the questions posed by students. He reflects,

> They [the students] ask some pretty difficult questions. Sometimes I just don't know the answer; other times they are asking questions that are about morals and values. The questions produce great class dialogue, but students often want a definitive answer, but with questions dealing with values, the students must come to their own resolution.

The second part of the post-visit lesson involves students meeting in their small museum tour groups to prepare for a jigsaw where they discuss the artifacts they chose with peers. Once ready, students meet in groups of four, with each group containing one person from each of the four assigned perspective pairs from the museum visit (perpetrators and liberators; survivors and rescuers; bystanders and resisters; collaborators and victims). In these larger groups the representative from each of the four perspectives presents the artifacts they chose and why they chose them. These discussions should build on the original background information learned during the pre-visit activity and should add personal perspectives and depth using the material collected during the visit. Mr. Jurel likes this activity because it often exposes students to artifacts they did not include in their own six artifacts, and students can express how they experienced the exhibit intellectually and emotionally. He finds the students split their discussion time between conversing about the events and people of the Holocaust and the more "meta" (big picture) issue of why they believe the USHMM staff included an artifact.

Next Mr. Jurel facilitates a class discussion focused not on the content, but on the exhibit itself. Students are asked to analyze and evaluate the purpose and effectiveness of the artifacts, narratives, images, etc., used to explain the Holocaust, and what decisions they might make differently if creating the exhibit. Mr. Jurel and the students draw on the discussion about the timeline activity from prior to the visit and their criteria for choosing timeline items as a way to think about USHMM staff choices. For Mr. Jurel, this segment is "way harder than the content piece. Students have much less experience doing this type of analysis and we only begin to deconstruct the work of museum staff . . . we need follow-up museum visits to continue the students' skill development."

The concluding activity requires students to use three of the six artifacts they chose from the exhibit to create a theoretical display with those artifacts as the centerpiece. Required elements include text to accompany the artifacts, a description of the physical layout, the intended impact on visitors, and an explanation of why these three artifacts were chosen for the display. Mr. Jurel began this activity after observing several students a few years ago who argued over an artifact in the exhibit and how it was displayed. They began creating their own mini-exhibit. The students were so engaged and had such a rich discussion that Mr. Jurel adopted the activity, which he calls the Matt–Julianne–Simone exhibit, after those students. Mr. Jurel finds that placing students in the role of museum staff is invaluable for understanding museum staff perspectives.

When time permits, which is only once every few years, Mr. Jurel includes various other activities in this unit including inviting a Holocaust survivor to speak, an activity using clips from various Holocaust films to consider how the Holocaust is remembered and presented through film, and/or an activity using video testimony from survivors such as those recorded and preserved by Spielberg's Shoah Foundation and the Fortunoff Video Archive for Holocaust Testimonies at Yale University.

REFLECTIONS ON THE CASE

The activities designed by Mr. Jurel are ambitious and require significant effort to plan and execute. They provide a model that demonstrates the key characteristics of effective museum visits to artifact and display museums.

Suggestions for Developing Activities for Artifact and Display Based Museums

This case suggests features of effective strategies for visits to artifact and display museums with students. These include developing clear learning objectives for students, visiting the museum and museum's website prior to the student visit, collaborating with museum staff, preparing students for the visit, following up with students after the visit, establishing high academic standards for museum visits, taking advantage of museum resources and activities that are not available in the classroom, and allowing students some freedom and choice while also keeping them focused on core ideas and objectives.

Developing Clear Learning Objectives for Students

The learning objectives established by Mr. Jurel focused on pre-, during-, and post-visit activities—not any one of these but all three. The objectives emphasized the human experiences during the Holocaust and the importance of understanding the Holocaust from multiple perspectives. These objectives were well matched to the USHMM resources and to the content of the Holocaust. The "Holocaust" exhibit at the USHMM tells a story of the past as one of human experiences using many personal narratives. Mr. Jurel's focus on liberators, bystanders, victims, etc., allows students to actively engage with the exhibit and meet the objective of identifying and explaining multiple perspectives. He is concerned that students could view the "Holocaust" exhibit as a series of disconnected artifacts, and thus aims to provide coherence and structure to the exhibit through his activities.

Visiting the Museum and Museum's Website Prior to the Student Visit

It was crucial that Mr. Jurel visit the "Holocaust" exhibit and the USHMM website prior to developing objectives and planning activities. The USHMM website provides extensive ideas for how to teach the Holocaust, and visiting the exhibit helps Mr. Jurel understand how his students might experience the visit, and thus how best to scaffold their learning experiences. For example, Mr. Jurel better appreciated how long to let students explore the exhibit, what types of behavior norms are appropriate, and what perspectives are included and/or left out of the exhibit so that he can meet his goal of exposing students to these perspectives.

Collaborating with Museum Staff

Rather than handing over his students to the museum staff once they arrived at the USHMM, Mr. Jurel collaborated with the education staff to plan the logistics and content of the students' experience. In this case Mr. Jurel planned the student activity for the main exhibit with the guidance and input of the museum staff, but he retained control of the objectives, implementation, and assessment. He then relied on museum staff as important resources to discuss the museum and the content of the Holocaust. While it is not always realistic to meet with multiple staff members, most museums are very accommodating, and excited to work with student groups. Collaboration allowed Mr. Jurel to blend his knowledge of the students, pedagogy, assessment, and historical understanding with the museum staff expertise in museum education and the Holocaust.

Preparing Students for the Visit and Following Up with Students after the Visit

Mr. Jurel exerted significant effort to prepare students for their visit and to build on the visit back in the classroom. In doing so he established high academic standards for a museum visit. Instead of viewing a field trip as a "day off" the students understood there would be lofty expectations. The pre-visit activities provided students with important background to understand the Holocaust as its own series of events, as well as within the context of WWII. The pre-visit work also set up students to consider multiple perspectives and to evaluate the museum's exhibits as historical narratives. Mr. Jurel prepared students for the emotional difficulty of the content, a unique feature of visiting the USHMM. The exhibit deals with human trauma through explicit photos and video, thus impacting students' experiences, but also influencing how their behavior might be received by other visitors. While there are always behavior management issues at a museum, they are acute at the USHMM, where unruly behavior could prove very offensive or upsetting to other visitors.

The post-visit activities permit Mr. Jurel multiple opportunities to assess student learning, connect the visit back into the classroom curriculum, and provide a forum for students to reflect on their own learning and to ask questions. Without follow-up activities it would be difficult to know if the objectives were met. They are also a mechanism to share across the assigned perspectives. Post-visit activities re-emphasize the academic norms of the visit.

Taking Advantage of Museum Resources and Activities that are Not Available in the Classroom

The whole point of visiting museums with students is that they offer experiences that are not replicable in the classroom. In this case the USHMM offered an extensive collection of artifacts, a multimedia format, a well-researched narrative on the Holocaust, the opportunity to consider multiple perspectives, expert museum staff, and the chance to examine issues of how history is represented at museums more broadly. Mr. Jurel took advantage of the museum's resources by creating an activity that moved beyond traditional lecture, textbook, and multiple-choice exams. Specifically, the explicit use of artifacts and the interactions with museum staff would be very difficult to duplicate in the classroom.

Allowing Students Some Freedom and Choice While Also Keeping Them Focused on Core Ideas

Research shows that a balanced approach to museum visits that allows students a degree of freedom while providing structure to support learning experiences is most effective (Bamberger & Tal, 2006). Mr. Jurel's students decided which artifacts to focus on, where to spend extra time, and at what pace to explore the exhibit. At the same time the students were not left floundering. They knew what to expect in the exhibit and, within the broad scope of the Holocaust, had specific ideas and questions to focus them.

Another way in which Mr. Jurel allowed freedom yet maintained focus was by asking the students to visit the exhibit in groups of three. Small groups permitted students to preserve some of the social interaction so important to that age group, while also forcing students to be responsible to each other and having others for intellectual and emotional support. The structure of the assignment helped to focus the groups, and Mr. Jurel (along with other chaperones) provided additional structure by informally monitoring the groups and formally checking in with them periodically. Mr. Jurel was active and supportive, but not intrusive.

At some artifact and display museums it may be appropriate for some portion of the activities to include a docent-guided tour. Such a formal tour is not appropriate in this case because it could be disruptive to other visitors, because it did not fit with the nature of the assignment to have different students focus on different aspects of the Holocaust, and because the exhibit is fairly easy to navigate. Incidentally, because of the disruptive nature of a formal tour, the USHMM does not offer docent-led programs for school groups.

This chapter focused on artifact and display museums through a case that explores the United States Holocaust Memorial Museum. The next chapter focuses on the nature and role of state history museums, and in particular the case of the Minnesota History Center. State history museums often share the design characteristics of an artifact and display museum, but also provide access to such resources as statewide educational programs, and state archives and genealogical records.

NOTE

1   We extend our gratitude to Peter Fredlake, Peter Black, Sara Weisman, Carly Gjolaj and other staff from the USHMM for their time and efforts to meet with us and provide information and resources to support the writing of this chapter.

RESOURCES

American Association of Museums list of accredited museums by state: www.aam-us.org/museumresources/accred/list.cfm?mode=state

The Fortunoff Video Archive for Holocaust Testimonies at Yale University: www.library.yale.edu/testimonies

Historical overview of the Holocaust: Bergen, Doris L. (2009). *War and Genocide: A Concise History of the Holocaust*. New York: Rowman and Littlefield.

The United States Holocaust Museum and education resources for teaching the Holocaust: www.ushmm.gov

USC Shoah Foundation Institute for Visual History and Education: http://dornsife.usc.edu/vhi

CHAPTER 4

State History Museums

The Minnesota History Center

Figure 4.1 The Minnesota History Center, St. Paul, Minnesota.

Source: With permission of the Minnesota Historical Society.

INTRODUCTION

Upon entering most history museums, the overall tone of the museum and how it is designed to engage visitors in exploring the past is obvious. When you enter the Atomic Testing Museum in Las Vegas, Nevada, for example, the faux blast doors and cut-out of Miss Atomic Bomb 1957 set a visitor to expect an interactive and engaging look at the history of atomic weapons and testing. The United States Holocaust Memorial Museum, discussed in the previous chapter, establishes a somber and reflective tone for a visitor with the cool physical building temperature, the architecture, the identification card, and transportation up and back in time with the elevator to the main exhibit, where you are confronted with powerful objects that construct a powerful story.

In this chapter, we explore the case of the Minnesota History Center, and the nature and role of state history museums, and the resources they provide in general. The History Center is designed for visitors to experience and interact with the past through exhibits based on oral and social histories of the people and events from Minnesota's past and present. Similar to most state history museums, the History Center's exhibits focus on the state's cultural, economic, social, and political history. The History Center is also a unique case among state history museums, however, as it closely resembles the interactive science museums that have gained popularity over the past two decades. A unique feature of this particular museum is that it is filled with primarily reproduction artifacts with which visitors can physically interact, and with simulations that engage visitors in experiencing events ranging from a 1965 tornado viewed from a recreated basement to the crash of a C-47 troop transport plane on D-Day that is housed in a reconstructed fuselage. Interactive museums such as the History Center often house fewer actual historical artifacts but instead rely on greater engagement with reproduction artifacts and experiences in order to help students and other visitors develop empathy and an understanding of social history through group or personal narratives. This interaction, however, also presents challenges for teachers as students may feel that they truly understand the experiences of those in the past as a result and then do not reflect on their experiences and the distance between them and the past.

IMPORTANT CHARACTERISTICS OF STATE HISTORY MUSEUMS

State history museums, or similar regionally focused museums, often hold some design or stylistic resemblance to the artifact and display museums described in Chapter 3. They often (1) include professional museum staff who make informed but subjective decisions about which objects to display and what to say (or not say) about these objects; (2) present numerous opportunities for students to analyze, interpret, and evaluate artifacts; (3) explicitly work to use evidence, space, and perspectives to create narratives; and (4) often have active and full-time education staff (see Chapter 3 for a more extensive discussion of these characteristics). State history museums also frequently include several other features that present unique opportunities and challenges for teachers to consider. They are often state-funded (in part or in full), house or have connections to state historical societies and state archives, have strong state-level educational programs, and feature exhibits that include a broad range of topics related to state history (social and cultural history, economic history, genealogy and property history, significant events or issues in state history, and the role of individuals from the state in important national and international events).

State History Museums Often Work Closely with State Historical Societies

As is the case with many state history museums, the Minnesota History Center is also home to the Minnesota Historical Society. The History Center is the heart of a larger system of museums and historical sites that are part of the Historical Society's educational mission. These other sites focus on events and earlier periods not explored at the History Center (e.g. Dakota War of 1862, French fur trade), while the History Center focuses on twentieth-century social history. In addition to the various educational and historical sites the Minnesota Historical Society operates, students, teachers, and the general public also have access to the archives that are housed in the Historical Society wing of the History Center building. State archives can be invaluable resources for students who are conducting research into family genealogy or other genealogical research, exploring the history of a piece of property or historic building, or looking for evidence contained in state reports, papers of former state officials, or other legal or historical documents.

Since state historical societies and history museums serve certain functions for the state, such as maintaining state archives and artifacts, and conducting educational programs, they are often funded at least in part by state governments. In the case of the History Center, the state funding covers much of the cost of the building and archive, but the History Center also relies on money raised from private donors, corporations, and through membership and visitor fees to support programming and the creation of new exhibits.

State History Museums Often Have Strong State-Wide Educational Programs

State history museums are founded with education at the core—not just the education of the K-12 students in the state, but of all state citizens and visitors. This means that the stories they tell often come from the perspective of state legacy, pride, or collective memory, and need to be examined in the same ways as the artifact and display museums discussed in Chapter 3. They also, however, often focus on the sometimes largely neglected stories of various groups of peoples who reside in the state, or events in the state's past that are lesser known but by no means insignificant.

State history museums also often have strong outreach programs for teachers and students who can't readily access the museum's exhibits in person. For example, the Minnesota History Center and Historical Society offer supplementary classes, such as a class on the role of the fur trade in Minnesota, that can be taught at the museum for school groups, out in the schools for those who can't come to the museum in person, or via distance-learning technology. State museums and historical societies often have "museum in a box" kits that can be distributed across the state, as the example of the Tennessee History Museum's program (discussed in Chapter 9) illustrates. The History Center and Historical Society also support the National History Day program for the state. National History Day is a competitive history research and presentation program modeled after science fair programs, and generally the strongest state National History Day programs have close ties to the respective state's historical society or state history museum.

State History Museums Focus on Broad Topics Related to State History

Unlike other theme-, issue-, or single-event-based museums, such as the United States Holocaust Memorial Museum discussed in the previous chapter, state history museums often focus on broad aspects of a state's history. One exhibit may focus on the indigenous people of the state, whereas another focuses on economic history. Most state history museums provide insights into the oral and social histories of the people or groups who immigrated, as well as more famous state citizens. In addition to providing insights on state history, state history museums also provide opportunities for visitors to contextualize larger events in U.S. history by providing a local or regional context, as well as to provide opportunities to explore the role of the state and its citizens in larger national and international events.

THE MINNESOTA HISTORY CENTER[1]

Unlike the USHMM and the Atomic Testing Museum, when visitors enter the Minnesota History Center, a beautiful structure located prominently in downtown St. Paul near the state capital building and St. Paul Cathedral, the intended experience is not immediately apparent. The center opened in 1992 and its building is constructed largely of granite, limestone mined in Minnesota, and local hardwoods. The exterior and main public spaces are filled with sculpture, etched glass, and windows that function both to allow copious amounts of natural light into the public spaces of the museum and to help reflect the sun to create a warm visual effect on the exterior of the building. The architecture inside is open, light-filled, and grand, and a replica of Minnesota native Charles Lindbergh's plane *Jenny* hangs over the second-floor atrium.

Upon entering the main exhibit space on the third floor, however, the expectations for your experience at the History Center change rapidly. In contrast to the building's architecture and formal appearance, and the ensuing expectations of an experience more reminiscent of a "traditional" artifact display museum, the main exhibit hall is anything but traditional. The volume of young people talking increases, and you see middle-grade students scurrying from room to room in excitement. The "Grainland" exhibit, which highlights the role of agriculture in the state's history, appears in front of you and sets the stage for what is to come—a physical and affective interactive experience of social and cultural history of Minnesota—where young people place themselves into actively constructing history. This is not a quiet museum setting. The activities described in this chapter build from this design and the unique attributes of state history museums to develop students' ability to recognize the perspectives of immigrants and other groups through social history and to set the stage for doing historical inquiry, particularly through conducting oral histories and inquiries into local historic buildings and structures.

Exhibits at the Minnesota History Center

The focus of all of the main museum exhibits is very much based on experiential education and social and cultural public history. Exhibits are designed for students to engage with the artifacts affectively, physically, and intellectually. The model for engagement is also reminiscent of the very successful and popular Science Museum of Minnesota, located nearby in downtown St. Paul. The History Center actively engages visitors in experiencing the museum through direct contact and interaction with exhibits beyond the cognitive or interpretive interactions found in more traditional archive and display-style history museums. The museum exhibits in the History Center lack significant numbers of authentic historical artifacts; instead, they emphasize interaction and affective experience.

The educational staff at the museum work closely with curatorial and museum staff to design the ongoing exhibits. One of the guiding principles in developing the exhibits is the desire to appeal to multiple intelligences (Gardner, 1993). In particular, the staff members believe that the exhibits should appeal to spatial, bodily kinesthetic, and interpersonal aspects of intelligence as a way to motivate students in the museum and to help students develop an understanding of people's experiences in the past. The artifacts guiding these exhibits are the histories of Minnesotans, many collected as part of oral history projects. Different forms of simulations are also present throughout the main exhibits to help tell these stories. Although there are still many actual historical artifacts in each exhibit area, they are more the supporting cast than the main show, with the stories and interactive exhibits taking center-stage.

This design is in direct opposition to what the center's designers and staff saw as aspects of traditional museums that fail to engage families and adolescents in particular—artifacts in glass cages with which they cannot interact. They acknowledge that this means that many of the exhibits include reproductions of artifacts and that visitors will have less interaction with actual historical artifacts, but they see active engagement for young visitors as providing benefits that outweigh the role traditional artifacts play. There is a tension in this kind of design between creating active exhibits that promote active engagement and creating exhibits that help students to thoughtfully reflect on the distance and space from the history they are engaging. This model presents a similar tension to the living history museums described in Chapter 7 on the historic triangle sites in Virginia, except that those are located on the actual historical sites, whereas this museum serves as a place to recreate experiences from a variety of time periods and locations in one space.

Here we describe four of the ongoing exhibits that are the core of the museum experience for students, and we outline activities for field trip preparation, the day of the visit, and ways to debrief or apply what students learn. The four exhibits—"Grainland," "Minnesota's Greatest Generation," "Weather Permitting," and "Open House: If These Walls Could Talk"—are long-term exhibits that will continue indefinitely at the museum.

Exhibit #1: "Grainland"

In "Grainland," visitors are given the opportunity to follow the course of grains, such as wheat and corn, both Minnesota agricultural staples beginning in the mid-nineteenth century, as they work their way through the grain elevator. The grain elevator, especially for rural Minnesotans of European descent, is a symbol of agricultural success and prominence as it reflects the history and value of agriculture to the state. When experiencing "Grainland," you do not watch a film or read cards. Instead, you physically follow the grain's path through a series of slides and chutes from a farmer's wagon to a railroad car headed for the grain market. The nature of this interaction is enjoyable for the young people playing the role of the grain. If they take a few minutes to reflect on their path and the tools involved, they will better understand how important the role of agriculture is to the state and the mechanics of how part of the process of getting the grain to market works. The exhibit will also help them to appreciate the many grain mills scattered throughout the small towns they may drive through.

Exhibit #2: "Minnesota's Greatest Generation"

This exhibit puts a Minnesota twist on the "greatest generation" phenomenon by looking at the influence of Minnesotans who grew up during the 1930s and participated in World War II. The exhibit includes a recreated 1940s-era soda fountain and theater, actual examples of an M-8 armored vehicle and a 1955 Ford Sedan (both produced in St. Paul's Ford plant), and simulations of an ammunition factory assembly line and a C-47 transport for paratroopers. There are also smaller parts of the exhibit that focus on social aspects of life during the period, featuring victory gardens and rationing and a 1950s house.

The two most interesting and interactive parts of the exhibit from a pedagogical point of view are the simulated assembly line, where visitors can work together to "manufacture" ammunition on a conveyer belt system, and the paratrooper simulation. The assembly line is designed to force students to work together as a team to pack ammunition casings with simulated plastic explosive charges and projectiles. One student has to crank the assembly line while others add in the different pieces to each shell. The simulation challenges visitors to produce six shells every fifteen seconds. A counter and clock are provided to help visitors meet that challenge. The sign with instructions on the simulated conveyer belt ends with the command to "repeat for 8 hours a day" to try to emphasize the laborious and monotonous process that their Minnesotan ancestors would have faced when working on one of these production lines. Although the simulation is designed to get students to reflect on their experience and develop empathy for the workers in munitions factories during the period, more often students simply crank the belt a few times, put together some shells, and move on to the next exhibit.

Figure 4.2 Artillery shell assembly line exhibit.

Source: With permission of the Minnesota Historical Society.

The paratroop simulation captivates students' attention a bit longer. In order to experience this episode from the past, which is captured as part of an oral history and then recreated inside of a C-47 fuselage turned theater, visitors must enter the plane and sit along the sideboards in the place of the paratroopers whose story they are about to hear. This particular plane had crashed—apparently into a barn or dwelling—as part of the massive paratroop drop the night before the D-Day invasion in Normandy, France, in 1944. Only three of the paratroopers inside, one being the Minnesota veteran who told the story, survived the crash by jumping out of the plane as it rapidly descended after being hit. Visitors experience the events through the voices of the paratroopers, the turbulence of the plane, and by seeing and hearing the explosions through the transport's windows. Much happens in the short time of the plane ride, but the dark and confined space provides more room to contemplate what is going on than the hectic environment of the rest of the exhibit where the assembly line is situated.

Exhibit #3: "Weather Permitting"

A very fitting topic for an exhibit in a Minnesota history museum, "Weather Permitting" focuses on the extreme weather conditions in the state and how the people have endured over the years. Parts of the exhibit include the topics of winter with demonstrations highlighting winter clothing, record winter extremes, and the winter pastime of ice fishing. Students can peek into an ice fishing shack or try on winter apparel. The most engaging part of the exhibit is again based on oral and media histories of a tornado that struck Fridley, Minnesota, in 1965. This exhibit invites visitors into a reconstructed basement of a house to experience the twister, complete with simulated sound effects of the stark silence and horrific roar of the "tornado" and the actual radio coverage of the weather event. Given the fairly universal topic of weather, it is easy for visitors to relate to and identify with many of the aspects of this exhibit, with the exception of the tornado simulation, which keeps students captivated (and captive) in the simulated basement room.

Exhibit #4: "Open House: If These Walls Could Talk"

In probably the most historically thorough and powerful exhibit, "Open House" invites visitors to literally walk through time as they explore the history of a particular east-side St. Paul house that has been recreated in the museum space. Each room in the house, which was home to approximately fifty families during its history, tells a different story from the perspective of one of these families based on archival and oral history evidence. The house is significant as its residents reflect the changing immigration patterns in the state over the past century, from German, Irish, and Italian immigrants, to African Americans, and later families of Laotian and Vietnamese origins. Similar to the Tenement Museum on the Lower East Side in New York City, the artifacts in each of the rooms reflect the period and experiences of its residents at the time.

The "Open House" exhibit provides a more personal touch than the Tenement Museum because curators had access to some of the house's former occupants through oral histories conducted as part of the project. These stories provide perspectives from the changing face of St. Paul's east side working-class and immigrant communities. Many of these occupants held jobs at the famous early factories and manufacturing facilities, including the meat-packing plant and brewery. Although most of the items in the rooms are recreations, the decorations and furnishings provide insight into the type of material

Figure 4.3 The entrance to the "Open House: If These Walls Could Talk" exhibit.

Source: With permission of the Minnesota Historical Society.

culture working-class families and particular immigrant groups would possess during different eras. Some of the oral histories are told through an audio recording that plays in the various rooms, while others are told through placards and artifacts around the room.

A few of these stories may seem trivial. For example, there is a story about a fire that once ignited in the attic and almost burned the house, and there is story of a Hmong family killing chickens in the basement. All of the stories are significant, however, as the experiences reflect the cultural histories of the occupants and of the state's citizens. In one room you hear how wine was made in the basement by an Italian immigrant family; in another, you see pictures and hear stories of a wedding that was held by a Hmong family for their daughter. In addition to these sentimental stories, some offer the perspectives of children. For example, one story tells of how a bed breaks, while the bed in the exhibit room crashes to the floor automatically to help illustrate the tale. All together, these stories provide a rich tale of oral histories of the lives of common Minnesotans from different backgrounds. The exhibit helps visitors to understand what Minnesotans' lives were like in certain periods as well as the diverse customs of the immigrants who chose to come to the state.

Minnesota History Center Educational Programs

Despite the explicit design for engaging visitors in the exhibits physically, intellectually, and emotionally, the museum provides very little structure when students visit the main exhibits. This is in large part because the exhibits are designed to be inherently engaging for students, and the staff believe the students should have the opportunity to explore and experience what the exhibits have to offer. They do offer three activities to visiting groups as a form of structure. The first, "Explore," is essentially a scavenger hunt that will push students to explore the exhibits. The second, "Museum Marvels," may be an interesting one for younger students. It asks students to seek out an object in the museum that they find to be particularly marvelous, take a picture of it (chaperones are provided with cameras), and then describe the reasons for their choice—which could be a nice follow-up activity back at school.

The final activity, and probably the most thoughtfully structured, is "Now on Display." This activity asks students to take the role of curator and asks them to essentially create their own exhibit using the various objects and artifacts that are in the History Center. They then use a booklet to sketch a design of their exhibit and explain the choices for their theme and design. Students could be issued digital cameras so that they could put together simple virtual museums as an assignment when they return to school to explain their own exhibit. This kind of activity may be useful to help students to understand how museums construct particular stories through the interweaving of stories, artifacts, and designed experiences.

Most of the school groups, however, spend their time exploring the museum with little structure. This is partially because of the logistical challenge presented when 400 middle-school students show up at once, as was the case on one visit. It is also in part because the museum staff assume teachers will provide structure for students and believe that, because of the design of the museum, little formal activity may be necessary for students to engage and learn. Although it seems to be the case that young visitors are very engaged during their visits, it is hard to tell what exactly they learned from the experience. What the museum does provide, however, is ample material to both engage students' motivation in the museum and opportunities to develop empathy skills in identifying perspectives through quality oral and local history projects that tell the story of Minnesota. These opportunities also provide a model for conducting similar projects when they return home.

ACTIVITIES FOR A VISIT TO THE MINNESOTA HISTORY CENTER

Here we describe two cases of pre-visit lessons, activities for visiting the History Center, and follow-up activities that were used after the visits. The first focuses on the visit and exploring the stories of immigrant and social history that are told throughout the History Center's many exhibits. The second uses the visit as a springboard for students to engage in their own local history projects. Both of these activities align with the overall museum goals of attaining social history and exploring the past through oral histories, local historic sites, and stories. The activities also use the museum exhibits in a powerful way to engage students in thinking about the past and how it is constructed and presented.

Activity #1: Experiencing Minnesota Immigrant and Social History

Overview

In this example, Ms. Swenson has her seventh-grade U.S. history students explore the powerful stories and oral histories told in the History Center exhibits and ties them to her history curriculum. One goal of the seventh-grade curriculum is to help students make explicit connections between the larger events of U.S. history and how these events connect to, or impact, Minnesotans and events in Minnesota history. For example, students need to know about immigration during the late 1800s and early 1900s, as well as in more recent periods, and to be able to explain how these waves of immigration impacted Minnesota. Similarly, they need to learn about the contributions of Minnesotans in the domestic and overseas efforts during World War II. Further, one of the skills objectives for the middle grades is the ability to recognize how the way history is presented, in different forms and using different types of evidence, impacts how history is told and understood.

Objectives

- Students will be able to describe the rich history of Minnesota immigrant communities and the contributions of specific immigrant groups.
- Students will recognize the perspectives of immigrant groups, their struggles, and their accomplishments.
- Students will be able to identify their affective reaction to the exhibits and how the design of the exhibit shapes what they learn about the stories being told.
- Students will learn about the key economic, social, and cultural contributions of Minnesota's residents during the twentieth century (and World War II specifically).

Pre-Visit Activities

In the days leading up to their visit, Ms. Swenson has her students explore demographic trends in Minnesota history, revisiting what the class learned about American Indian groups, such as the Ojibwe and Dakota, and the arrival of immigrant groups from northern European and Scandinavian countries during the nineteenth century. She uses this lesson to examine the arrival of later immigrant groups, such as the Irish and Italian immigrants of the early 1900s, African Americans that arrived as part of the Great Migration, and the most recent immigrants from east Africa (e.g. Somalia, Ethiopia) and southeast Asia (e.g. Hmong, Vietnamese).

After providing a general overview and timeline, Ms. Swenson breaks the class into groups and has them explore demographic information from GIS and census maps on the arrivals of different immigrant groups. She provides some guiding questions for this research activity, including: when did this group arrive in Minnesota? Why did they emigrate from their home countries or other parts of the U.S. (e.g. conflict, occupations)? Why did these groups select Minnesota as their new home? What are the particular group characteristics (e.g. what part of the state did they settle in? Are there particular customs or occupations?)? Finally, what contributions have these groups made to the larger Minnesota history and culture? The student groups then present their findings.

These presentations provide background and insights into the reasons for both emigration and immigration for the different major groups. For example, students learned that many of the Germans who came to Minnesota in the mid-1800s were fleeing religious persecution; that many of the Hmong and Vietnamese who came in the 1970s were refugees of the Vietnam War, and were sponsored by Christian aid groups and the federal government; and that more recent groups of Somali and Ethiopian refugees were fleeing violence and famine in their home countries. These presentations added depth to the common story of Minnesota as the destination for primarily Scandinavian farmers. The group presenting on the different American Indian nations also uses maps to show the shifting and then shrinking territory these groups called home over the past two hundred years and ties it back to topics they discussed earlier in the year.

In addition to looking at various ethnic groups in Minnesota, Ms. Swenson reviews with students the major events and milestones in Minnesota history that they studied during the year, including the participation in various wars, the role of the state economically (e.g. grain production, agriculture in general, manufacturing), and important Minnesotans who had an impact on a national level (e.g. Hubert Humphrey). This activity helps students to prepare for the different stories and groups of Minnesota residents they will encounter at the History Center, and it provides insights into the major demographic and historic changes in the state in general. She also ties the demographic activity to the history of the students' suburban community and the history and population shifts that have occurred. During these preparation activities she uses some of the archives from the Minnesota Historical Society website to prep students for engaging the types of media and oral histories that they will encounter.

During-Visit Activities

During their visit to the History Center, Ms. Swenson asks students to explore the museum with a particular purpose. She instructs students to keep a record of their reactions to each of the major exhibits, "Minnesota's Greatest Generation," "Open House," and "Weather Permitting," in a museum journal. In particular, she asks students to pick out one particular story or object from each exhibit that they find most interesting. Ms. Swenson explains to the students that they are to fill out their journals as they work through the museum by describing the object or story and their reaction to it, how it made them feel, what it made them think about, and what they found interesting about it. They also need to record a description of the actual object or exhibit and how it was designed.

This journal activity provides a record of the students' experiences in the History Center and allows students to choose what they find interesting while also assuring that they make it to each of the major exhibits. As these exhibits are designed around particular stories that the History Center has collected, the exhibits provide insights into the Minnesota social history and events in which Minnesotans have been involved. For example, some students selected the C-47 paratrooper experience as the object for the "Minnesota's Greatest Generation" exhibit and explained why they found this interesting. One student, who also mentioned that he had seen the HBO series *Band of Brothers* (2001), said, "The paratrooper simulation helped me to think about how scary it would have been to be a paratrooper . . . just sitting in the plane waiting to drop into gunfire." Other students found a personal connection to one of the stories in "Open House," as they had relatives or neighbors who once worked at the same factories as one of the house's former residents. One student, whose mother works at one of the newer St. Paul microbreweries, noted that it was interesting that St. Paul had a long history of brewing and "how much bigger that brewery seemed to be than the one my mom works at."

Post-Visit Activities

The day after their trip to the museum, Ms. Swenson polls students to see which exhibits they found to be most interesting and creates a list of them on the board. She then places the students in small groups and asks them to talk about one of their selected objects or stories and explain why they found it interesting and how it made them feel. In particular, she asks what aspects of the story or object really pulled them into the exhibit. As part of this, she also has them describe the object or story in some detail—who told the story or what did the object represent? She then leads the class in a larger discussion of some of the most popular exhibits and the reasons students selected them. This activity helps students to both tie the stories and objects back to what they had learned about Minnesota and U.S. history, and also to understand that different students experienced the exhibits differently and found particular stories more or less interesting.

This project could also be used to begin an investigation of the experiences of a local group or the history of a local industry or event that impacted the area (e.g. tornado, closing of a factory). This extension of the social history inquiry sparked by the museum visit could focus on how an event may have impacted different groups of people in the state or local area. Or, similar to the "Now on Display" activity described above, students could design their own small exhibit that explains a story that is significant either to them personally or related to a larger historic event, or the experience of a relative, neighbor, or friend. They could use what they learned about the emotional reaction to the exhibits at the History Center to design their own engaging object-based exhibit.

Activity #2: Local and Oral History Projects

Overview

In this case, Mr. Ibrahim uses the museum field trip both as part of his curriculum and as a way to jump-start his juniors in their local history project for his U.S. history class. The general focus for the project is for students to conduct an original inquiry into a local history topic (e.g. oral history of local residents, the history of local buildings or structures, or the history of important local events). As the History Center exhibits reflect what he sees as ideal examples of what he hopes students will attain, he uses a visit to the museum from his Twin Cities high school as a way to get his students started on their projects. Some of these projects are also used as part of the National History Day in Minnesota competition. As the History Center exhibits fit in with teaching twentieth-century social history, he takes them early in the spring when they begin studying immigration and industrialization at the turn of the century. This way, the visit is also an introduction to life during and after World War II, which comes later in the semester. This also provides time for students to do their projects in time for the National History in Minnesota regional competition for those who want to compete. National History Day is sponsored by the Minnesota Historical Society and the University of Minnesota and is very popular across the state.

Objectives
- To develop skills in doing local and oral history projects (e.g. analysis, interviews).
- To be able to recognize perspectives of different cultures and from different time periods.
- To understand the social history and culture of Minnesotans.
- To develop empathy for the experiences of others in the past.

Pre-Visit Activities

As preparation for the visit, Mr. Ibrahim, much like Ms. Swenson in the earlier example, has students investigate the various immigrant groups that have come to Minnesota, focusing in particular on groups represented in the Twin Cities area. He also has students look at their own family histories and how they came to arrive in the Twin Cities. As the visit is also a way to help students learn about doing oral and local history, Mr. Ibrahim often has had a local public historian or a staff member from the historical society come out and talk about the methods used for doing oral history and the history of buildings, including the types of evidence or data collection that would be used, the types of questions to ask, the sources or evidence to search for, and where the students can find them (e.g. historical society, state or county government archives). When he cannot arrange for a historian to speak to the class, he uses resources from the historical society website. The website provides materials for conducting oral and building history, and examples of these projects for students to use. Of course, both of these models are used heavily in the History Center exhibits. In the past, he has also arranged for his students to meet with a member of the historical society staff, whose offices are in the History Center, to talk about techniques and show the resources available for students and their projects.

The goal of these pre-visit activities is to encourage students to think about the experiences and backgrounds of Minnesotans in history and to encourage them to think about the work of historians in doing these types of local history projects. Mr. Ibrahim finishes the pre-visit activities by having students start a list of local topics, events, people, and buildings that they may want to investigate more closely for their projects. He notes that many of these initial ideas transformed into their local history projects as students are often already interested in the history of a relative or neighbor or a building in their neighborhood.

During-Visit Activities

As part of their visit to the History Center, Mr. Ibrahim has students do a critique of the exhibits. He asks them to pick out the exhibit or a portion of the exhibit that they think is most compelling and well presented, somewhat similar to Ms. Swenson. However, instead of just thinking about how it engages them, he asks his students to evaluate the story being told, the evidence used, and the overall aesthetics of the exhibit. He provides them with the following questions to help guide their critiques:

- Which of the stories/objects/exhibits do you find most compelling? Why?
- What is significant about the story being told?
- Who is the story about? What larger group narratives or histories does this story illustrate (if any)?
- How does this story fit into larger national or global stories and histories?
- What evidence is used?
- How is the story structured (e.g. visually, sound, simulation, interactive objects)?
- What is missing? What is not convincing about the exhibit?
- What might you change to make the exhibit more compelling?

Many of Mr. Ibrahim's students are themselves first- or second-generation immigrants of southeast Asian or African descent, and they are particularly interested in the "Open

House" exhibit. Many compare their personal stories with the stories of the Hmong immigrants in the "Open House" exhibit, but also find many parallels to the stories of early European immigrants. For example, a student named Rahman, whose family are immigrants from Bangladesh, talks about how his family came to St. Paul because a relative was able to get his mother a job at a local manufacturing facility, and how similar that is to the experience of the early German and Italian immigrants who worked in different industrial jobs.

Post-Visit Activities

After their visit, Mr. Ibrahim has students share their experiences and critiques, first in smaller groups and then a selected number of students present larger themes to the whole class. Students then discuss their reactions and the similarities or differences to their critiques. Finally, Mr. Ibrahim has the students reflect on the overall nature and goals of doing local history. The final assessment for the museum experience includes both their written exhibit critique and a short essay that responds to the following questions:

- Is this history? Why?
- Why is this kind of history important?
- Why might it be important to capture and store these stories from the perspectives of ordinary people or the history of local events and places?

Mr. Ibrahim then uses this activity as a springboard into the students' own local history projects. The students use what they learned from the oral and local history workshop and their analysis of the History Center exhibits prominently as they conduct and present their projects. Students have the option of choosing (as a group or individually) to embark on one of the following projects: an oral history project to understand perspectives and experiences of a relative, neighbor or acquaintance who participated in or experienced a significant historical event; an inquiry into a local historical event (e.g. a labor strike) that was significant in shaping the history of the area or community; or the study of a historic building in town (e.g. historic meaning old, visible, or maybe even infamous) to understand its original purpose, who lived or worked there over the years, and its importance to the local community. Many of his students end up making a return visit to the History Center to access state history archives housed there by the Minnesota Historical Society as part of their research.

REFLECTIONS ON THE CASES

The cases of Ms. Swenson and Mr. Ibrahim illustrate two approaches to using the strengths of a state history museum to work in a way that aligns with both the content and skills they want students to develop in their classes. Both rely on a body of knowledge and experience, as well as resources, but most of these can be easily attained through working with the History Center or historical society staff. It is also important to recognize, similar to the case in Chapter 3, that these activities take time, and that all aspects of the preparation, day of visit, and post-visit activities are important for an effective experience. The models presented here, however, encourage students to both experience aspects of perspectives on the past and provide windows for their own development in conducting historical inquiry, as well as understanding the nature of history and how it is constructed.

Suggestions for Developing Activities for State History Museums

State history museums present many of the same attributes and challenges to the artifact and display museums described in Chapter 3. The effective strategies outlined at the end of that chapter readily apply for a visit to a state history museum, and generally to any museum visit. These include developing clear learning objectives for students, visiting the museum and museum website prior to the student visit, collaborating with museum staff, preparing students for the visit, following up with students after the visit, establishing high academic standards for museum visits, taking advantage of museum resources and activities that are not available in the classroom, and allowing students some freedom and choice while keeping them focused on core ideas and objectives (see Chapter 3 for an in-depth discussion of these features).

In addition, state history museums and the specific case for the Minnesota History Center require some further considerations. Both Ms. Swenson and Mr. Ibrahim have taken advantage of the vast resources available at the History Center and Historical Society. Similarly, many state history museums also house state archives or access to archives, and have the resources and expertise contained in a state historical society. These resources are vital for teachers who want their students to conduct research into state, family, or even local topics. These state records and historical archives provide data and insights into the past through documents and other materials that may not be accessed in other ways. They also provide the opportunity to engage with materials that historians use regularly, from census records to copies of property deeds, but that students will often not engage with in a history class.

Because of its unique design and emphasis on interactive exhibits and social history, the Minnesota History Center presents enormous opportunities for history teachers, but it also presents some challenges. It is easy to get excited and go from exhibit to exhibit— experiencing a tornado in a basement, trying on winter clothes, making ammunition, working behind the counter of a 1940s-era soda fountain—and fail to reflect on the stories being told and how you understand them as history. It is easy to view these exhibits through our experiences today and not place them into the context of the time. For example, what did the paratroopers really feel as their plane went up in flames? Or what was it like to live in tenement housing at the turn of the century? The level of interaction and affective appeal of the exhibits presents a challenge for teachers. Reproduction artifacts present many advantages as well as challenges. They provide the opportunity for students to get hands-on experience and the opportunity to construct historical understanding through the interactions. It is key, however, to help students recognize the limits to what they can learn from those artifacts based on what they know about their origins, purposes, and contexts. These artifacts can and should be used, however, to dig deeper into inquiry into the past and to generate questions. Teachers can similarly use "museum in a box" types of programs to bring reproduction artifacts into their classes to engage their students (see Chapter 9 for more on museum kits).

Separate Engagement from Authenticity from Interpretation

The strengths of the interactive model used at the Minnesota History Center are easily apparent, especially when it comes to motivating and engaging visitors. It is also a model that lends itself to the types of social history, empathetic understanding, and the recognition of perspectives that are the goals for the History Center. There are also challenges for museum staff, and particularly for teachers, in making sure students go beyond the immediate physical and mental stimulus provided in the exhibits and move into the intellectual, reflective, and analytical stances that will help them develop a better understanding of the rich history that the exhibits illustrate. As the exhibits are designed around general theories about learning and motivation, such as multiple intelligences, they are less focused on engaging students in authentic disciplinary-based historical thinking practices. This is a major tension that museum educators and teachers face with this style of a museum—the tension between motivating and engaging students actively with artifacts and the represented past, and helping students to recognize the limits of their own understanding of the past.

In order to help students recognize how these exhibits construct the past and promote particular narratives through visitor engagement in these exhibits, both Ms. Swenson and Mr. Ibrahim asked students to collect specific types of information related to their goals. This provided some focus and structure so that students would reflect on what they were experiencing during their visit without detracting from the engagement. The debriefing of the visit is also critical. Both teachers engaged students in reflection and discussions on the content they wanted students to learn, as well as an examination of the exhibits and work of the museum staff in designing the exhibits. By asking students to think about the design of the exhibits, and decisions the museum designers made to engage them, students begin to think more meta-cognitively about the experience. They begin to separate their excitement in the moment in order to examine the power of the exhibits to engage them with the past in particular ways. This allows students to see how the museum's decisions influenced what they learned at the museum. This is similar to a historiographical analysis of historical writing, with the exhibits and the stories they tell being analyzed as a form of "text."

Both of the museums discussed thus far—the United States Holocaust Memorial Museum and the Minnesota History Center—provide emotional and affective-generating experiences. The USHMM uses the power of its story, artifacts, and architecture to draw in visitors and tell a compelling story that is visceral and engaging, even horrifying. The History Center also draws in visitors emotionally and affectively, but it is a more physical and kinetic emotional experience, different from that of visiting the USHMM or most other artifact and display museums. For educators, both museums present a similar challenge. They are not designed to encourage critical reflection on the part of visitors, nor do they. In addition, they do not require vast amounts of interpretation, as the stories are told visually, through audio soundtracks, and even with film or special effects. This makes the experience all the more authentic for visitors, but may also lead young people to believe that they have a fuller understanding of the events or issues being explored than is actually possible.

Aim to Develop Empathy, Not Sympathy

The challenge these museums pose is that they make students sympathize with those whose story is being told as a result of the emotion and even adrenaline the museum engagement causes. This is why Barton and Levstik (2004) use the term "perspective recognition" versus empathy or perspective taking. The emphasis in the debriefing of a visit is to help students recognize the perspectives of the people or groups whose stories were told in the museums while also recognizing that they can never fully know what it was like to be a victim or even bystander of the Holocaust, nor can they understand what it would have been like to live during the Great Depression or work in a World War II munitions factory.

This does not mean students cannot relate to some of the artifacts and stories told in these museums and develop empathy. This notion of empathy instead should focus on aspects of the decision-making and experiences of people that are more easily understood and for which there is evidence to provide their perspectives. State history museums have the potential to provide powerful experiences for students in thinking about and understanding the past of their local area and the people who live there. These institutions also help visitors to understand the role of the state and its citizens in world and national events, and to help place these larger events within a local or regional context. For example, Ms. Swenson's students will be able to place their understanding of immigrant groups who came to Minnesota within the larger waves of immigration to the United States and the worldwide events that triggered these mass migrations. This is a particularly poignant goal for a visit to a state history museum, as the ability to recognize the perspectives and contributions of the various groups who reside in the state (or next door) is fundamental for young citizens. It is the teachers' job to help them make sense of their experiences and develop a complex understanding of their engagements in these museums. This is a common theme that carries through the remaining chapters, and becomes even more relevant when students participate in living history or explore an actual historic site.

NOTE

1   Thanks to Wendy Jones and the Minnesota History Center staff for the information and materials they shared. Also thanks to the Minnesota Historical Society, the History Center's parent organization. Founded in 1849, the Society is a non-profit organization that serves as the chief caretaker of Minnesota's story.

RESOURCES

Minnesota Historical Society—State Archives: www.mnhs.org/preserve/records/index.htm

Minnesota History Center: www.minnesotahistorycenter.org

Resources for conducting a building or house history: www.mnhs.org/localhistory/bldghistory/househistory.htm

Resources for conducting oral history: www.mnhs.org/collections/oralhistory/oralhistory.htm

Tennessee State Museum Traveling Trunks: www.tnmuseum.org/Teachers/Traveling_Trunks

CHAPTER 5

Historic Forts

The Fort at No. 4 and Fort Ticonderoga

Figure 5.1 The outer wall at Fort Ticonderoga.

INTRODUCTION

From the historic 1672 masonry walls of the Spanish Castillo de San Marcos in Saint Augustine, Florida, to the US Air Force's 1963 Minuteman Missile launch facilities near Rapid City, South Dakota, the United States bristles with historic forts. Each of them marks a formerly crucial site of defense, conflict, and/or intercultural contact in American history. There are forts that cover every chronological period of the American past, every significant conflict, every avenue of westward migration and expansion, and every effort to put an "American" (or British, French, Spanish, or Dutch) stamp on a continent and its people. Historic forts survive today in a variety of modes: as archaeological sites, as original structures, as partially preserved historic sites adapted to modern usages, and as imaginative reconstructions. But no matter what their form, historic forts are exceptionally productive sites for helping students understand historical narratives, view the past from multiple perspectives, connect the past to the present, explore the nature of and dimensions of conflict, and appreciate the ways in which geography influences history. These advantages are sometimes offset by a triumphantly and uncritically patriotic interpretive approach, but even at such forts, a skillful and alert teacher can turn the most biased, mono-dimensional interpretation of history to students' advantage.

This chapter focuses on two specific forts as cases highlighting some of the student learning experiences forts and related historic sites can provide. The Fort at No. 4, along the Connecticut River at Charlestown, New Hampshire, is a modern reconstruction of a garrison compound that originally stood a short distance south of the present-day site. A palisade-enclosed area of interconnected wooden structures with a guard tower, it was associated with the defense of English settlers during the French and Indian wars of the 1740s through 1760s.

Fort Ticonderoga, located at the portage between Lake Champlain and Lake George in upstate New York, was built by the French as Fort Carillon between 1754 and 1757. It was captured and renamed Ticonderoga by the British in 1759. During the American Revolution, control of it was sought by both the British and American armies, and the fort changed hands several times.

Both Ticonderoga and the Fort at No. 4 provide unique opportunities and pose special educational challenges for teachers. Together they exhibit many of the features common to historic forts that make them such fruitful places for education and provide a rounded example of beneficial ways forts and related historic sites can assist K-12 student learning. We begin this chapter with a brief review of the background of historic site preservation in America, and then turn to a discussion of the attributes and the pedagogical issues and opportunities forts raise. We follow with the two cases and detail examples of how teachers are taking pedagogical advantage of their visits to these forts. Finally, we close with suggestions on how to use forts effectively as laboratories for student learning.[1]

Historic Site Preservation in America

The historic site movement in America began during the last decade of the nineteenth century, when powerful veterans' organizations, concerned in part about the preservation of their Civil War legacy, began to press the federal War Department to protect and conserve major battlefields and military posts. A decade later, the federal Antiquities Act of 1906 authorized the president to reserve as national monuments "historic landmarks, historic and prehistoric structures" and other historically significant sites (Mackintosh, 1985, p. 1). Spurred by the creation of the National Park Service in 1916, the 1920s and early 1930s witnessed the preservation of an array of archaeological sites, battlefields and forts, among them the Colonial National Monument (see Chapter 7, on Jamestown and Yorktown) and Morristown National Historical Park in New Jersey. In 1935, the federal Historic Sites Act called for a thorough survey of all historic sites in the country to determine those sites "which possess exceptional value as commemorating or illustrating the history of the United States." Such sites would then be preserved by the National Park Service (Mackintosh, 1985, p. 120).

The actual survey began in August of 1936, and by 1943 it had inventoried 560 historic places, 229 of which were found to be nationally significant and 18 of which had been formally designated national historic sites. World War II brought a suspension of the survey and it was not reinitiated until 1956, when its restart dovetailed with the establishment of the National Historic Landmark program. Recognizing that it would be impossible to bring every significant historical site into the National Park system, a program was established to provide federal recognition of a place's importance without obligating the government to fund its operation or maintenance. An initial 92 historic sites were placed on the national register of historic landmarks in October of 1960. By early 1961, 213 sites were newly designated National Historic Landmarks, including the U.S. Capitol, Monticello, Fort Larned, Fort Bowie, and the Springfield Armory. In the years since then, the selection of historic landmarks has continued apace. By 1984, the total number of landmarks had expanded to 1,600, and in the years since then the definition of what constitutes a historically significant site has been expanded to include virtually every type of facility we have denoted in this book as a museum. Today, the number on the national register of historic landmarks sites exceeds 80,000 (Mackintosh, 1985).

Although "historic landmarks" as currently defined is an expansive category, we have chosen in this chapter to focus on historic forts. Not only are they one of the most common types of historic sites, they offer exceptional opportunities for teachers seeking to incorporate museums into their teaching. Other types of historic sites (e.g. historic houses, monuments, artifact museums, archaeological sites) are covered in other chapters.

IMPORTANT CHARACTERISTICS OF HISTORIC FORTS

Regardless of their location, or the reasons for their existence, historic forts share a number of inherently useful attributes that make them excellent teaching places. Forts can help students to understand the role of geography in history, to explore power and authority, to see history through multiple perspectives, to explore the differences between history and heritage, to engage with archaeological evidence, and to examine the role of women in history.

Forts Highlight the Importance of Geography in History

People who build forts take pains to locate them at places that provide military or politically strategic advantages. For that reason, they are superb places to get students thinking deeply about geography. Using maps and on-site observation, students and teachers can ponder questions such as: Why was this site chosen instead of various alternatives? What military or political advantages did this location and its geographic features (rivers, mountains, forests, plains, etc.) provide? From whom were the fort's occupants seeking protection? What groups and places did the fort protect or control? Why did the builders use the materials they did (e.g. stone, wood, dirt) and why did they use a particular shape? From Fort Sumter (built to defend the seaborne approaches to Charleston Harbor from foreign assault, but later seen as a site of Northern aggression by South Carolina secessionists) to Fort Machilimackinac in northern Michigan (site of the first land battle of the War of 1812) to Bents Old Fort in LaJunta, Colorado (where traders, trappers, and Plains Indians came together to exchange goods in the 1840s), historic forts are literally landmarks of geographic learning.

Forts are Expressions of Power and Authority by One Group over Others

From Fort McHenry in Baltimore Harbor (the place where Francis Scott Key wrote "The Star-Spangled Banner" in 1814) to Fort Caroline in Jacksonville (where French colonists laid claim to the Florida peninsula in 1564), no structure better expresses one group's assertion of authority over others than a fort. Forts are always built to assert or defend control at a place where challenges to that control are anticipated. For that reason, they are excellent sites to explore questions about the nature of power and governmental authority. Why did the builders of a fort believe they should control the area in which they built their fort? Who did they expect to oppose them? Which group had the best claim to authority at that place? Why? Such questions often are very useful in preparing students to think about fort visits in a broad historical context.

Forts Provide Opportunities to Examine the Past From Multiple Perspectives

Because forts are located at the nexus of anticipated conflict between groups competing for control over a region, they are excellent locations to teach students to think about history from multiple perspectives. At Civil War Fort Donelson, for example, students can examine how the construction in 1861 of a Confederate fort to defend the Cumberland River approaches to Tennessee and Kentucky was perceived by both Southern sympathizers and the citizens of the border state of Kentucky. Students can then examine how the same people felt about the fort's occupation by Northern forces following its defeat and subsequent capture by Union forces under General Ulysses S. Grant in February 1862. This type of analysis of multiple perspectives is inherent in the history of many forts. How did the fort's builders feel about the site they built? Was it adequate to defend the claims their government was making about the region? What was life like for the fort's occupants? How did the people living near the fort feel about its presence? Did attitudes about the fort in question change over time? As sights created to meet anticipated challenges or conflict, forts readily lend themselves to the useful analysis of multiple (and often competing) perspectives.

Forts also promote an understanding of multiple perspectives because during the centuries of American expansion, forts were often built on the margins of settlement, at places that brought peoples of many different cultures into contact, and sometimes conflict. Fort Vancouver National Historic Site in Vancouver, Washington, fur-trading headquarters of the Hudson Bay Company during the years before America acquired undisputed control of the Oregon Territory in 1848, is a classic example (Davison, 2010). The polyglot community of the fort and surrounding environs brought Scottish, Irish, Hawaiian, Chinook and other indigenous groups of people into close contact for many decades. Many forts were similar sites of intercultural contact and exchange, and offer important opportunities for teachers to lead student inquiry into the coming together of different cultures. How did different people communicate? What motives brought these different groups together? Did one group have advantage or authority over another? How did they resolve conflicts? Forts that produced significant contacts among people from numerous cultures are excellent places to examine in microcosm the kinds of questions that will be crucial to understanding life in a future "global village."

Forts Can Be Used to Explore the Differences Between History and Heritage

Because many historic forts and related sites were the focal points of significant loss of human life and memorable acts of courage, they often become "sacred ground"—a place where survivors and descendants gather to commemorate and remember the actions of those who fought. Such commemorations are usually patriotic and celebratory, focused on a perspective that honors and valorizes the participants. Washington's Revolutionary War winter encampment at Valley Forge, Pennsylvania, is described by the US National Park Service as such a place: "Few places evoke the spirit of patriotism and independence, represent individual and collective sacrifice, or demonstrate the resolve, tenacity and determination of the people of the United States to be free as does Valley Forge" (National Park Service, 2011). These expressions of pride in *heritage*—a particular perspective that promotes patriotism and appreciation for the courageous actions of one group's predecessors—provide a useful service. Often, too, they are marked by the placement of monuments to signify the importance of the battle or events within the battle (see Chapter 8 on monuments). They impose a duty on present and future generations to continue to honor past sacrifices and to be willing to endure such sacrifices in the service of the nation if called upon to do so in the future.

Yet celebrations of heritage, which often take an uncritically positive view of the complex causes and effects of conflict, should not be allowed to overpower or substitute for a nuanced and critical examination of causes and effects. The winter weather endured by Washington's army at Morristown, New Jersey, two years after the 1777 winter at Valley Forge, for example, was decidedly harsher than the one we commemorate. Teachers can help develop students' ability to think critically and realistically about historical events by supplementing heritage-focused interpretations of historic forts with study of the attitudes of others affected by the conflict (e.g. military opponents, civilians affected by the battle, etc.), even while celebrating acts of heroism and courage in the national interest.

Forts are Often Accompanied by Archaeological Artifacts that Serve as Historical Evidence

One of the important sources of knowledge about many historic sites comes from the archaeological artifacts found during excavations of a fort and its surrounding environs. At St. Augustine, Florida, for example, much of the knowledge we have about the ten sixteenth- and seventeenth-century wooden forts built prior to the 1672 construction of the masonry-walled Castillo de San Marcos comes from the extensive archaeological excavations conducted on and around the 20.5 acre site. The artifacts found in these digs have provided crucial evidence in helping determine the pattern of activities of the site's residents, and the food and lifestyles that evolved in the fort's unique environment (Manucy, 1997). The presence of archaeological artifacts at forts offer students two effective learning opportunities: (1) exploring artifacts in relation to the places in which they were found for the evidence they contain; (2) exploring artifacts in combination with written evidence to determine how these two categories of evidence support or refute each other. The importance of archaeological artifacts is also discussed in Chapter 7 on living history museums.

Forts Can Advance the Study of Women in History

Historic forts, because they were usually occupied primarily by male military personnel, are often thought of as bastions of masculinity and male social relations. Yet in the historic period virtually every military camp relied heavily on the services of many women to support the logistical needs of the garrison as cooks, nurses, seamstresses, laundresses, wives, and (occasionally) sex workers. The efforts of these women were often overlooked in past histories that focused primarily on soldiers' memoirs and official records. Today historians have proven quite adept at gathering evidence in diaries, letters, and other sources of the crucial importance of women's activities at historic forts. These artifacts offer important opportunities to engage female students in the study of a place they might otherwise see as male-centered and less engaging. At historic Fort Snelling, in St. Paul, Minnesota, for example, field trips include significant exposure to the crucial roles played by women in supporting the logistical needs of the fort, as well as learning about the often unheralded role of Mrs. Dred Scott (an antebellum resident of Fort Snelling) in that crucial pre-Civil War Supreme Court decision.

THE FORT AT NO. 4

The Fort at No. 4 was originally constructed in 1743, in anticipation of renewed hostilities between English settlers and French troops from Canada and their Native American allies. This northernmost English fortification and settlement along the Connecticut River was a crucial site of international conflict, intercultural contact, trade, and expansion until well after the French and Indian War ended in 1763. It is closely associated with the 1759 military exploits of Robert Rogers, whose Ranger troops were the predecessors of today's Army Special Forces. It is also remembered as the site in 1754 of the captivity of Susannah Johnson by Abenaki Indians, whose subsequent account of her ordeal became one of the period's most widely read captivity narratives. Following the American Revolution, the fort site fell into disuse and evolved into the town of Charlestown, New Hampshire.

In 1948, a group of patriotic descendants of the region's original settlers created a non-profit organization to preserve the history of the fort by constructing a replica of it as a living history museum. Fort drawings, maps, letters, and even powder horns were used to design the replica as close to the original as possible. Construction began in 1960 with the building of a palisade and single house at a site along the Connecticut River a short distance north of the original fort. It continued intermittently into the mid-1990s. Today the Fort at No. 4 consists of a number of interconnected houses and lean-tos within the palisade, each staged to represent the status and employments of the house's original occupants. The reconstructed Fort at No. 4 not only reflects historians' best understanding of the design of the original, it displays various changes in reconstruction techniques as they evolved during the fort's development.

The Fort at No. 4 is open seasonally from May through the end of October, and is staffed entirely by unpaid volunteers, most of whom dress in period costume and tell visitors about life and crafts as practiced in the eighteenth-century fort. Most present in the third person, as costumed-but-contemporary narrators, describing the history of the fort. Some, especially on special occasions, present in the first person as "living history" interpreters, simulating a real person or type of person resident at the original

Figure 5.2 The Fort at No. 4.

Source: Photo courtesy of James Lawyer Photography.

fort. The Fort at No. 4 hosts special events such as an annual French and Indian War encampment, and eighteenth-century prayer services on a few Sundays during the summer.

Activities for a Visit to the Fort at No. 4

Overview

For Bruce Patten, a 34-year-old middle-school social studies teacher in an independent school in central New Hampshire, the Fort at No. 4 is an ideal place at which to help his students understand the importance of the French and Indian wars of empire in United States history. A Massachusetts native who spent his summers kayaking along the Connecticut River, Patten had always appreciated the importance of the 410-mile-long river as a corridor of migration, culture, trade, and war. His seventh-graders' field trip to the Fort at No. 4 is the culminating event of a unit in which he teaches the colonial history of New England by focusing on the river. Patten begins his unit with a two-day geography lesson focused on settlement and migration up the river valley in the seventeenth and eighteenth centuries.

Objectives

His goals for this unit are ambitious and include:

- Students will understand the importance of river systems (and particularly the Connecticut River) as channels of commerce, conflict, contact, and intercultural communication during the seventeenth and eighteenth centuries.

- Students will understand how geography shapes the way in which people meet their needs for food, clothing, and shelter.
- Students will know the general sites of settlement of the major indigenous tribal bands in New England prior to their contact with Europeans.
- Students will understand the pattern of English and French settlement in New England and Canada in the 1600s and 1700s, and how these influenced relations with Native peoples.
- Students will explore the general chronology and spatial dimensions of European settlement along the Connecticut River from 1635 to 1763, the conflicts that ensued following that settlement, and the impact upon intercultural relations.
- Students will analyze the personal experience of settlement and conflict from the perspective of a variety of participants—Native American and European, military and civilian.

Pre-Visit Activities

Mr. Patten begins the lesson by showing a relief map of New England, highlighting its rivers and mountain ranges. He shows areas occupied by different indigenous groups at the moment of first contact with Europeans. Using images representing different tribal encampments, he leads the students in a discussion of similarities and differences among different Indian groups, including sedentary agriculture versus hunting and gathering, seasonal occupations, reliance on game versus fish and shellfish, and how these differences were the product of geographic differences such as coastal, river, or interior settlement. At the end of the conversation he gives each student an outline map of New England showing the Connecticut River, and has the students write the names of each of the Indian groups (e.g. Mohegan) in its relative area of settlement along the Connecticut River.

In part two of this lesson, Mr. Patten displays the outline map with tribal locations and notes the locations and dates of settlement of the following Connecticut River towns: Saybrook, Connecticut (1635), Hartford, Connecticut (1636), Springfield, Massachusetts (1637), Northampton, Massachusetts (1654), Deerfield, Massachusetts (1673), Fort Dummer, Vermont (1724), and the Fort at No. 4, New Hampshire (1743). He queries students as to why the settlers would have preferred to settle along the river, and why the pattern of settlement over time was distinctively south to north. He also asks the students to speculate as to why there were fairly long gaps between the settlement of the towns formed after Springfield. He concludes the lesson by having the students add the English settlements to their outline maps of tribal settlements.

The next day Mr. Patten asks students to re-examine the outline maps they have made of early settlement and to revisit the question of why there were such long gaps in the settlement of upriver towns. Patten lists the students' responses on the class whiteboard. Usually, the students suggest the slow northern settlement was the result of logistical issues: distance from the ocean, slow population growth, and abundance of untaken land. Only rarely do the students suggest that Native American resistance to English expansion was a cause.

This allows Mr. Patten to transition into the subject of Native American resistance to English settlement. He asks the students to discuss how the Native people might have felt about this expanding English settlement. When prompted, the students generally agree the Native Americans would not have liked English expansion. When asked what the Native Americans would have done to resist expansion, some students suggest they would have fought against the English. When asked whether they did fight the English, the students are invariably unsure in their responses.

Patten next distributes a copy of Narragansett sachem Miantonomi's 1640s call for war against the English: "these English having gotten our land, . . . cut down the grass . . . fell the trees; their cows and horses eat the grass . . . their hogs spoil our clam banks, and we shall all be starved." The students read this aloud, and then are asked to enumerate Miantonomi's objections against the English and whether these warranted going to war against them, a question that often provokes spirited discussion. "The students are moved by Miantonomi's eloquence," Patten reports, "but are sharply divided on whether this is justification for war. What's important to me is that they now are really engaged in thinking about these issues."

Patten briefly describes and gives the dates of the first two intercultural conflicts in New England—the Pequot War (1637) and King Philip's War (1675–1677)—and asks how these wars might have been both related to and affected by expanding European occupation of native people's lands. Students are asked to examine their maps, and consider where dispossessed Indians might have gone after the wars. Patten notes that they ultimately resettled to the north and west of English settlement, and has the students draw new Indian settlements in the northern sections of their maps. The map now clearly shows that the northern border lands are slowly becoming the new homeland of dispossessed Indian groups, and sites of ever-increasing hostility to English expansion.

Comfortable that his students understand the patterns of settlement and native resistance to English expansion within New England, Mr. Patten shifts the scale of his geographic focus. He shows students a map of eastern North America depicting French and English settlement through 1763, and describes the settlement of Canada along the St. Lawrence river system. He notes traditional sources of conflict (e.g. religious and political) between England and France, and also how the French population of North America was much smaller than the English population, leading the French to establish early alliances with the Huron and Abenaki nations. He invites students to consider how the French desire for alliances might have affected their relations with those Indians dispossessed by English settlement. He then brings the students' attention back to their maps of the Connecticut River watershed and asks them to consider why the two northernmost (and last-settled) places along the Connecticut River were called "forts" instead of towns. "By this point in the unit," Patten notes,

> students have developed a fair understanding of how geography, settlement and expansion, Native American dispossession, and international politics shaped the lives of New England and its people during the colonial period. They have a visual sense of how these factors shaped the political geography of the region. Moving forward, I work to help them understand the personal dimensions of this era of conflict—how it felt to live along a river of war.

Mr. Patten follows the two-day geography mini-unit with lessons designed to show his students that for nearly a century, the Connecticut River was a theater of imperial struggle. European conflicts between England and France produced nearly continuous warfare between French Canada and New England. In an image-rich PowerPoint lecture he shows the chronic series of imperial wars between the French and British—such as King William's War (1689–1698), Queen Anne's War (1702–1713), Graylock's War (1723–1725), King George's War (1744–1748), and the French and Indian War (1754–1763)—and the Native American/European alliances that made these conflicts intercultural as well as international.

Shifting focus again from the continental perspective to the local, Patten asks his students to consider how the Connecticut River factored into these conflicts, and what effects nearly a century of warfare would have on Indians and Europeans. As a case study of this period he uses the 1704 French and Indian winter raid on Deerfield, Massachusetts. Patten guides his students through the "Raid on Deerfield: Many Stories of 1704" website (see Chapter 9 for a more detailed discussion of this online resource) and has them consider the events surrounding the attack on the English village of Deerfield by French and Indian forces from the different perspectives of the English, French, Mohawk, Huron, and Abenaki people involved in it. He distributes three primary-source accounts of the raid, and gives each student a card with the name of a person who experienced the raid. Students are to read the primary-source accounts, and then write an account of the attack in the first person using what they have learned about their character from the primary-source accounts. "This is usually a dramatic moment in our study of this period," Patten notes. "Some students are powerfully affected by imagining what this attack was like for their assigned person, and it comes out in their stories. It makes the patterns on the maps come alive in powerful and moving ways."

Mr. Patten follows this lesson on the Deerfield raid with one devoted to the experience (not uncommon among the English) of being taken captive by Native Americans and marched overland to Canada. Those who survived this grueling ordeal experienced a variety of futures: incorporation into Native American groups as adoptees or servants, integration into French communities, or ransom back to their English families. Patten uses clips from the film *Captive: The Story of Esther*, which documents the story of Esther Wheelwright, a young girl taken captive by Abenaki warriors in 1703. In Canada, Esther ultimately converted to Catholicism, refused to return to her family, and became an Ursuline nun. Patten contrasts Wheelwright's story with primary-source accounts of another captive, Susannah Johnson, taken just outside the Fort at No. 4 in August, 1754. Johnson gave birth to a daughter on the March to Canada, was held prisoner in the Native American town of St. Francis, then sold to a French family in Montreal, and finally was ransomed in 1757, returning to her home at the Fort at No. 4. "Johnson's vivid account is an excellent preparation for our field trip," Patten notes. 'She gives students a real glimpse of what life on the New England frontier was like and the captivity experience." Just prior to the field trip, Mr. Patten focuses student attention on the French and Indian War and the exploits of Robert Rogers and his rangers, a military unit closely associated with the Fort at No. 4. Patten says,

> By the time we visit the fort, my students have a very good sense of how it fit into the larger context of war and politics in early North America. But what they don't have is that experiential feel for what life on the New England frontier was like.

During-Visit Activities

Mr. Patten believes his students' visit to the Fort at No. 4 is a crucial moment in their historical understanding. "Here is where the abstractions we have been reading and

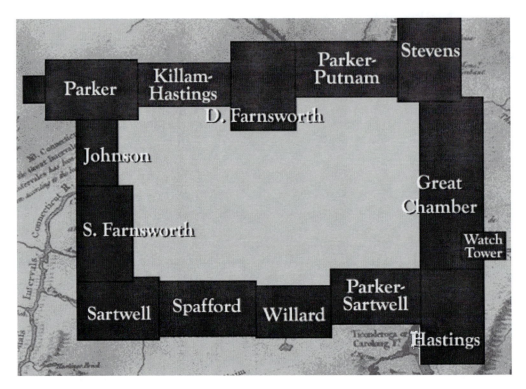

Figure 5.3 Residents of the interconnected structures at the Fort at No. 4.

Source: From the Fort at No. 4 Website.

talking about in class suddenly become material and very real. It's an eye- and mind-opening experience for students I can't imagine duplicating in class," he says.

Prior to entering the fort itself Mr. Patten walks his students into the Great Meadow between the fort and the Connecticut River to give them a feel for the wooden stockade and its geographic setting. He questions them as to why the fort would have been located so close to the river and why the fort's watchtower appears to only provide a clear view of the river side of the fort. This materializes for them the point he has been stressing in class about rivers as corridors of trade and conflict. Moving toward the fort itself, Mr. Patten asks them to speculate on why each of the posts in the stockade were set five inches apart from each other (answer: to prevent the French and Indians from easily setting fire to the fort).

Mr. Patten next leads the students and chaperones into the fort, where they gather in the interior courtyard and are met by the fort's volunteer guides. Prior to beginning the guided tour, Mr. Patten instructs his students to make note of three things they find most interesting about the tour that they will later be expected to share with their classmates.

The guides divide the students into groups of six to eight, and lead the students on a tour through each of the connected rooms/houses of the forts. Each of the residences—which range from plank-floored and plastered two-story houses to dirt-floored lean-tos, all interconnected—is staged to reflect the lifestyle, status, and occupation of the persons who occupied it in the 1740s and 1750s.

The Captain Phineas Stevens house, for example, in the southwest corner of the fort, is staged to reflect the life of a frontier merchant-trader, with trade goods (e.g. pipes, molasses, flour, salt, cloth), account books, and storage shelves. The John Hastings house is staged to reflect his occupation as the fort physician, with a variety of medicines and medical instruments. The lean-to of James and Susannah Johnson (the captive students read about prior to the trip) reflects the rustic temporary quarters of those who would have retreated to the fort from homes outside the stockade when attacks seemed imminent. Other areas focus on eighteenth-century textiles, cooking techniques and daily lives, while the Lieutenant Isaac Parker house reflects the upscale refinements of a relatively well-to-do frontier family. One of the lean-tos is staged as a Native interpretation area, with artifacts, birch-bark canoe, and a temporary wigwam—reproductions that enable guides to describe the lifestyle of the region's Abenaki peoples.

One of the advantages of the fact that the Fort at No. 4 is a historical reproduction is that it is a very student-friendly environment. Rather than protecting historically significant artifacts by roping off areas or enclosing them in cases, students are given free access to the fort and its interior rooms. Guides are of course careful to protect valuable reproduction artifacts, but there is a different atmosphere that encourages students to really experience the spaces of the fort, and try to imagine themselves as fort residents. In one of the houses, for example, students are encouraged to sit at the dining-room table and practice learning reading from the reproduction "horn books" that were the colonial equivalent of primary readers. Because the fort, like the original, is free of modern conveniences such as lighting, running water, heating, and air conditioning, students quickly gain a feel for the relatively dark, sometimes inclement places in which colonial people lived their lives.

While discussing the aspects of colonial life for which a particular room is staged, guides also often include interesting biographical details about the original residents of the room. Because many of them were at one time or another and in one way or another casualties of the river's imperial conflicts between the English, French, and Native Americans, this helps students gain a cumulative sense of how perilous life at Fort No. 4 was, and the interconnected lives of the European and native peoples of the region. "The overall impact of the Fort at No. 4 experience is often transformative," Patten notes. "I sometimes feel my students get more of a sense of what the colonial period and its conflicts were like in this two-and-a-half-hour visit than in the weeks of lessons preceding it." He hastens to add, though, that the preparation for the visit is instrumental to the power of the on-site experience.

Post-Visit Activities

The day after the field trip, Mr. Patten has his students write brief descriptions of their three most interesting items from the field trip, and then discusses these with the students, making sure to put the local and particular into the larger historical context of New England's imperial wars. His final assignment for the unit consists of giving students one of ten biographical data sheets of a person who was actually associated in the historical record with the Fort at No. 4 during its most active period (1740–1776). The biographies are of men and women, English, French, and Native American, for whom a well-documented association with the fort can be established. Patten obtained biographical information from the Fort at No. 4 website, and supplemented it over time with primary source accounts by or about the characters. Reprising the activity he had

Figure 5.4 Table where students read from horn books.

students do for the Deerfield raid, he asks students to use the knowledge they gained in class and on the field trip to do two things: (1) write a brief outline of English, Native American and French relations along the Connecticut River from early colonial settlement to the establishment of the Fort at No. 4; (2) write a first-person account of a significant event that occurred at the Fort at No. 4, as seen through the eyes of their assigned biographical character. The event must be one in which the biographical character is known to have participated. Patten reports being consistently surprised at how his students are able to create vivid descriptions of events at the Fort at No. 4, and connect them to the larger flow of inter-colonial and international history.

FORT TICONDEROGA

If it were ever possible to say that a place had too much history, it might be Fort Ticonderoga in upstate New York. Located at the portage between Lake Champlain to the north and Lake George to the south, this strategic choke point along a water corridor that stretches from Quebec and Montreal to Albany and New York City has witnessed two extended wars involving three different nations, during which it changed hands four times. Long before a fort was built there, the Ticonderoga peninsula also witnessed the first recorded battle involving Europeans and Native Americans, when the French explorer Samuel Champlain fought in a battle between Mohawks and Algonquians in 1609.

Originally named Fort Carrillon, the masonry military bastion was built from 1754 to 1757 by the French to protect Canada from invasion. From here, the Marquis de Montcalm launched his famous siege against the English at Fort William Henry in August 1757 (subsequently fictionalized in the book and film *The Last of the Mohicans*). The following year, Carillon witnessed one of the bloodiest battles ever fought in North America, when 2,500 casualties were suffered in a futile attempt by the British to seize the fort. A second British attempt the next year proved successful, and the fort changed both hands and names, from Carillon to Ticonderoga. With the transfer of Canada to Britain at the conclusion of the French and Indian War in 1763, the strategic importance of Ticonderoga was diminished, and by the outbreak of the American Revolution it was garrisoned with fewer than fifty British troops. At that time, the fort's cannons outnumbered the fort's defenders by nearly two to one, which made it immensely attractive to American troops following the battles of Lexington and Concord in 1775. What they needed to drive the British out of Boston were cannons, and Fort Ticonderoga was a place where they could acquire them. On May 21, 1775, Ethan Allen and his Green Mountain Boys and Connecticut troops under Benedict Arnold captured the fort in a nearly bloodless fight.

The Americans, realizing that Britain was likely to try to crush their revolution by sending an army down the Lake Champlain–Lake George–Hudson River corridor to isolate New England from the rest of the country, rushed to defend their new capture. They expanded the fort's defenses to add a companion outpost (Mount Independence) on the Vermont side of the lake, and by the summer of 1776, American defenders numbered 16,000, far more than the 12,000 defending Boston. By the summer of 1777, American forces had been substantially drawn down, and when British General John Burgoyne's engineers successfully mounted cannons atop nearby Mount Defiance, the Americans abandoned the fort, and it changed hands for the third time. Three months later, in October 1777, following Burgoyne's disastrous defeat at Saratoga, the fort changed hands again, remaining thereafter an American possession. In the 1790s, the United States government turned possession of the fort, now in disrepair, over to the State of New York, who later sold the fort to William Ferris Pell, a descendant of Loyalists in the American Revolution. Pell's great-grandson Steven Pell and his wife Sarah began restoration of the fort in 1908, a project that continued until Steven Pell's death in the 1950s. Today Fort Ticonderoga exists as a non-profit corporation, dependent on income from admissions and related sales, support from its "friends" organization, private benefactors, and public and private grants.

Fort Ticonderoga's commitment to education is significant. Each year approximately 5,000 students visit the fort on field trips, and hundreds of teachers and amateur and professional historians participate in Ticonderoga-sponsored workshops, professional development courses, and annual Revolutionary War and French and Indian War week-long "colleges." In 2007, the fort opened the Deborah Clark Mars Education Center, which has allowed them to develop expanded and year-round educational programs.

A teacher seeking to use Fort Ticonderoga as a teaching tool faces the dilemma of deciding which aspect of Fort Ticonderoga's two-war, three-nation, four-occupation history to make the focus of his or her visit. While it is possible to use the fort and its environs to expose students to the broad outlines of the fort's French and Indian War and Revolutionary War history, any effort to do so in detail can be confusing. The average student field trip visit is two-and-a-half hours. "In that time," Fort Ticonderoga's Director of Educational Programming reports, "students can get an overview of the two wars, but our experience has shown it is best to focus on either the fort's Revolutionary War or French and Indian War history in a way that makes it really memorable."

Activities for a Visit to Fort Ticonderoga

Overview

For Sharon Jackson, a fifth-grade teacher in South Burlington, Vermont, choosing which story to focus on is easy. Ethan Allen and his Green Mountain Boys are icons in Vermont history and fixtures in the Vermont social studies curriculum. Like many Vermont teachers, Mrs. Jackson focuses on the capture of Fort Ticonderoga from the British by Ethan Allen and Benedict Arnold in 1775. Yet, as a Burlington native who loves her region's history, and a teacher who has voluntarily participated in two summer professional development workshops at Fort Ticonderoga, Mrs. Jackson wants her students to appreciate the larger history of conflict involving the fort. Therefore, she works to show Ticonderoga's importance both before and after its capture by Ethan Allen and company.

Objectives

Mrs. Jackson's goals for the Ticonderoga unit are as follows:

- Students will understand why taking Ticonderoga was so important for the Americans at the start of the Revolution, and will learn how the taking of the fort occurred, using primary sources to assess the conflicting accounts about the takeover.

- Students will consider the experience of being a soldier in 1776, and will learn first-hand the requirement for teamwork in military units.
- Students will analyze the role of women and African Americans at Ticonderoga, and assess the limits of existing evidence concerning them.
- Students will explore historic objects and artifacts as primary sources, and will explore their connection to the fort's history.
- Students will evaluate the central role that Fort Ticonderoga played in both the French and Indian War and the American Revolution.

Pre-Visit Activities

Mrs. Jackson's students are first exposed to Fort Ticonderoga as the French Fort Carillon, in a short unit she does on the French and Indian War. In that unit she uses her students' knowledge of Lake Champlain and maps of the larger watershed from New York to Quebec to help her students understand the importance of these rivers as superhighways of communication, trade, and war, and the strategic position Fort Carillon/Ticonderoga had as a major portage point on that highway. Mrs. Jackson emphasizes that even before the French and Indian War, Anglo-colonials had been conditioned to fear attacks coming from the north, and she highlights the security they felt when the British conquered Canada in 1763. This is useful context to which she returns later when she begins her discussion of the American Revolution.

Next, Mrs. Jackson turns her attention to the American Revolution with lessons on the events leading up to the war itself. She starts with colonial reaction to the British Stamp Act and continues through the Boston Massacre in 1770, the Boston Tea Party in 1773, and the Intolerable or Coercive Acts of 1774.

Mrs. Jackson spends a full day on the battles of Lexington and Concord, the rush of patriots to the defense of Boston, and the appointment of Washington as the Continental Army commander in June of 1775. Using replicas of eighteenth-century maps of Boston, she shows students the topography of Boston harbor, underscoring the hills around the occupied city. As an imaginative writing exercise, she asks students to assume the role of George Washington, having just arrived near Boston and having assessed the military situation there. She asks them to write down as many things as they can think of that Washington and his army might have needed. Students work together in small groups to consolidate and to prioritize the top five items from their lists. Mrs. Jackson consistently finds these lists to be varied and interesting. Students readily think of more soldiers, food, and munitions as items Washington would need, and often include tents and housing, horses, and even doctors. Only a few suggest cannons as a priority need. But when she reminds students of the map of Boston, and points out how effective cannons could be in driving the British out of the city, they readily concede that cannons should be at or near the top of the list. Mrs. Jackson closes by asking the students to think overnight about where the Continental Army might get cannons from.

In the next class, which takes place just prior to the field trip, she revisits the question of where they could acquire cannons to defend Boston. Either through a few students' prior knowledge, or through Mrs. Jackson's prompting, the possibility of Fort Ticonderoga as a source of armaments soon becomes clear. Mrs. Jackson next discusses the question of who should be sent to get the cannons and who could authorize them to do so. This allows her to point out the difficulty of managing a conflict before there was a government to do so. She notes that both Ethan Allen and Benedict Arnold considered themselves authorized (by different authorities) to seize Ticonderoga, and that each set out to do so independently of the other. Knowing the students will learn more about the capture of the fort on the next day's visit, Mrs. Jackson provides only a summary account of the taking of the fort, noting that Allen and Arnold agreed to work together and that on the morning of May 10, 1775, they captured the lightly defended fort. As one of her unit goals is to help students understand the experience of being a Revolutionary War soldier, she spends much of this class discussing with students what qualities a soldier might need and what they thought it would be like to be a soldier under Ethan Allen. Using materials provided by Fort Ticonderoga's education department, she talks about the process of enlistment in the patriot militia, and ends the day inviting the students to sign a replica of an eighteenth-century document "enlisting" in the American army for one day—the day of the field trip. The lesson ends with the students signing up for service.

During-Visit Activities

At Fort Ticonderoga, the students participate in "America's First Victory," an award-winning seventy-five-minute experiential lesson developed by the Fort Ticonderoga education department for primary school students. In this lesson, students are greeted by costumed educators and their "enlistment" in the colonial militia is confirmed. Their prior knowledge of the Revolution is assessed by questions such as "Have you heard of Ethan Allen and his Green Mountain Boys?" and "Do you know why New Yorkers called them the 'Bennington Mob?'" Each student is assigned a role in the upcoming activity and given an appropriate costume. Students are then taken to view the fort's cannon, and to discuss their strategic importance. Next, the educator leads the students through a re-enactment of the taking of the fort, which ends at the actual door from which the British commander DeLaPlace (now a student assuming his role) surrenders. The re-enactment follows the sequence of events described in the account of Jocelyn Feltham, a British lieutenant at the fort during its capture. The fort is taken. America has its first victory, and the students "Huzzah." But their experience is not over.

Having taken the fort, the militia are now resident soldiers, untrained, undisciplined, and hardly fit for service. The educator now becomes a drill instructor, and during the remainder of the program the participants are instructed in military discipline; given the rudiments of marching, turning, etc. Importantly, Mrs. Jackson and the students' chaperones are participants in these activities. The educators at Ticonderoga believe their inclusion signifies to the students the importance of the activity they are participating in.

Depending on her assessment of students' overall interests, Mrs. Jackson leads her students through one of several activities following the experiential lesson. She asks some classes to tour the fort's museum, looking specifically for objects associated with Ethan Allen or Benedict Arnold and the taking of the fort. Other times, she will lead students back to the cannons and have them find and write down the three numbers on the cannons' barrels. These numbers can be used with a formula to determine a cannon's weight. Mrs. Jackson likes this activity because it accomplishes two goals: it teaches students to examine artifacts as sources of evidence; and it reinforces lessons from a discipline outside of history. In another activity, Mrs. Jackson leads students through a guided discussion of the museum's Ticonderoga artwork, helping students assess images as constructed evidence.

Mrs. Jackson believes her students' participation in the "America's First Victory" program and the other field trip activities are crucial to their overall learning experience. It breaks the mold of something she says has been called "2 × 4 education"—the knowledge gained from two books within four walls. "Re-enacting history at the place where it actually happened gives students a new appreciation for the reality of history, the fact that the things they read about 'actually happened.'" This historical empathy prepares them to eagerly participate in the follow-up activities she conducts following the field trip.

Post-Visit Activities

In the class immediately following the field trip Mrs. Jackson debriefs the students, asking what parts of the field trip they found most meaningful. Invariably the re-enactment is considered the highlight of the trip by most students. She uses this as a platform to deepen her students' understanding of what happened, by having them read accounts of the capture of Ticonderoga by three different participants in it: Jocelyn Feltham (the British lieutenant); Ethan Allen (an account in which Benedict Arnold is not mentioned); and Benedict Arnold (an account in which Allen's role is minimized and criticized). Mrs. Jackson provides both the original sources, and a simplified "translation" of the source accounts into modern English. The students are grouped together to discuss the similarities and differences in the accounts, and then are asked to determine which account is right. Jackson finds this to be an exceptionally effective way of teaching students about multiple perspectives of historical events, as well as the challenges of interpreting historical evidence.

In another follow-up lesson, Mrs. Jackson helps her students try to assess the role of women and African Americans at Ticonderoga. After describing the reinforcement of Ticonderoga (because of fears of British invasion from Canada) and its companion Fort Independence, located across the lake, in 1776, Mrs. Jackson asks her students if they think there were any women among the 16,000 Continental troops. She then points out the limited and conflicting evidence for women's presence at Ticonderoga: the appearance of only one woman by name in records relating to the fort (Eliza Kingsbury); and an order from General Anthony Wayne that one woman from each Pennsylvania regiment be assigned to hospital duty. Wayne's order, if extended to the entire complement of troops at Ticonderoga, could mean that as many as 1,000 women were present there in 1776. Mrs. Jackson sees this as a lesson in interpreting and assessing primary sources, and as a platform from which to discuss women's roles in supporting troops in the field during the Revolution.

The evidence for the presence of African Americans at Ticonderoga is also slim and ambiguous. Mrs. Jackson uses a letter by a soldier to his wife in Pennsylvania describing an encounter with "Jacob Drown our former servant who ran away" (and enlisted in the Massachusetts militia) as an opportunity to discuss whether Drown might have been an indentured servant or a slave, which allows her to discuss the larger role of African Americans in the Revolution. "By connecting broader issues associated with the American Revolution back to the experience they had at Fort Ticonderoga," Mrs. Jackson says, "students are more engaged, and much more able to identify with the reality of the historical past." Her field trip to Fort Ticonderoga is, in her own assessment, the lynch-pin in students' understanding of the Revolution.

REFLECTIONS ON THE CASE

Both Mr. Patten and Mrs. Jackson use visits to a historic fort as a keystone experience for understanding large and complex historical periods. Mr. Patten's students visit the Fort at No. 4 following a long and layered development of a Connecticut River-centered approach to colonial history. He uses geography and personal narratives to focus students' attention on the trajectories of historical development, to help them develop historical empathy, and to see the past from multiple perspectives. His exercise of having students assume a role of one of the participants in the 1704 raid on Deerfield, Massachusetts foreshadows the culminating activity of the field trip to the Fort at No. 4, the first-person account of a fort resident's experience accompanied by a larger historical overview of Anglo, Native American, and French relations along the Connecticut River valley. In a similar fashion, Mrs. Jackson uses her students' experience at Fort Ticonderoga as a reference point from which to engage them in broader issues surrounding the American Revolution. If the Fort at No. 4 trip is a culminating activity for Mr. Patten, the Ticonderoga trip is a kind of starting point for Mrs. Jackson, an experience from which she can reference a number of subsequent points about the future course of the American Revolution.

Both teachers understand that forts are excellent places to emphasize the role of geography in history. Both also use the forts as vehicles for exploring the contested nature of authority in situations of multicultural contact. Through their incorporation of primary sources into their lessons, they help students acquire historical thinking skills, particularly the ability to critically analyze and assess sources as historical evidence. Yet the grounding of these sources in an actual physical setting keeps students grounded in the reality of history and helps avoid the abstraction that can distract students' attention.

Stories and structures seem critical to both these teachers' use of forts. Perhaps because forts are inherently sites of contest and conflict, they seem to generate powerful and compelling narratives that engage students' imaginations and hold their attention. Because they are real, physical settings and often sites where important things *actually happened*, they have the power to give the past a presence that is vivid, memorable, and capable of providing a foundation upon which larger historical understanding can be layered.

Suggestions for Developing Activities with Historic Forts

Teachers who want to use historic forts as teaching tools have a remarkable profusion of sites to choose from. These range from barely visible archaeological ruins to National Park Service historic landmarks. It is highly likely that there are one or more sites to complement your teaching curriculum well within field trip range. Yet maximizing the value of a historical fort's educational potential can be enhanced by following these guidelines.

Choose the Most Appropriate Site

Not all forts are equally useful teaching tools. The historic fort or forts incorporated into teaching should serve, as in the case of Mr. Patten and Mrs. Jackson, as more than examples of a particular historical moment. They should offer rich education content and serve as a platform for discussion of, or reference to, larger historical issues and periods. In considering potential sites, the following questions are useful to consider:

- What power relations or struggle for authority does this historic fort represent?
- How will this particular fort help me represent the study of history from multiple perspectives?
- Does this site embody a historical or a heritage-based approach to the past, and is it useful in helping my students distinguish between the two?
- Does this fort provide opportunities to view history from the perspective of groups normally under-represented in the written historical records: women, marginalized racial and ethnic groups, the poor, and the uneducated or under-educated?
- Is there archaeological or artifact based evidence available at this fort useful in teaching historical thinking skills?
- Is there a clear lesson in the historical influence of geography at this fort?

Though most of these questions do not come with ready answers at any historical site, keeping them in mind when thinking about possible historic forts to incorporate into teaching can be most helpful.

Connect a Fort's Local Story in the Context of National History

Some of the power of historical forts comes from the status and importance they lend to the places where they are built. The mere presence of a fort demonstrates that at one time a location was thought to have strategic significance that was worthy of protection. Students respond well to the idea that their locality or region has historical importance; it encourages interest and engagement. But for that local historical connection to be most important, the fort's story also have perceptible connection to broader national or global historical forces. The best fort sites have deeply embedded local significance; but the events that happened there can be clearly connected to the history of the nation.

Find the Engaging Stories Presented by the Fort

Forts that teach well teach with stories. The presence of an edifice, no matter how massive or imposing, is merely a symbol until it is brought to life by the stories of the people who occupied or interacted with it. In selecting a fort to teach with, find the relevant stories connected with it. Often, if the fort has an education department or director, they will know and use these stories already. Their websites may have reading lists or primary source selections or links. If not, the rewarding job of story-finding is up to you. Library and web searches are likely to reveal a number of personal narratives, memoirs, or stories written by people associated with the fort during its most important years. Historic newspapers are also excellent sources of material related to forts. Images, including art, photographs, and drawings of the fort and its people or the events associated with it can also be excellent teaching tools. The decision to use a historic fort in teaching should be based in part on the availability of multiple sources to teach about that fort.

Layer the Fort into Your Curriculum

The right fort field trip, used effectively, should be a culminating experience giving life to a detailed and layered curriculum (Mr. Patten and the Fort at No. 4), or it should serve as a reference point to a series of inter-related lessons connected to a broader historical theme or topic (Mrs. Jackson and Fort Ticonderoga). This is accomplished by careful and thoughtful planning about the kinds of issues a fort visit can underscore and clarify, followed by a thoughtful effort to develop a layered teaching unit to make use of that capacity.

Visit the Fort, Collaborate with Staff, and Participate in Professional Development Offered by the Fort

At some point, each chapter in this book stresses the need for teachers to visit museums and contact museum educators when developing field trip activities for their students. Forts are no different. In fact, more than most other types of museums, good use of forts requires that a teacher know the site and the educational possibilities provided by its staff. Every fort, as a result of its history, location, artifact mix, staffing, and mission, has a unique educational story and a unique approach to telling that story. By informing oneself of those attributes, visiting the fort and its website, talking to the museum educators, and participating in the professional development programs they may offer, teachers can virtually ensure that their fort field trip will be a sparkling moment in a deeply meaningful teaching experience for their students.

NOTE

1   We wish to thank Wendalyn Baker, Director of the Fort at No. 4, and Richard Strum, Director of Education at Fort Ticonderoga, for their invaluable assistance in learning about their institutions' education programs, and in gathering materials for this chapter.

RESOURCES

Architect of the Capitol, Washington, D.C.: www.aoc.gov

Bents Old Fort National Historic Site, CO: www.nps.gov/beol/index.htm

Brumwell, S. (2007). *White Devil: A True Story of War, Savagery and Vengeance in Colonial America*. New York: Da Capo Press.

Castillo de San Marcos National Monument, St. Augustine, FL: www.nps.gov/casa/index.htm

Colonial National Historic Park, VA: www.nps.gov/colo/index.htm

The Fort at No. 4, Charlestown, NH: www.fortat4.com

Fort Bowie National Historic Site, AZ: www.nps.gov/fobo

Fort Caroline National Memorial, FL: www.nps.gov/timu/historyculture/foca.htm

Fort Donelson National Battlefield, TN: www.nps.gov/fodo/index.htm

Fort Larned National Historic Site, KS: www.nps.gov/fols

Fort McHenry National Monument and Historic Shrine, MD: www.nps.gov/fomc/index.htm

Fort Machilimackinac, MI: www.mackinacparks.com/fort-mackinac

Fort Sumter National Monument, SC: www.nps.gov/fosu/index.htm

Fort Ticonderoga, Ticonderoga, NY: www.fortticonderoga.org

Fort Vancouver National Historic Site, OR: www.nps.gov/fova/index.htm

Historic Fort Snelling, MN: www.historicfortsnelling.org

Historic Forts of Maine: www.travel-maine.info/historic_forts.htm

Johnston, S.W. (2009). *A Narrative of the Captivity of Mrs. Johnson, together with a Narrative of James Johnson: Indian Captive of Charlestown, New Hampshire.* Westminster, MD: Heritage Books.

Miantonomi, "So We Must Be One . . .": http://historymatters.gmu.edu/d/6227

Minuteman Missile National Historic Site, Rapid City, SD: www.nps.gov/mimi/index.htm

Morristown National Historic Park, Morristown, NJ: www.nps.gov/morr/index.htm

National Register of Historic Places, "Teaching with Historic Places": www.nps.gov/nr/twhp/descrip.htm

North American Forts 1526–1956: www.northamericanforts.com

"Raid on Deerfield: Many Stories of 1704": http://1704.deerfield.history.museum

Springfield Armory National Historic Site, MA: www.nps.gov/spar/index.htm

Thomas Jefferson's Monticello, Charlottesville, VA: www.monticello.org

Valley Forge National Historic Park, PA, "History and Culture": www.nps.gov/vafo/historyculture/index.htm

CHAPTER 6

Historic House Museums
The Johnson County Historical Society and the Mark Twain House

Figure 6.1 The Mark Twain House.

Source: Photo courtesy of the Mark Twain House and Museum, Hartford, CT. Photo by John Groo.

INTRODUCTION

On almost any school day in Charleston, South Carolina, school buses wind their way along Ashley River Road, bringing students to experience their state's history at Middleton Place, an eighteenth-century rice plantation that has remained under the stewardship of the same family for over 320 years. The educational activities for students at Middleton Place are diverse and multi-disciplinary. Some of them center on the plantation's two historic house museums: the South Flanker, the one surviving wing of the great plantation house burned by the Union army in 1865, and Eliza's house, a modest two-family duplex once occupied by former Middleton family slaves. Between these two houses—the elegantly furnished South Flanker (with its Benjamin West portrait of Arthur Middleton, signer of the Declaration of Independence) and the modest former slave quarters (the site of Middleton Place's permanent exhibit on African American history)—there is a social, cultural, and economic contrast, and a centuries-long history that powerfully underscores both the range and educational importance of historic house museums.

Historic house museums and similar single-focus, small-scale historic properties are among the most common and accessible museums available to teachers. Most towns—no matter how small—boast at least one cherished historic house or old school museum, while larger towns may offer historic properties associated with a variety of time periods, themes and events. Although house museums offer special logistical and pedagogical challenges to teachers conducting field trips, they are also ideally suited for helping students connect the past to the present, acquire historical empathy, understand historical narratives, develop appreciation for objects and artifacts as primary sources, and acquire the ability to examine history from multiple perspectives. Everyone, after all, has some understanding of what a residence is and does. Historic houses offer a compact, clearly focused comparison between those understandings and the ways residences and similar sites functioned in other times (Donnelly, 2002).

This chapter focuses on two cases: (1) the historic properties of the Johnson County Historical Society (JCHS) in Coralville, Iowa; and (2) the Mark Twain House and Museum in Hartford, Connecticut. These two cases highlight some of the particular strengths of teaching using house museums and related sites: the ability to provide students with accessible and tangible connections to history that often seems distant and abstract in the classroom; and the ability to simultaneously make connections and distinctions between the present and the past, by relating historical experience to spaces and activities that students readily understand.

After discussing the history and growth of historic house museums in America, we cover the different approaches to educational programming such museums offer, and their advantages and disadvantages for educators and students. From there we turn to our case histories, reviewing some exemplary educational experiences offered at both JCHS and the Mark Twain House. Finally, we provide some specific guidelines useful for teachers planning to incorporate historic house museum experiences into their pedagogy.[1]

IMPORTANT CHARACTERISTICS OF HISTORIC HOUSE MUSEUMS

History and Growth of Historic House Museums

The historic house museum movement in America extends back to the mid-nineteenth century, with the successful preservation in 1850 of the Hasbrouck House in Newburgh, New York, site of an important headquarters of George Washington during the American Revolution. This was followed in short order by other preservation efforts, including: Andrew Jackson's Nashville, Tennessee, plantation home, The Hermitage, in 1856; Carpenter's Hall in Philadelphia in 1857 (site of Benjamin Franklin's Library Company and the First Continental Congress); and Washington's Mount Vernon home in 1858.

These early sites set the pattern for preserving houses associated primarily with famous figures, a trend largely followed into the mid-1930s, by which time there were approximately 500 historic house museums in America. The movement received great impetus through the founding of Colonial Williamsburg by John D. Rockefeller during the same decade (Builder, 2002).

After World War II, the rise of automobile culture, increased governmental support for museums, and a new focus on history "from the bottom up" stimulated a rapid increase in historic house preservation. This time, rather than focusing only on the famous, the concern was with preserving places reflecting the diverse experiences of race, class, and gender in American life. Between 1960 and 2000, a new house museum opened in America on average every three days; more than 6,000 historic house museums were added to the American legacy (Builder, 2002).

Today there is an astonishing array of house museums available to support American public education. They represent an equally astounding number of subjects, themes, approaches, and capacities (Young, 2002). From the Pappy Thornton Farm Museum in Clovis, New Mexico, to Bacon's Castle in Surry, Virginia, the Sod House Museum in Aline, Oklahoma, or the Louis Armstrong House in Corona, New York, America's house museums provide insight into every aspect of United States history from the founding to the present. Yet for all their diversity of subject matter and approach, there are certain aspects of education in a historic house museum that remain constant. (Walker & Graham, 2000).

Historic House Museums Present Unique Challenges and Possibilities

All history museums face the challenge of finding effective ways to help students cross the cultural bridge that separates them from that past. The past really is, in this regard, a foreign country. Historic house museums possess unique characteristics that both support student learning and create barriers for visits. But because the physical spaces (e.g. hall, kitchen, bedroom, classroom) of historic house museums and related sites are readily understood by visitors, such museums have an inherent advantage in helping students connect the present to the past. Visitors can readily compare their understandings of how a particular room looks and functions in the present to the way it is being represented at the museum. But the same floor plan that can facilitate historical comparisons also presents logistical challenges, especially for students on field trips. Many historic house museums and related properties lack classroom-sized spaces in which to conduct educational programs; many also lack defined areas for students to use to eat lunches or snacks in inclement weather. Restroom facilities for class or grade-size groups may also be limited, and portions of historic houses may not be accessible for students with physical disabilities. None of these need pose serious limitations to field trips, provided teachers are aware of such limitations and have planned workarounds in advance.

The defined and confined spaces of historic house museums often limit the number of people who can access a given area at one time, and so dictate the way the museum delivers its information. When only a few students can be in any room at once, the interpretive narrative regarding a site's importance must be delivered in carefully timed and segmented portions. House museums have long worked to determine which methods best accomplish this. A few approaches have become standard; each has some particular advantages and disadvantages for visiting school groups. These include a third-person-led tour, a self-guided tour, a recorded tour, and a first-person-interpreted tour.

Third-Person-Led Tour

The most common form of historic house museum tour consists of a guide leading the group through the house, describing and interpreting the historical significance of the rooms and objects on the tour. Groups are relatively small, and the house and furnishings are the "eyewitnesses" to the past. The advantages of such a tour are in the museum's ability to shape the experience and assure that students receive the same basic messages consistently throughout their visit. Also, the tour guide can facilitate student interaction and answer student questions. However, a distinct disadvantage is that such a tour is very dependent on the abilities of the interpreter.

Self-Guided Tour

Often used in museums with large numbers of visitors or those with very small staffs and limited budgets, self-guided tours do not utilize museum staff. Students learn about the site from labels or text panels stationed along the tour. Objects and furnishings are frequently screened off or protected under Plexiglas. A shortcoming of the self-guided tour is that it places a significant burden on the teacher to define the learning experience for his or her students.

Recorded Tour

Site interpretation is delivered through audio recordings, accessed through some form of technology (e.g. in-room speakers, audio headsets, cell phone dial-up) by students as they tour the site. Such devices allow museums total control over the content of the visit, as well as the ability to enhance the presentation through background music, sound effects, and narrated vignettes. Drawbacks include the fact that the recording, once completed, can be cost-prohibitive to alter. Students also miss the opportunity for immediate interaction with live interpreters.

First-Person-Interpreted Tour

In this tour, costumed guides assume the role of historical characters associated with the site and conduct the tour as if they were living in the past they represent. By using the site as a set, this form of tour, especially in the hands of a skillful educator–actor–guide, can be thoroughly entertaining. A bad guide, however, can make the experience painful. Establishing effective first-person educational experiences, as discussed in Chapter 7 on living history museums, requires an institution to invest substantial sums in training persons to enable them to fully make use of the vocabulary, mannerisms, mores, gestures, and cultural attitudes of past times (Levy, 2002).

THE JOHNSON COUNTY HISTORICAL SOCIETY

Each year, 20,000 visitors—adults, educators, and students—take part in the programs and activities of the Johnson County Historical Society (JCHS) in Coralville, Iowa. These programs take place primarily at four sites owned and/or managed by the society: the JCHS Museum, which houses 10,000 artifacts covering all periods of the county's history, and three house museums: the 1876 Coralville schoolhouse; Plum Grove, the 1844 residence of Iowa territorial governor Robert Lucas and his wife Friendly; and the 1855 Johnson County Poor Farm/Asylum. The society conducts its programming through the efforts of two full-time employees and a dedicated staff of volunteers and seasonal staff. It receives funding from memberships, the government of Johnson County, the city of Coralville, and the State of Iowa. In this section, we will briefly review the educational offerings at the 1844 Plum Grove and 1855 Poor Farm and Asylum sites, before concentrating on the experiences of Heather Williams' fifth-grade class at the 1877 Coralville School House.

Home, Gardens, and Archaeology at Plum Grove

The 1844 residence of territorial governor Robert Lucas, his wife Friendly, and several of their children and grandchildren is typical of many historic house museums. Listed on the National Register of Historic Places, Plum Grove is furnished (courtesy of the National Society of Colonial Dames) to represent the antebellum period during which the Lucas family occupied it. The ample three-acre site surrounding the home enables Plum Grove to present the history of mid-nineteenth-century Iowa land use, as well as home life. Gardens maintained by the Johnson County Master Gardeners organization produce historic kitchen garden crops from Smithsonian heirloom seeds, and a prairie landscape section, reflecting Iowa's original open space, is also maintained. Numerous archaeological excavations at Plum Grove by the Iowa state archaeologist and others since 1974 have provided a clear view of changes in structures and land use over time, which are nicely documented graphically on the house's website. From Memorial Day through October, tours of Plum Grove are conducted in the third person by volunteer guides under JCHS direction. School groups visiting the site usually do so as part of their study of Iowa history and/or westward expansion, and most of them are fifth-graders. The visits are structured to help students understand how early Iowa settlers lived, and how that lifestyle differs from that of contemporary Iowans. Artifacts such as horsehair couches, recordings of a melodeon playing period music, and territorial maps showing that Iowa territory reached into modern Minnesota help students see that Iowa "then" was very different than it is today.

As in many house museums, the relatively small and highly compartmentalized size of the house dictates the way in which student tours are conducted. Classes (the average size is thirty) are divided into two groups. While one group is given a room-by-room tour of the house, the other tours the gardens and archaeological sites. The site does not have a classroom, so an orientation is given, and students' questions are fielded by guides as part of the tour. In case of inclement weather, students are divided into upstairs/downstairs tour groups, further emphasizing the site's physical restrictions. Nevertheless, educators report the site as a highly effective way for helping students realize that Iowa was once a much more isolated and difficult setting in which to live, and that it also was, for many years, a significant focus of American westward expansion.

The 1855 Poor Farm and Asylum is another site managed by the Johnson County Historical Society. In 1859, Johnson County became the first Iowa county to centralize care for the poor and mentally disabled at a county poor farm and asylum. Today, though much of the original site is gone or repurposed, the original six-cell asylum wing and subsequent ten-cell addition remain intact, along with a small adjacent cemetery. This

Figure 6.2 Social services, circa 1859: The Poor Farm and Asylum.

Source: Photo courtesy of the Johnson County Historical Society.

Figure 6.3 "An award-winning day in school . . ." (in 1877).

Source: Photo courtesy of the Johnson County Historical Society.

site is interpreted by JCHS for high school and college students with an impact that many find profoundly affecting.

Classes visiting the Poor Farm and Asylum are often high school or college Psychology, American Studies, or Nursing classes. These groups visit the site to reflect on the differences in attitudes toward, and treatment of, mentally ill persons in this century compared to the nineteenth. Before entering the Asylum area, museum educators provide students with historical background and information about the establishment of the Poor Farm and Asylum, and the treatment and classification of mental disorders in the nineteenth century. By connecting concepts of the "worthy" and "unworthy" poor to then poorly understood categories of mental disease and deficiency, important issues about the relationships among cultural values, social concerns, and medical care are brought into sharp relief.

But while these raise thought-provoking issues, the key to the Poor Farm and Asylum's impact on students is the physical space itself. "The power of the experience," one educator explained, "is in the isolation, the crowding, the lack of climate control. It's not a comfortable place to be." Once inside, students are most moved by the barred cells, closed-in spaces, and the dates, poems, and incoherent sentences written on the wall by former "inmates." These invariably prompt a flood of questions that make it obvious students are emotionally moved by the site. Some teachers further capitalize on this impact by having students spend a bit of intentional quiet time within the cells as preparation for writing post-visit reflections on their experience.

Activities for a Visit to the Johnson County Historical Society

Overview

The Johnson County Historical Society's signature educational program is the "Country School Experience," the subject of this case. Heather Williams, who has taught for nine years in the Iowa City Community School District of which Coralville is a part, has integrated this comprehensive unit into her fifth-grade Iowa history curriculum since it was introduced several years ago. The fifth-grade district curriculum revolves around Iowa history. The "Country School Experience" gives her students the opportunity to learn about early Iowa and local history in the context of larger national history. They do so by conducting in-class research on early Iowa history, as well as the life of a representative student who attended Coralville's first non-graded single-class school in 1877. This research is facilitated through Ms. Williams's use of pre-visit materials and activities provided by the Johnson County Historical Society educational staff. In a culminating activity, each student assumes the identity of the student he or she has been researching through spending a day in school in 1877 at the Coralville school.

Objectives

During this unit, Ms. Williams focuses on the following learning and historical thinking objectives, each of which is aligned with the Iowa Core Curriculum for Social Studies:

- Students will understand the 1877 school in historical context, by studying the major historical trends changing Coralville, Iowa and the nation in the 1870s, and how these changes in turn affected the composition of the 1877 Coralville school.
- Students will understand the diversity of Iowa's early population and develop a multi-perspective understanding of how different groups (Czech, Swedish, Anglo, Bohemian) approached their schoolroom experience.
- Students will evaluate and synthesize primary sources as evidence documenting what 1877 Iowans considered newsworthy and important.
- Students will consider the effect of gender and age on the status of children in 1877 Iowa and today.
- Students will gain historical empathy by comparing their contemporary educational experience to their 1877 classroom experience.

Pre-Visit Activities

To facilitate student preparation for their visit, the Johnson County Historical Society furnishes Ms. Williams with an activities trunk that arrives at the school several weeks in advance of the field trip. The trunk contains biographical information on forty students who are representative of the ages, capacities, ethnicities, and family composi- tions of students from the 1877 class. It also contains thirteen lessons/activities that provide students with background knowledge about post-Civil War history and nineteenth-century school life. JCHS requires that the students receive some of the lessons as preparation for the trip. Ms. Williams tailors others to meet the interests and capacities of her class.

Ms. Williams begins by matching biographies to students. Unlike today's schools, the ungraded 1877 school taught students of numerous ages, ethnicities, educational attainments, and intellectual abilities, all within a single classroom. The historical identities that Ms. Williams's students assume before their visit reflect those different capacities. Some of the biographical students are younger (and will be asked to do less rigorous work during their 1877 school day) while others are more advanced (and will be asked to demonstrate greater knowledge). By carefully matching the biographies of the 1877 students to the abilities of her present day fifth-graders, Ms. Williams helps assure that the educator playing the role of nineteenth-century teacher approaches each student at his or her level of attainment. This differentiation, which both Ms. Williams and the JCHS educators see as a very important part of the program, helps assure that the Country School Experience remains a positive and enjoyable learning activity for every student.

Once Ms. Williams has assigned each of her students the identity of one of the 1877 students, she gives each student a biographical statement giving them essential information about that student: name, place of origin, number of siblings in their family, and occupations of family members. These characters are not actual historical characters, but composite characters based on students who would have attended the school. Importantly, Iowa in 1877 was a land of immigrants. And the biographies reflect the Czech, German, Bohemian, and Ohioan backgrounds prevalent among Iowa's late-nineteenth-century population.

For students, the biographical statement of the student whose identity they will assume is just the beginning. Their job now is, with Ms. Williams's guidance, to do research that will tell them more about their character so they will be more adequately prepared to assume his or her identity at the school house. For this task, Ms. Williams uses several of the pre-prepared lessons included in the JCHS traveling trunk. In one exemplary activity, students pore over a variety of included primary source materials (newspaper articles, baseball line scores, letters, photos) to create a newspaper focused on the important news events for 1877 Coralville readers. In another, students study the various occupations of people in 1877 Iowa, as a way of coming to understand how the occupations pursued by their assigned character's father (or mother) fit into the social and economic fabric of the community. Ms. Williams supplements these activities with lessons on the importance of railroad transportation in attracting people to Iowa, and the effort by the state to recruit immigrants from northern Europe in the 1870s. One reason Ms. Williams is highly committed to the Country School Experience is because the effect on students of having to research a person they will soon portray is remarkable. "They become connected to the [historical] person. They want to know more. This curiosity is amplified by the fact that they are researching how life was for a person more or less their own age." By the time the actual visit to the 1877 school arrives, students are both knowledgeable and enthused about the character they will portray.

During-Visit Activities

The actual on-site visit to the 1877 Coralville School is, by most fifth-grade field trip standards, a long one. It begins at nine in the morning and ends just after a post-lunch debriefing session at around 1:30. From the moment they arrive, the students, who role-play in character as the person they have studied, are exposed to the differences in education circa 1877 versus today. They are greeted by an 1877 teacher in period garb (a JCHS volunteer educator, who is almost always a retired primary teacher), who separates boys from girls and lines them up to enter the school by gender through two different doors. Once inside they find the seat with their name tag on it, put on the name tag, and become their 1877 character. They stand and introduce themselves as their character, which often prompts an in-role response or question from the teacher ("Yes, Jacob, I saw your father fixing Mr. Harness's wagon yesterday. How is your sister? Feeling better?") Students are instructed in the rules of 1877 classroom discipline, which include raising your fingers to talk and standing up when you speak. As in 1877, the students then begin the school day with a patriotic song ("My Country 'tis of Thee") and a reading from the biblical book of Proverbs.

During the rest of the morning the students are exposed to the elements of the 1877 curriculum. They are given exercises in spelling, ciphering, geography (using a local map produced in the 1880s), a reading exercise from *McGuffey's Reader*, and additional work in memorization and elocution. For these lessons, pre-classifying the students through their biographies is very useful to the educator/teacher. It ensures that few if any students will be given an assignment too difficult for them to respond to adequately. The students operate under 1877 classroom discipline until lunchtime.

A Learning Lunch

Though students bring their own lunches from home, just prior to the lunch break each student is given a lunch pail, stocked with artificial food items indicative of a lunch that would have been eaten by an 1877 student of their character's ethnicity and family's economic status. A Czech immigrant, for example, might have sausage and bread in his lunch box. Students from more prosperous homes have many items in their lunch pail; poorer students may have only a few. Students are invited to reflect on the different food items and the disparities in quantity before breaking character and eating their own lunches. The food pails have proven very effective in reinforcing the existence of ethnic diversity and economic disparities within country schools, and in creating historical empathy in ways that students can easily relate to their present school circumstances.

The Debriefing

After lunch, the students return to the classroom, not in character but as themselves, and are invited to ask questions and make comments on their 1877 classroom experience. They also are taken to another portion of the building where they view exhibits about the school's history. This debriefing is very effective in drawing out contrasts between the disciplinary approaches and curriculum of the past compared to that experienced today. Students not only understand that school in the past was quite different, they gain a new appreciation for some of the more relaxed (but no less committed) approaches to learning in use today. Ms. Williams conducts a second debriefing with her students the morning after the field trip, to identify and clarify any lingering questions/misconceptions about the experience.

Post-Visit Activities

Ms. Williams has her students complete two follow-up activities subsequent to their visit to the 1877 Coralville Day School. First, they enter into their notebooks responses to two prompts: (1) What did you like about your 1877 school experience and what did you not like? (2) How was school in 1877 different than school today? In what ways was school in 1877 similar to today? Finally, for extra credit, they are invited to interview a family member about their school experiences, and record reflections on that report in their notebooks.

THE MARK TWAIN HOUSE AND MUSEUM

The Mark Twain House and Museum in Hartford is in many ways typical of historic house museums associated with an important figure in American life and culture. The somewhat quirky Victorian mansion's architecture reflects the personality of the author/satirist who built it, and who wrote within its walls many of the novels for which he is most widely remembered: *The Adventures of Tom Sawyer*, *The Adventures of Huckleberry Finn*, *The Gilded Age*, and *A Connecticut Yankee in King's Arthur's Court*. The continuing popularity of Twain and his works makes the house a magnet for visitors from all over the world. Each year, an average of 12,000 students in grades three through twelve come to the site for educational tours and activities. Unlike many historic houses, the Mark Twain House and Museum is fortunate to have an adjacent visitor center that provides space for many of the logistical and educational functions associated with the high volume of student visitors.

Given the need to maximize the efficiency of its education programs, the Twain House carefully focuses its programming mission on two historical themes that the house and its famous resident best exemplify, and which are of significant importance in United

Figure 6.4 The Mark Twain House kitchen.

Source: Photo courtesy of the Mark Twain House and Museum, Hartford, CT. Photo by John Groo.

Figure 6.5 The Mark Twain House billiard room.

Source: Photo courtesy of the Mark Twain House and Museum, Hartford, CT. Photo by John Groo.

States history, social studies, and American literature. These themes, according to the Education Program Manager, a veteran high school history teacher, help the Twain House provide the best learning experiences for visiting students.

The first theme is "Mark Twain as Provocateur". Through his writings, Twain consistently challenged Americans to realize their cultural inconsistencies and to face hard questions about the relationship between American ideals and realities. Whether it's analyzing the challenge to Jim Crow racism posed in *The Adventures of Huckleberry Finn* or exploring the critique of unbridled excess in *The Gilded Age*, educational programs analyzing Twain's literature, informed by his life in Hartford, are a core component of the Twain House educational programs.

The second theme is "The Gilded Age". Although Twain critiqued the Gilded Age of the late nineteenth century, his home and standard of living in many ways exemplified the lifestyle he critiqued. Focusing on the history of the Gilded Age as seen through the Twain House, its residents, and the community that surrounded it allows exploration of critical historical issues such as immigration, industrialization, racism, and late nineteenth-century gender and class roles.

Activities for a Visit to the Mark Twain House and Museum

Overview

Each year for the past three years, Murray Hall, a high school teacher from a large town near Hartford, Connecticut, has guided his students through a unit designed around a tour of the Mark Twain House and servants' wing, followed by focused writing activities conducted in coordination with Twain House educators. Each year Mr. Hall tailors the activities to his students' relative abilities at interpreting visual (as opposed to written) primary source information. However, all of his activities use the experience of the Twain House's family, and their Irish American and African American servants and acquaintances, to humanize the social and economic stratification in Gilded Age America.

Objectives

Mr. Hall's goals for this unit are:

- Students will understand the industrial success of inventors Eli Whitney and Samuel Colt as representative of the industrial transformation of America in the nineteenth century.
- Students will learn that industrialization prompted widespread immigration from Europe to America, especially in the second half of the nineteenth century.
- Students will evaluate the ways in which industrialization raised standards of living, produced economic stratification, and exacerbated class and racial divisions.
- Students will analyze how historic homes emulate economic, class, and racial divisions.

Pre-Visit Activities

Prior to their field trip to the Twain House, Mr. Hall leads his students through a study of American industrialization and immigration as it took place in nineteenth-century Hartford. Mr. Hall's preparatory classroom activities occupy the week prior to the field trip. As part of these activities, he provides image-rich lectures showing the industrial, social, and economic transformation of Hartford in the nineteenth century. He leads his students in guided deconstruction of photographs and has students read short primary-source documents written by Samuel Colt and Eli Whitney, as well as newspaper accounts about the lives of immigrants and factory workers, and short excerpts from Twain's *A Connecticut Yankee in King Arthur's Court*. Collectively, these documents present a picture of Hartford as a dynamic, progressive, and wealthy city whose character and population characteristics are being transformed by Yankee ingenuity expressed through industrialization. Students are asked to assess the changes described in the documents and their effects on both the city and its people. Then they are asked to consider how that nineteenth-century image contrasts with what they know about the city today (it is one of the poorer mid-sized cities in the U.S.). After discussing the social, economic and cultural changes to the region during the Twain era, Hall asks his students whether and where the nineteenth-century industrial expansion of Hartford still leaves visible effects on the city. He prompts their responses with images of the still-extant factories (frequently vacant) and public architecture that reflected the wealth of the city in the nineteenth century, and contrasts these with images of the industrial worker housing built by Colt and others that still lines many Hartford streets.

During-Visit Activities

The day of the field trip students participate in the following activities at the Twain House. After arriving at the museum, students are divided into groups of sixteen for a tour of the living quarters of both the Twain House and the servants' quarters. The tour is conducted by museum educators, well trained in working with student groups. Their goal is to impart useful and clear information about the house and its residents, while keeping within the time constraints imposed by the need to move small groups of students through the house in an orderly manner. This requires the educators to control the pace and content of the tour, though at each stop there is a brief time to answer student questions. While tours are carefully time managed, they do not give the feeling of being rushed.

The family spaces of the twenty-five-room, 11,500-square-foot Victorian Gothic house are staged as they were when the Twains lived there (with many original furnishings), and reflect the lifestyle of a modern and very prosperous nineteenth-century family. The elegant Louis Comfort Tiffany-designed interior includes elaborate stenciling and carved woodwork. The plush furnishing and spacious social areas show that the Twains moved in and were part of Hartford's social elite. At the same time, amusing touches such as cigar-and-pool-cue stenciling in Twain's billiard room and the portrait of a cat dressed in an Elizabethan ruffled collar in the living room reflect the sense of humor of the resident author. Students touring the family's living quarters are given an extensive sense of the daily lives and activities of the entire Twain family. The guides also suggest, but do not overly emphasize, the amount of labor by others that was required to support the Twains' upper-class lifestyle.

The house and servants' quarters tours are conducted as separate but related activities, so that museum educators can underscore the contrasts between the lives of the Twains and those who served them. Students view the kitchen, butler's pantry, and other behind-the-scenes areas necessary to maintain the Twains' lifestyle. The massive cast iron stove, large and well-stocked pantry shelves, and other features such as the great copper hot-water tank hint at the effort required of the six or seven servants that kept the household functioning. Guides introduce students to well-documented Twain employees such as George Griffin, a freed slave who was the Twains' butler, and Katy Leary, their Irish American maid. The comparatively spartan servant quarters, contrasted with the opulence of the Twain living areas, demonstrate dramatically the class divide that was such a prominent feature of life in the Gilded Age.

After the tours, students reconvene in the visitor center classroom, where they are divided into small groups and participate in a primary-source analysis and writing exercise using images and documents. Each group is given two folders. The first contains numerous primary source images of the tools and appliances used by servants in the Twain household to perform their daily activities. Twain House educators guide the students through the analysis of a few of these objects, helping them to think about the object's function and the effort required to use each object efficiently. The second folder contains primary and secondary source materials related to one of the servants employed in the Twain household. The documents help the students develop a sense of both what that person was like and how he or she interacted with the Twain family members. Mr. Hall and the museum educators guide the students in analysis of one of the documents.

For their writing assignment, the student groups are instructed to use both the images and the biographical information in their folders to develop a collectively written short story about the servant whose data they have received and his or her relationship to the Twain household. The goal of this exercise from the standpoint of developing historical thinking skills is to help students understand the challenges of constructing history from primary and secondary sources. The goal in terms of historical knowledge is to help them understand the difficulty of working-class employment during the period and social and economic stratification caused by industrialization.

Post-Visit Activities

A critical component of the students' field trip writing activity is their knowledge that the story they write will be read and graded by Mr. Hall and reviewed after the visit. Mr. Hall, having then read each of the students' papers, uses them to conduct a guided debriefing of the entire Twain House visit, considering what the students learned ("found most surprising or interesting") from the house, and then from the writing assignments. He then ties these findings directly to the subjects of industrialization, immigration, and social stratification with which he began his unit. Why did the Twains' servants choose to work in the Twain household rather than in one of Hartford's many factories? Was life better for a house servant than an industrial worker? What might the differences have been between them? Did the Twains see their servants as social equals or inferiors? How did the servants view the Twains? How do those attitudes stack up against American democratic ideals?

What Mr. Hall likes best about incorporating the Twain House into the unit on industrialization and immigration is that, similar to the Country School experience at the Johnson County Historical Society, it humanizes and personalizes for his students abstract historical concepts. "It's one thing to talk about the class distinctions present in the Gilded Age," he says. "It's quite another to see them through the eyes of a servant such as George Griffin or Kate Leary." Students are much better at remembering macro-social and economic concepts, Hall believes, once they have been able to connect them to the experience of a historical character to whom they can relate. Such "personalization of the abstract" is a benefit many historic house educators and teachers point to as one of the primary reasons for incorporating house museums into curriculum.

REFLECTIONS ON THE CASES

The JCHS Country School Experience is a model example of museums and teachers working in partnership. The project requires a commitment from teachers like Ms. Williams both in time and effort, but JCHS has clearly taken pains to provide materials, such as the biographies and the trunk-based pre-visit lessons and source materials, that help students become deeply engaged in the assignment. Moreover, the assignment is fully integrated into the Iowa Core Curriculum for Social Studies, a fact that makes it easy for teachers such as Heather Williams to commit to using it.

As the Education Coordinator for JCHS underscored, the value of such a program is that it allows students to interact with history in a more personal way—to get physically into history through a hands-on, total immersion experience, completely in harmony with their in-class studies. It takes the abstractions present in a textbook and puts a personal element to them that is highly memorable.

The Twain House is fortunate in having an education director with a prior career as a history teacher. This has enabled them to integrate a classroom teacher's perspective into the student post-tour activity. It capitalizes on the site's mission-related themes: teaching the Gilded Age; and presenting the life and works of Mark Twain as informed by his life in Hartford. Mr. Hall is careful to give his students an appropriate context with which to consider their field trip experience through his pre-visit lectures on the industrial revolution and immigration in nineteenth-century America. By incorporating Twain-related primary-source activities into this pre-visit experience, he further "preinforces" the links between the historical changes he highlights in class and the expressions of those changes on view at the Twain House.

An important aspect of the post-tour program is the fact that students know their work will be collected and graded. Without the knowledge that their efforts really "count," some students will not take the post-tour activity seriously. The key to the success of Mr. Hall's field trips' learning experiences is that they are part of a sequenced learning unit involving pre-visit, field trip, and post-visit exercises, all carefully designed around important historical themes that are, through the on-site activities, connected to powerful historical stories and characters.

Regardless of which interpretive format a historic house museum makes primary use of, all successful house museum tours exhibit the same underlying qualities. First and foremost, they are based on excellent scholarship and rooted firmly in historical evidence. Historians' knowledge of and understandings about the past are subject to continuous revision. Museums must take these changes into account and incorporate them into their interpretations. The reputation and the credibility of museums' programming depend on this. Implicit in this scholarship-based interpretation is a commitment to presenting the site's stories within their broader historical context. At JCHS, for example, the Country School Experience is carefully linked to the study of the larger trends of immigration and national expansion that framed the lives of its 1870s students. The Mark Twain House's servants' quarters tour and related activities were the product of years of research on both the Twain household and the scholarship of social relations during the Gilded Age. Excellent historic house experiences embed their interpretations solidly in the history of the period they represent, and not just the life experiences of the historic residents. They also relate history in meaningful and understandable ways to the present.

The best house museum programs recognize that their sites held different meanings for individuals in the past, and will have different meanings for visitors in the present. The way a plantation house was experienced by slave-holding masters, for example, was different from the way it was experienced by their overseers, wives, children, house servants, field slaves, and visitors, just as the experience of Samuel Clemens at the Mark Twain House was different from that of his butler. Visitors, too, will view the site based on their personal interests, backgrounds, and perspectives. The most effective house museum tours capitalize on these multiple angles of engagement to present the past from a number of different perspectives.

Effective house museum tours are structured around a limited number of themes—usually three to five—that are crucial to understanding the site's history. Both JCHS and the Mark Twain House utilize this kind of focused theme-based approach to educational programming, one of the keys to their effectiveness. These themes emerge out of the stories of the inhabitants, the history of the time in which they lived, and the artifacts and documentary sources available to aid interpretation. Artifacts are carefully selected to support these themes, and the tour and guide interpretation also remain focused on the key thematic messages.

Historic house museums and related sites are almost always connected to specific people, whose biographies become central to the site interpretation. This is a strength of historic house museums. People like to hear other people's stories, and the best house museum experiences communicate their themes through a historically contextualized retelling of people's narratives. At the Twain House, everything is ultimately connected to the biography of the author, but the institution has done a superb job of amplifying Clemens's life through the stories of those with whom he was associated.

Finally—and this is unusually important for school groups—the best house museum tours provide a well-organized and carefully planned visitor experience. This includes structuring the tour to accommodate the size of the class or classes visiting, the logistical requirements of school groups, and assuring that the tour is structured in ways that maximize educational opportunities and assure visitor comfort (Levy, 2002; Donnelly, 2002). Many historic house museums provide educational experiences specifically designed for school groups. These may depart from the institution's standard interpretive approach. They also may supplement site visits with significant pre- and post-visit resources made available via their website or through classroom visits by museum personnel prior to the field trip (see Chapter 9 for ideas). Teachers considering incorporating house museum visits into their curriculum should always think holistically of the experience, and seek museum cooperation in establishing effective pre-, during-, and post-visit educational resources and experiences.

Suggestions for Developing Activities for Historic House Museums

Teachers wanting to maximize the learning opportunities provided by historic house museums and similar single-focus small-scale historical properties should keep a number of considerations in mind as they consider planning the experience. These include: the unique opportunities provided by historic houses, the house's strengths and logistical challenges, the importance of pre-visits, the benefits of providing a human dimension to the house visit, the connection of the visit to specific learning goals, and the need to assess students and follow up with staff.

Historic Houses Are Abundantly Available

Except for monuments, historic house museums are the most common type of museum in America today. No matter where you teach, it is likely that there are a number of historic house sites nearby that will be eager to help you connect your students to the past in powerful, meaningful ways.

Historic Houses Have Special Strengths and Pose Special Logistical Problems

Everyone can relate to a residence, and make clear connections between the rooms in a historic house and those serving similar functions today. That is a particular strength of historic house museums and similar sites. But familiar, family-oriented spaces often mean that students must experience them in small groups through guided and linear room-to-room tours. There also may not be class-sized waiting rooms, adequate restroom facilities, or appropriate lunch spaces available, and they may not be fully accessible for disabled students. Teachers should consider these factors when planning for chaperones and making provisions for inclement weather.

Teacher Pre-Visits Are Virtually Mandatory

Any teacher considering taking students to a historic house museum or related site should visit the site well in advance and meet with that site's education personnel about the visit. Find out what education programs they offer for students at your class level, and which educators will teach your students. Museum educators at house museums are unanimous in noting that some guides are excellent teachers and others not as capable. If possible, go along on a tour with the actual guide who would be conducting your class visit. Make notes on the themes he or she stresses and how you might integrate them subtly into pre-visit activities. Teachers should also think about how to handle classroom management issues while at the museum.

Make the House Museum a Place Where What Is Already Known Takes on a Human Dimension

The best field trips involve students who have been prepared by pre-visit lessons that help them understand the larger historical changes that affected the occupants of the visited site. Without a historical framework in which to embed the field trip experience, the trip can devolve into a kind of anecdotal history or "day off from class." If possible, time your field trip visit to coincide with the time in which you will naturally be studying the relevant period in your course. If this is not possible, be sure to set aside enough time to set the historical stage for your students prior to the visit. Doing this will help students see the lives of the site's former residents or occupants as exemplary of the historical forces and changes taking place during the period under study.

Have Learning Goals for the Field Trip Experience

These can often be developed in collaboration with the museum's guides or education director. The key to success in this regard is having prior knowledge of what the museum will be presenting to your classes. If a pre-field trip site visit is simply not possible, study online course descriptions carefully, and develop activities that will coincide with the experiences described. Check the museum website for pre-visit materials. Many institutions make them available on the web. If online materials are not adequate for your needs, email or call to talk about what they might be able to make available.

Follow Up the Visit with Students and Assess Their Learning

Once the field trip is completed, debrief students for their responses to the field trip and conduct activities that will help you assess the degree to which that experience helped reinforce their historical knowledge of the period you have been presenting.

Follow Up with the Museum Educators

Good museums of all kinds pay careful attention to teacher comments regarding their programs. Take the time to let them know your reaction to their education programs. What worked for your students? What didn't? Such information is welcome and invaluable to the museum.

In Coralville, Hartford, and cities and towns across America, teachers and historic house museums are working together in remarkable ways to make history vital and memorable for a rising generation of students. Teachers who make best use of these experiences are the ones who integrate the stories brought to life at the historic site into the context of larger historical periods and transformations.

NOTE

1   We wish to thank Megan McCollum from the Johnson County Historical Society and Craig Hotchkiss from the Mark Twain House and Museum for the time and assistance they gave us on this project, and especially for the benefit of their knowledge about teaching with museums.

RESOURCES

Johnson County Historical Society: www.jchsiowa.org

Mark Twain House: www.marktwainhouse.org

Bacon's Castle, Surrey, VA: http://preservationvirginia.org/BaconsCastle

Carpenters Hall, Philadelphia, PA: www.ushistory.org/carpentershall

Hasbrouck House, Newburgh, NY: http://nysparks.state.ny.us/historic-sites/17/details.aspx

The Hermitage, Nashville, TN: www.thehermitage.com/mansion-grounds/mansion/preservation

Louis Armstrong House, Corona, NY: www.louisarmstronghouse.org/visiting/overview.htm

Middleton Place, Charleston, SC: https://www.middletonplace.org/house-museum.html

Mount Vernon, Mount Vernon, VA: www.mountvernon.org/index.cfm?

Pappy Thornton Farm Museum, Clovis, NM: www.discoverourtown.com/NM/Clovis/Attractions/old-homestead-museum-pappy-thornton-farm-museum/54183.html

Plum Grove, Iowa City, IA: www.uiowa.edu/~plumgrov

Sod House Museum, Aline, OK: www.okhistory.org/outreach/homes/sodhousemuseum.html

Living History Museums
Colonial Williamsburg, The Jamestown Settlement, Yorktown

Figure 7.1 Sign welcoming visitors to the Historic Triangle.

INTRODUCTION

It is late June. The midday sun is hot and high in the sky, and the humidity practically drips from the trees. All of a sudden the quiet afternoon is broken by shouts of "The British are coming!" Soon, the sound of horse hooves grows louder, and a troop of dragoons (British Cavalry) appear on Duke of Gloucester Street. Within hours, the town is filled with British soldiers who harass the shopkeepers and townspeople, and declare martial law.

This is not a scene from a Hollywood film, but it is what you might witness as a visitor to Colonial Williamsburg during the "Under the Redcoat" weekend. This weekend-long program marks the anniversary of the occupation of Williamsburg by Cromwell's British forces before their retreat to Yorktown, Virginia, and the final major battle of the American Revolution. British military re-enactors from all over the U.S. and Canada come to town to participate with Colonial Williamsburg's staff of historical interpreters. Over the course of the weekend, notable events such as the declaration of martial law and Cromwell's address to the troops are re-enacted. In addition, interpreters demonstrate aspects of daily life for visitors from the perspectives of soldiers, escaped slaves who have joined Cromwell's forces to gain their freedom, and camp followers who take care of the needs of the army (e.g. seamstresses, cooks, surgeons). Visitors to Colonial Williamsburg interact with these re-enactors, watch military drills and staged events (such as Cromwell's address), and then retire to one of the colonial taverns for dinner by candlelight (but luckily with air conditioning).

This chapter examines living history museums through exploration of the three sites that form Virginia's "Historic Triangle": Colonial Williamsburg, Yorktown, and Jamestown. Colonial Williamsburg is the site of a living history museum housed in Virginia's colonial capital and set at the time of the American Revolution. Yorktown, the site of the final major battle of the American Revolution, is home to a National Historic Battlefield, which is run by the National Park Service, and the Yorktown Victory Center, a living history museum centered on the time of the battle. Two sites are also located at Jamestown. They include Historic Jamestowne, the actual site of the first English permanent settlement, run by a partnership of the Park Service and Preservation Virginia, and Jamestown Settlement, a living history exhibition and museum located nearby.

In addition to the hundreds of thousands of tourists who visit each year, the three sites play host to thousands of elementary and secondary students. Although the bulk of student visitors are from Virginia and the mid-Atlantic region, these sites host student visitors from all over the United States as a stopping point for groups whose destination is Washington, D.C., or other cities along the east coast. Through these museums, students experience the excitement and engagement of examining the past through the historical interpreters and living history model. In addition to experiencing these recreated historic sites through interacting with the historical interpreters that occupy them, students can also try their hands at archaeology and historical interpretation. The two cases highlighted in this chapter focus on the practices of historical interpreters and historical archaeologists, and how both help young students to start to understand not only the history presented at these sites but also the methods and evidence historical interpreters and archaeologists use to do their jobs.

IMPORTANT CHARACTERISTICS OF LIVING HISTORY MUSEUMS

The term "living history" is used broadly, but generally refers to museums that focus on civilian and military re-enactors, trade and occupation demonstrations (e.g. farming, blacksmith), experimental archaeology, and first-person historical character interpretation or theatre performances based on historic events. Generally, the museum experience includes some kind of live presentation or facilitation. Living history museums have emerged as a major form of historical and heritage tourism. Although there have been living history sites, such as Colonial Williamsburg, in operation since the 1920s, living history museums have become especially popular since the 1970s (Crang, 1996). These sites have strong proponents and strong detractors within the history and museum community, and they are often critiqued for being ahistorical and a form of cultural tourism more than thoughtful historical interpretation and research (e.g. Kirshenblatt-Gimblett, 1998; Stover, 1989). When done well, historical interpretation can engage visitors in rich interactions with the past and help them construct an understanding of life from an earlier time (Leinhardt, Crowley, & Knutson, 2002). Of course, interpretation of the past is always tenuous, even when based on the best historical research. Living history museums not only attempt to describe the past or place artifacts in a narrative, but they also present a physical, historical, and conversational reconstruction.

For teachers, there are several features of living history museums to consider when planning visits with students, or even in selecting living history museums to visit. These features include the quality of living history museums and the organizations that run them; the tension between their need to entertain and engage visitors, and their desire to educate and adhere to the historical record; the role geography plays in a living history site; and the need to help students understand that these sites represent particular interpreted perspectives on the past and that these perspectives are hard to separate from our present-day experiences.

Quality Matters in Living History Sites

The term "living history" is used broadly, but living history sites represent a wide range in quality of representation and research. Living history sites and historical interpreters are often criticized within the field of museum studies for focusing too much on aesthetics and not enough on authenticity, a critique similar to one discussed about Hollywood film (e.g. Stoddard & Marcus, 2006). Crang (1996) notes, however, that this form of interpretation is not that different from other forms of interpretation at historic sites and museums. In fact, it may provide more opportunities for visitors' self-reflexivity than a static exhibition because of the potentially active nature of engagement between visitors and interpreters. This self-reflection is going to be impacted by the quality of the educational and historical programming, and the quality of the staff at the living history museum.

There are two particular characteristics that help in determining the potential quality of the history at a living history museum: the nature of the organization and its financing, and the depth of historical work being done at the site. For example, living history sites that are tied to a historical society, preservation or heritage group, or a national park, will generally be better funded and have better long-term support than a smaller organization. The exception is an organization like Colonial Williamsburg, which is run independently but has a large endowment managed by the Colonial Williamsburg Foundation. In addition to financing, higher-quality living history sites will have historians on staff and will often have ongoing historical or archaeological work being done at the site (if it is also a historic site). The historians' depth of expertise often results in having well-trained historical interpreters and interpretation programs, as well as some academic components to the museum's programming. The quality of the historical interpretation that occurs at these sites is paramount to the success of your visit and the historical understanding that students will develop as a result. Of course, there are limits to even the best historical interpretation, as it is impossible to know exactly how life was or the views of people from the past; however, in terms of its educational mission, it is much more useful to have staff who can answer students' questions based on evidence they have studied in a nuanced way, rather than having staff that just look the part in historical costume with a limited understanding of the perspectives they portray.

Living History Museums Manage a Tension Between Entertainment and Education

There is a constant tension between engaging and entertaining visitors, and providing as well-warranted a historical experience as possible (Chhabra, 2008; Handler & Gable, 1997; Kirshenblatt-Gimblett, 1998). This is easily the strongest critique of the representation of the past in living history museums, and one of the challenges that living history staff face. As noted above, organizations with strong research departments and resources, such as Colonial Williamsburg and Plimoth Plantation, have their historical interpreters go to great lengths to research and prepare their roles, including personal narratives and trades. This research and preparation takes great amounts of money, time, and resources. Even with great research, the interpreters must find ways to engage visitors in the stories they tell or the trades they share, balancing an exciting story with an accurate context. For educators, it is important to recognize the tension between entertainment and intellectual pursuits at living history museums, and to structure activities accordingly to help students recognize and make sense of this tension.

This question of quality and authenticity raises the question broached by many historians—can living history museums be accurate and still fit their mission? Is it possible to recreate the world of the past in a way that is appealing to visitors and historically accurate? Similar to the production of history-related film (or any historical work, for that matter), there are always issues of veracity, narrative, and perspective when constructing a historical account. This problem is expanded, however, when the account is a place where visitors can walk through and experience life from the past. Of course, there are real limits to how closely this can be done.

Living History Museums Highlight the Importance of Geography

The sites in this chapter are all located on or near the actual historical sites they represent, but other living history museums are constructed on sites that have no historical importance or do not align with the focus of the living history museum. For example, American Village is a living history museum in Alabama that has living history exhibits that present key moments around the American Revolution, including the Boston Tea Party and the battles at Lexington and Concord. As we discuss in Chapter 5 with historic forts, geography does matter in terms of authenticity. For example, the Battle of Yorktown or the Boston Tea Party would make little sense in a spot away from water or a harbor. More often, the best sites are located at the historical site they interpret, or at least in the same region, so that the conditions faced add to the experience and help visitors comprehend the history being portrayed. For example, it would not make sense to students to hear that Founding Fathers such as Thomas Jefferson loathed Williamsburg's tropical summer and mosquitoes if it were located somewhere cooler and away from salt marshes.

Living History Museums Present Particular Views on the Past

Similar to any historical work, text, or museum, living history museums present particular views on the past that are guided by a number of factors. Their sites and the perspectives of historical characters they employ are influenced by the historical evidence they have available. Similar to any issue with history, the records, letters, and materials of the wealthy are going to be more abundant than those of the lower-class, indentured, or enslaved peoples who likely could not read or write at the time. This is also true of period furnishings. At Colonial Williamsburg, the Dewitt Wallace Decorative Arts Museum displays fine examples of eighteenth-century furnishings. These items were originally donated or collected to be included in the reconstructed buildings, but it was realized that all of the pieces were ones that an upper-class family would have owned. Most of the people who resided in Williamsburg would not have owned such fine furnishings. Instead, Colonial Williamsburg built replica furnishings based on the best historical information they had. Of course, this type of interpretation based on evidence is always a challenge in history.

Two other factors are more specific to living history museums. These are the importance of the need to make money and the need to appeal to the school curricula. In order to sustain themselves, many museums market toward education groups; however, living history sites are often designed with families and educational visitors in mind. In fact, many historic sites, such as Fort Ticonderoga and Fort Snelling, have expanded the living history aspects of their sites in order to have a more robust and appealing educational program. For the most part, these programs provide an entertaining and engaging experience for students, yet sometimes the need to attract visitors or the need to align with state curriculum standards in order to help teachers justify the field trip can lead living history museums into areas that do not necessarily fit their missions or contexts. For example, the tours at Colonial Williamsburg are designed to align with state history standards that may or may not fit the strengths of the living history program they employ.

Our Contemporary Context Limits Authenticity at Living History Museums

As noted above, complete historical authenticity is impossible. So, what can be expected of a living history museum? Will the population look just as it did? No, of course not. The population today is much older due to increased life expectancies, and this would likely be reflected. Further, the inclusion of a slave market, the role of indentured servants, or a presentation of the treatment of the disabled or infirmed during the period being interpreted could cause many visitors to be turned off, so these aspects of life are often downplayed or absent at living history museums. For example, a re-enactment of a slave auction in Colonial Williamsburg in an effort to expand its African American interpretation program made national news and caused such an outrage that it was not repeated (Janofsky, 1994). It is the challenge all history museums face—the need to attract visitors with engaging programming while not offending them, especially when challenging aspects of the past may be most educational, accurate, and inclusive.

In addition to painful aspects of the past, there are simple sensory issues, such as recreating the smell, feel, and sounds of the past. Tourists would not want to spend their days at Colonial Williamsburg or other history sites in the South in the summer without air conditioning. They would also not want to spend time around the historical interpreters if historically accurate in their odor, as most would rarely have bathed. The romanticism of living history sites is in part by design, as what museums portray has been selected to appeal to visitors, but it is also in part out of necessity, as visitors would not want to experience true authenticity when it comes to life in a different time and the hardships that were present. For educational visitors, it is important to have objectives that take advantage of what a living history site can offer while recognizing the limits that will always be present in terms of authenticity and accuracy.

COLONIAL WILLIAMSBURG, JAMESTOWN, AND YORKTOWN[1]

Colonial Williamsburg

Located on the site of the colonial capital of Williamsburg, Virginia, Colonial Williamsburg is a living history museum set on just over 300 acres. Colonial Williamsburg is run by the Colonial Williamsburg Foundation, and was started in the 1920s with help from the John D. Rockefeller family and other wealthy donors. The heart of this reconstructed town is Duke of Gloucester Street, which is the main thoroughfare, and runs between the campus of the College of William and Mary's historic Wren Building and the colonial capital building. Along Duke of Gloucester Street's mile-long stretch are original and recreated buildings designed to mirror what the town looked like on the eve of the American Revolution. Hundreds of buildings make up the historic area, and most of these are reproductions of buildings (such as the Williamsburg Inn) that serve a hospitality function. Of the reproduction buildings, some are replicas of actual shops and have historical interpreters sharing their trades with visitors. Others are recreations of actual buildings or are in the style of period buildings that house other functions for the museum, such as the hospitality functions run by the foundation, places for employees to cool off in the summer, or as housing for some of the employees. Eighty-eight of the more than 500 buildings are eighteenth-century structures that have been preserved.

In addition to the research around who lived in or would have visited Williamsburg in the 1770s, the historians are very interested in the architecture and material culture of the time. At Colonial Williamsburg, they use archaeology to find out as much as they can about the buildings and structures that existed, and this assists them in their reconstruction of these buildings. For visitors, the dig sites provide insights into how these living history sites do their work and provide some transparency into the interpretation that occurs. New construction sites at Colonial Williamsburg are especially popular as they are done with hand-made bricks and construction techniques from the past, at least as much as is allowed today (e.g. the required hardhats are not colonial issue). These sites provide a glimpse into the interpretation process as visitors can see artifacts being pulled from a dig site or the nature of the construction going into the "new" buildings being built.

Figure 7.2 Children from a school group participate in eighteenth-century militia activities during their school's trip to Colonial Williamsburg.

Source: Photo courtesy of the Colonial Williamsburg Foundation.

Colonial Williamsburg's programming includes the following: (1) various themed guided tours of the historic area on foot and via horse-drawn carriage; (2) the many interpreted trade shops and buildings, including the governor's palace, jail, and gunpowder magazine (with military demonstrations); and (3) episodes of street theatre that present interpretations of historic events related to the Revolution that occurred in Williamsburg. In all of these programs interpreters invite visitors to ask questions or even join in and become part of the re-enactment. Unlike many museums or historic sites, anyone can walk through the historic area for no charge. Tickets need to be purchased for those who want to enter the historic buildings and shops, or take part in the street theatre, but anyone can wander, walk, or even run through the historic area and still experience the sights, sounds, and smells. For school groups, the primary mode of engagement is special guided tours with expert guides and opportunities for the students to try their hands at playing colonial games, learning about the lives of colonial kids, and even wearing colonial dress.

The training for the approximately forty educational tour guides is intensive, lasting up to four months. Guides must be able to talk about every inch of the historic area, answer questions, and engage the various age groups on the tours. The tours are very informative and provide a good survey of the colonial town, a sampling of the trade shops, and one of the major buildings, as well as an explanation of some of the major events that occurred. The guides are adept at customizing tours to fit group needs and interests. In addition, the Colonial Williamsburg website provides numerous resources for teachers, including pre- and post-visit activities, lesson plans using the museum's artifacts and primary sources, a virtual tour, and electronic field trips that provide some insights into the museum and its programs.

Jamestown

Jamestown is the site of the first permanent English colony in North America, established in 1607. There are two historic sites related to Jamestown. The first, Historic Jamestowne (using the historic spelling), is operated by the National Park Service in partnership with Preservation Virginia, a historic conservation group. This site is located on the original Jamestown fort site, which later expanded to become a town, and the first Virginia capital. Most historians believed that the original fort site was lost to the James River until its wall posts were discovered during archaeological excavations in the 1990s. Today the site includes an outline of the fort, active archaeological dig sites of the major buildings, a historic church that includes a tower built in the seventeenth-century, and the Archaearium, a museum that houses many of the artifacts that have been excavated and that tells some of the story of Jamestown along with the process of unearthing and interpreting the site. In addition to the archaeological focus of the site, there are also historical interpreters who portray individuals who inhabited Jamestown and provide insights into life there.

The educational programs are run through a partnership between the Park Service Rangers, who guide groups primarily around the historic town site, and Preservation Virginia guides, who focus on the original fort and the archaeological work being done, as well as providing a visit to the Archaearium Museum. The Preservation Virginia program focuses in particular on archaeology and the role of historical archaeology in answering many of the questions that were left open in the history of the Jamestowne settlement, as well as the broader role archaeology can play within historical interpretation. Preservation Virginia archaeologists continue to dig at the site, and visitors can see and hear about the methods they use and the artifacts they have discovered. An exposed shell of a building structure stands on the footprint of one of their former dig sites to show both the construction methods and the approximate size of the building that formerly stood there.

The second Jamestown site is Jamestown Settlement, which comprises an interactive display museum that shares some similarities with the Minnesota History Center discussed in Chapter 4, and tells the story of Jamestown through the perspectives of the English, the local Powhatan people, and the first Africans brought to the colony as slaves. The site, which was originally built in the 1950s as a commemoration park for the 350th anniversary of the Jamestown settlement, and was renovated and expanded for the 400th anniversary, includes a living history museum that is comprised of a recreation of the original fort, a Powhatan village, and the three ships that brought the first settlers across the Atlantic. Jamestown Settlement is operated by the Jamestown–Yorktown Foundation, which also operates the Yorktown Victory Center, described below.

Similar to Colonial Williamsburg, Jamestown Settlement provides guided tours for educational groups along with demonstrations of life at the settlement, in the village, or on the ships. Specialized "hands-on" programs focus on themes such as life on the ships or life in the settlement. Here the interpreters are in place more for education and less to play a role of a specific historical agent. They are in place to show how to build a wooden canoe or fishing net, or to show how the crew of the *Godspeed* or one of the other ships used period navigation tools. The historical interpretation here is not focused as much on specific historic people who lived at Jamestown, or on the types of street theatre employed at Colonial Williamsburg. Instead, they use their historical interpreters to explain the jobs, customs, and processes that settlers and local Powhatan people adhered to at the time. For example, the interpreters show visitors how settlers built canoes to explore the rivers and salt marshes, how they learned to grow tobacco, or how the Powhatan tribe grew and ground corn for flour.

Both Jamestown sites offer online curriculum materials for teachers to use prior to visiting, including lesson plans, primary source materials, and educational videos. Both also offer opportunities for teachers to come to summer institutes to help develop their content knowledge and prepare them for bringing students on field trips. These institutes provide a preview of the programming Jamestown offers, more in-depth insights for the teachers on the site, and, in the case of Historic Jamestowne, the work of the archaeologists there. As the recommended tours and programs last roughly two to three hours at each site, groups are often encouraged to split their day between two sites. For Historic Jamestowne, which is partnered with Colonial Williamsburg, groups often spend the morning at Jamestown and the afternoon touring Colonial Williamsburg. For Jamestown Settlement, groups often then visit Yorktown Victory Center, the other site managed by the Jamestown–Yorktown Foundation.

Yorktown

Yorktown is the least developed of the three historic triangle destinations. Historically, it is the site of the last major battle of the American Revolution, where the mixed colonial and French forces under the command of General Washington, General Rochambeau, and Admiral de Grasse besieged Lord Cromwell's British army. A large portion of the actual battlefield is now run by the National Park Service, and parts of the downtown historic Yorktown village contain historic buildings that cater to tourism. In addition to the driving and walking tours of several key redoubts, or fortifications, on the battlefield, the Yorktown Victory Center was developed to provide a more comprehensive living history perspective on the events to supplement the park service's programs.

The Yorktown Battlefield National Park site consists of a small museum and both walking and self-driving tours of different parts of the battlefield. There are placards throughout the park that provide information about each site, as there is little actually left of the battlefield other than some surviving fortifications. The Park Service Rangers provide guided walking tours and some military demonstrations for tour and school groups. There are also tours and activities in some of the historic village buildings.

Victory at Yorktown is located alongside the Battlefield Park and provides a living history experience of the soldiers who fought at Yorktown. They demonstrate camp life and military drills for visitors, with other themed demonstrations such as military medicine during the Revolution. They also have a small museum on site that provides a chronology of the war and explanation of the Yorktown battle. Similar to its partner institution, Jamestown Settlement, Victory at Yorktown provides guided tours and demonstrations for school groups, along with some curriculum materials and other resources for teachers.

ACTIVITIES FOR A VISIT TO WILLIAMSBURG, YORKTOWN, AND JAMESTOWN

Activity #1: Exploring the Trades and Perspectives of Williamsburg

Overview

Ms. Sampson's sixth-grade classes visit Colonial Williamsburg each year between their units on the colonies and the American Revolution. The field trip helps her students experience and learn about what it would have been like to live during the period, and it also sets up study of the causes and ideas that led to the Revolution. A middle-school teacher for seven years, Ms. Sampson has participated in Colonial Williamsburg's Summer Teacher Institute and has a good understanding of the resources and activities that are available during a visit. She also tries to help her students get the most out of the visit by teaching them about the people who lived during the colonial era, and their diverse perspectives and views on the eve of the Revolution.

Objectives

Ms. Sampson's objectives for the visit to Colonial Williamsburg are for her students to be able to:

- Describe a colonial era trade or occupation, including who commonly held the position, what training or education was needed, and what a typical day of work was like.
- Identify and describe common views for and against the American Revolution in Virginia and the perspectives of people who held them.
- Conduct a historiographical analysis of historical interpretation.
- Develop questions for interviewing historical interpreters and tour guides.
- Present the information they have gathered on a colonial occupation to their class.

Pre-Visit Activities

As part of their study of the colonies, Ms. Sampson's students learn about the different origins, religions, customs, economies, and politics in the different colonies. In order to take advantage of the living history aspect of Colonial Williamsburg, Ms. Sampson has students explore the different trades and aspects of living during the period as the major goal for their visit. She also uses the visit to help students understand the issues on the eve of the Revolution and realize that colonists had many different views on the separation from Britain, and how the separation might impact their lives and businesses. Early in the week of their visit, as they finish up their unit on the colonies, she posts a list of the different trades and occupations that students can choose to examine during their visit. She tells the students to "identify a job from colonial times that you want to learn more about during our visit to Colonial Williamsburg," and she provides more information on each job from the Colonial Williamsburg website. For some less-known jobs, she asks if students know what the job may be—for example, "What do you think a cooper does?" The list of jobs varies from year to year depending on her students' interests, but often includes the following: printer, jailor, farm worker, gunsmith, weaver, shoemaker, carpenter, merchant, domestic cook, housewife, planter, soldier, and blacksmith. She selects occupations that she knows will provide different perspectives on the Revolution and also represent the social groups living in Williamsburg (e.g. indentured servants, gentry, enslaved Africans, women).

The next day students rank their top three most interesting trades or occupations, and Ms. Sampson sets up groups for the visit. In preparation for their investigation of a particular perspective of a trade or occupation, students do some investigatory work using materials Ms. Sampson has collected over the years (e.g. primary accounts, images). In small groups they generate a number of questions. Ms. Sampson makes sure all groups ask a few standard questions so that they can report back to the class when they present after their trip. These questions include:

- What groups of people are usually in this trade (e.g. indentured servants, educated gentry, enslaved African Americans, lower-class women)?
- What preparation or skills do you need for this trade (e.g. apprenticeship, education, class, rank)?
- What do you do in a typical day?
- How would the Revolution with Britain affect you and your trade?

These questions are on the board for students to put into the field trip journal charts that they are required to use during the visit. Many of the student-generated questions are pretty basic and relevant to a sixth-grader's life. For example, students ask, "How old were you when you started this job?", "Do you make a lot of money?", and "How much do you work?" Other students, especially those that have more prior knowledge about the occupation they select, have more specific questions. For example, one student who is interested in guns was prepared to ask "How long does it take you to build a whole gun?" and "What is the difference between a musket and a rifle?" Another student interested in farm workers and the experiences of enslaved or indentured workers prepares to ask, "Do you ever get time off?" and (for an indentured worker) "How long do you need to work in order to gain your freedom?"

As part of their preparation, students also do a virtual tour of Colonial Williamsburg, and Ms. Sampson provides background information on what they will likely see, showing images from the Colonial Williamsburg website and the virtual "Tour the Town" site. Ms. Sampson describes the history and purpose of Colonial Williamsburg and is explicit about the nature of the historical interpretation that is done there. She tells her class, "They [Colonial Williamsburg] have gone to great lengths to try to present the past as accurately as possible, but it would be impossible to make everything exactly as it was." She also explains the limitations of what they can expect, including that the people may be from different ethnic groups or of different ages than the original colonists they portray, that their accents are likely different, and that many people died at a young age in colonial times or would have had diseases that we rarely see today. Ms. Sampson notes that the interpreters are limited to the evidence that they have, and there is more evidence from the wealthy and powerful people who were educated than from many of the common colonists. She also discusses the different views that existed on the eve of the Revolution and reads some excerpts from primary sources that represent these different perspectives. These primary sources also model the types of materials used to develop the historical interpretations. They include the perspectives of the Randolph family, whose members were split between loyalist and patriot viewpoints. Ms. Sampson downloaded the resources from the Colonial Williamsburg website for teachers. Next, Ms. Sampson asks students in their trade groups to come up with two or three questions for the tour related to the Revolution or what was happening in Williamsburg at the time, based on the activities and virtual tour.

Ms. Sampson carefully structures the visit logistically so that the field trip goes smoothly and students are intellectually engaged during their visit, while also enjoying some free time and being able to select what they want to see. She has set an initial plan for their visit based on her previous experiences through the School and Group Tour Office. This allows the tour guides to plan in advance for the main buildings and sites Ms. Sampson would like her class to visit. Some of the visits to buildings, such as the capital building, needed to be scheduled in advance. She has four other chaperones accompanying her group of forty-eight students for their visit, including two parents, another teacher, and a special education aide, and she assigns three trades to each chaperone. Each chaperone has a group of about nine or ten students, and Ms. Sampson provides the chaperones in advance with instructions and information about the trades or occupations they are going to investigate with their groups, and the major questions students should ask on the visit. Ms. Sampson makes sure to assign each student to one of his or her top three choices, and often students end up visiting two of their top three because of the related interests in the groups. For example, many students who are interested in the gunsmith are also interested in the blacksmith, or those interested in the life of a soldier are also interested in the job of a jailor at the Gaol (jail).

During-Visit Activities

During the morning of the Williamsburg experience, the students take guided tours with Colonial Williamsburg educational tour guides. This tour provides a look at many of the highlights of Williamsburg, and includes a visit to the capital building and a demonstration of period clothing and games. Upon their arrival at Colonial Williamsburg, Ms. Sampson meets with the tour guides to make last-minute changes to their tour based on what events are occurring that day that align with her objectives. She let the guides know which trades students will be exploring in the afternoon so that they do not spend a lot of time at those places as part of their tour. She asks that they visit the capital building so that they can discuss the role of the Virginia delegates and the issues that arose in the 1770s. She also asks that they spend a little time walking through the Great Hopes Plantation section so that they get a sense for the role of agriculture and the fact that the population of Williamsburg at the time was roughly 50 percent African American, most of whom were enslaved. Finally, she asks the guides to explain the major events in Williamsburg leading up to the Revolution and the differing perspectives of the colonists, in addition to talking about the various buildings and trades. The tour guides accommodate these requests, especially as their tour explicitly works to meet the Virginia standards that examine the Revolution.

As students go with their tour guides in groups of sixteen, the tour guides answer questions and prompt students with some questions of their own. This is largely a didactic model, but Ms. Sampson's students ask their prepared questions along the way. The capital building seems to be particularly interesting to students as they learn about the role of the Virginia Delegates, who they were (white, male, land owning), and their rather limited power in what happened in the colony. The tour guides use students as examples to re-enact an actual trial held in the court room. The guides point out that "of course only white male property owners could serve on the jury," much to the chagrin and a chorus of boos from Sampson's female students. The guides also discuss the role of the delegates in Colonial Virginia and the lack of power they had relative to the king's appointees. This sets up questions about the causes of the Revolution as well as the fact that some delegates were against splitting from Britain because they profited from the relationship.

After the morning tour, the students eat lunch on the lawn at the Governor's Palace and play some colonial games. They then split into their groups in the afternoon to explore their trades. Students keep journals to record information—both about the views they hear on the Revolution from different historical characters they meet and also about their selected trades. The groups also take photographs. Some students bring along cameras, and Ms. Sampson has two digital cameras she lets students use if they do not have their own. The images then become part of the presentations they give when they return to school.

As the shops and locations for the trades are all over Colonial Williamsburg, Ms. Sampson sets up the groups to explore two trades that are close to each other. For example, one group goes to the site of the Great Hopes Plantation to talk with a slave who works in the fields and a planter or carpenter, while another group visits the blacksmith and gunsmith shops. The chaperones help prompt students to ask questions and also ask some follow-up questions of their own to make sure students receive the information they need. Students in the groups share notes along the way. After each group visits their three assigned trades, they have free time to decide as a group what else they want to do. Some groups opt to take pictures in the pillory, while others watch military drills near the powder magazine or attempt to pet the horses in one of the many pastures.

Post-Visit Activities

The day after their visit, Ms. Sampson begins her class with a discussion of the American Revolution and what students have learned from their visit, focusing on the perspectives of people for or against separation from Britain. She charts out this discussion on the whiteboard in the form of a modified KWL (Know, Want to know, Learned) chart. Students identify different reasons for colonists wanting to break away, such as "taxes" and "no representation." They also identify reasons for desiring to remain a colony, such as the view that they were "all British subjects" and loyal to the king, and that there were important economic considerations (such as ties merchants had to the British Empire). Ms. Sampson uses this discussion in following classes to teach the causes of the American Revolution and what happened during the war.

Following the discussion, the students move into their groups and put together a presentation for the class describing the trade they studied and using the questions identified above. In addition to the information they have collected during their visit, Ms. Sampson asks students to corroborate their answers with other sources that she makes available. This is a part of the activity that she has added most recently because she wants her students to be more analytical of the history they encounter and to develop their view of history as an interpretation or construction using different types of evidence. Therefore, she put together packets of primary and secondary materials, including graphics, maps, and other types of evidence that she knows will support what the students experienced at Colonial Williamsburg, but might also challenge some of the interpretations they saw. She also asks students to identify any remaining questions they have. This latter part of the activity is done to prompt them to think about how realistically the living history could be portrayed and how it differs from other historical accounts. During the student presentations, it is obvious that the groups identify the aspects of the occupation that are very grounded in the historical record with other items that they find to be missing or contradictory. For example, the group who studied the print shop at Colonial Williamsburg noted that the historical interpreter in the role of the apprentice in the shop was "much too old," and explained that they discovered this through records that list the ages of boys working in similar shops at the time (part of the materials provided by Ms. Sampson). Similarly, the group who studied the farm laborers at Great Hopes Plantation explained that up to 50 percent of the Williamsburg population at the time of the Revolution were either free or enslaved African Americans, and they felt the population they encountered did not match this census data. All of the presentations include images and basic information the students have collected about the trades, including answers to the questions identified above, and critiques that highlight both the strengths and limitations of the history presented, based on their own analyses.

The experience, and class session, ends with a class discussion of what the students have identified in their presentations, primarily what they thought the strengths and weaknesses were of Colonial Williamsburg's interpretation and presentation of the history. In particular, students brought up strengths such as the knowledge of the trades the interpreters had and the look of the shops and materials. Weaknesses identified by the students include the language, which differed from the documents they or Ms. Sampson had read, and the ability of people to portray the roles of enslaved or indentured people without knowing what it felt like. Ms. Sampson notes later that this discussion was important because it helped them gain some of the distance from the past represented at Colonial Williamsburg, and also because it allowed them to think more critically about our ability to really know the past.

Activity #2: Exploring Jamestowne's Mysteries Through Archaeology

Overview

The second case in this chapter highlights Mr. Smith's fifth-grade class visit to Historic Jamestowne. This visit aligns with the Virginia History course Mr. Smith teaches and helps students to understand what it was like to live during the seventeenth century in the first English colony in the New World. It also engages students in the disciplinary lens of archaeology, how it provides evidence of the past, and how it can provide answers that the analysis of historical documents and other evidence cannot provide. Mr. Smith was an anthropology and elementary education major and has visited the Jamestown archaeological dig site several times over the years to watch archaeologists unearth artifacts—from armor breastplates or bits of pottery to ship ballast stones from a foundation in the original fort.

Objectives

One of the goals for Mr. Smith's Virginia history class is for students to know about the origins of Virginia, including the first permanent settlement at Jamestown. He also uses the visit to help students learn the process of inquiry and to understand the role that archaeology plays in understanding the past. His specific goals for the visit include:

- Students will be able to describe the difficulties faced by the first English settlers at Jamestown.
- Students will be able to identify and describe the role of archaeology in understanding the past.
- Students will be able to describe the basic methods used by archaeologists to unearth and analyze artifacts.

Pre-Visit Activity

Prior to their visit, Mr. Smith explains the reasons behind the decision to establish the Virginia Company and the timeline of events of European exploration and colonization of the Americas. In particular he focuses on the competition between the English and Spanish for raw materials and wealth from New World colonies, and the desire to find trading routes to India and China. He reads from John Smith's accounts as well as those from other settlers and investors. In particular the class focuses on the "Starving Time" at Jamestown in 1609–1610 and the various explanations that exist for what caused it. He also uses videos from a Public Broadcasting Service special on the Jamestown archaeological dig that discovered the actual site of the original fort and found evidence of the real causes of the Starving Time. This part of the activity lays the foundation for their visit and the role that archaeology has played in helping to answer some of the mysteries of the Starving Time. He also has students look at some documents that describe the nature of the crew and settlers from the initial Jamestown exploration, and why the Virginia Company sent people skilled as goldsmiths, soldiers, and gentlemen instead of farmers and carpenters.

In order to prepare them for the archaeology aspect of the field trip, Mr. Smith lays out a gridded map on his floor with different artifacts hidden in sectors of the grid. He then explains to students that when archaeologists do a dig, they grid an area to track where they find artifacts. This system helps them to better piece together what the artifacts are and what they can tell us about life in the past. Students then play the role of archaeologists in working on the different grids, "discovering" artifacts and working with a group of students to attempt to interpret the nature and uses of the artifacts. Some of the materials for this activity came from Colonial Williamsburg's archaeology simulation kit and a lesson plan on teaching about Jamestown (see pp. 130–131 for more information). He supplements these artifacts with items such as an oyster shell. This activity provides some initial insights into the role and work of archaeologists, in particular their methods of systematically investigating a dig site and the interpretation process. At the end of it, Smith has students brainstorm questions to ask the tour guides and archaeologists they will meet during their visit about their work.

During-Visit Activities

Mr. Smith asks his students to answer several questions during and after their visit: what role does archaeology have in our understanding of the past? How does your new

Figure 7.3 Jamestown artifacts in the Archaearium Museum, Historic Jamestowne.

Source: Photo courtesy of Preservation Virginia.

understanding of Jamestowne help us to understand early Virginia? And why is the settling of Jamestowne a significant historical event? This latter question is discussed around the struggles of the early colonists in particular, but also concerns the many firsts for the colony in terms of agricultural advances, early manufacturing, and the transition from a venture of the Virginia Company to the establishment of a relatively independent and self-governing colony. Specifically, he asks students to be able to name some particular artifacts or interpretations to add to what they have discussed about early Virginia so far or about their prior knowledge of Virginia history. Mr. Smith feels that these questions help to frame the visit toward the objectives while also providing some freedom to enjoy the visit.

The class's two-hour visit to Historic Jamestowne is comprised primarily of the tour by a Preservation Virginia educational staff member. The tour focuses on the role of archaeology and some of the major discoveries at Jamestowne. It also helps to tie the story of Jamestowne to the material culture found at the site and other elements of forensic archaeology that helped to explain the major events in the early years of the colony, such as the Starving Time. For example, on archaeological evidence, many historians and archaeologists now believe that the Starving Time came during a severe drought in Virginia, and this drought led to a number of factors that could have caused the mass starvation. One is that the local Powhatan people had less surplus corn to trade with the colonists, leading to some hostilities. The drought also caused the already suspect water supply to become more brackish and could have led to salt poisoning. As part of the tour, students are able to see an active dig site of a basement and hear stories of major finds in the old wells that have been uncovered. They then see examples of those artifacts and the processes of the archaeologists in the Archaearium.

During the tour students are most engaged in the Archaearium, where they see how archaeologists create a reconstructed image from skeletons they have unearthed of early Jamestown colonists and learn about their investigations into how they died. One famous example is of the skeleton of a settler known as "JR" who the archaeologists discovered died of a musket ball to the knee. Students can see the cast of the JR skeleton with musket ball intact and hypothesize why the settlers may have turned to violence toward each other. The museum also shows many of the forensic techniques and technologies used to analyze and interpret the material they have unearthed. Mr. Smith plays an active role during the tour and museum visit by asking students questions and pointing out particular items he thinks certain students will find interesting. He also pushes them with questions to get them to think about the interpretation methods used by the archaeologists.

One exhibit shows a digital reconstruction of a colonist whose skeleton was found at Jamestowne. These digital technologies are used heavily to reveal the archaeologists' interpretations visually, and the students find these digital reconstructions to be quite interesting. The students not only comment on the digitally remastered colonist and skeletal remains, but they also jockey for their turn to use the "virtual viewers." These viewers look much like the telescopic viewers used at tourist sites to see views from tall buildings, but they show both the actual view and a semi-transparent digitally recon-structed view of what Jamestown archaeologists believe the fort and buildings looked like during the time of the settlement. This digital overlay also provides more information about the fort, buildings, and locations of important archaeological finds, such as in one of the wells. Mr. Smith asks students what they think of this digital recreation and if there are any other factors that would have changed the physical landscape of the site over the past 400 years, including the remaining mounds of earth that once served as Confederate artillery batteries during the Civil War.

Post-Visit Activities

As a debrief to their visit, Mr. Smith asks his students to write out their answers to the three questions he posed for the visit. He then leads a discussion with his class on what they have learned from their visit and asks them to share their answers to the questions. Some students compare the work of archaeologists to the work of forensics experts on television shows such as *CSI* and also point out how they can answer some questions that historians cannot, especially when it comes to explaining diseases that may not have been understood at the time they occurred. One student, who thought the JR skeleton (the one with the musket ball) was "cool," also questioned how archaeologists are able to know what the settlers would have looked like just from the bones. Other students noted that some things, such as recognizing the rank of a colonist because he was buried with a particular artifact that noted rank or class (e.g. a "captain's pike"), are more believable interpretations than some of the digital reconstructions.

Similar to Ms. Sampson, Mr. Smith wants his students to understand the events that occurred at Jamestown and the hardships the colonists faced at the time. He also wants his students to understand both the methods used to investigate the past, in this case through archaeology, and how these methods are used to present the history with which they engaged on their visit. He asks students how it has been possible to rebuild the wall of the fort in the right place and how the archaeologists know the reconstructed building is the same as it was four hundred years ago. Students answer that "the fence posts were placed in the same places where they found the old holes," and that the "building was based on something in England." Mr. Smith elaborates that the building was based on some construction that still exists in England from the period and area where many of the colonists came from, and that it represents the best guess they could make about what the building would have looked like. Making these aspects of the site and the interpretation that occurs more transparent is helpful for students to develop an epistemic view of the past as something that is constructed based on evidence, but is also always an interpretation with limits. Most of the students, however, think that both the reconstructed fence and building and the digital viewer that shows a recreation of the fort give them a better sense of what the settlement would have looked like. They note that these seemed much more reasonable than the graphic in their textbooks.

REFLECTIONS ON THE CASE

Taking large groups of K–12 students to often wide open living history museums at which visitors could spend literally days presents a number of logistical and instructional challenges. The nature of living history museums also presents challenges of helping students reflect on how they view the past through a contemporary lens, the nature of interpretation, and their ability to fully understand the past, similar to those encountered by the teachers described in previous chapters. As Ms. Sampson reflected, however, "teachers use field trips as extensions of their classrooms—as a different way of getting to reflect and think about history. The challenges are worth the experience."

Suggestions for Activities with Living History Museums

There are several keys to a successful field trip to a living history museum. These include extensive teacher preparation for a visit, balancing education and entertainment, and avoiding strictly didactic tours.

Preparation for a Visit to a Living History Museum is Critical

As also advocated in other chapters, it is important to be in contact with museum educators well in advance of your trip and to effectively prepare your students for their experience based on curricular objectives. It is imperative, especially at a site as large and complex as Colonial Williamsburg, to make a pre-field trip visit, if at all possible. If you have only a morning, or even a whole day, scheduled for your visit, you will need to plan and prioritize to make sure your students experience the particular events, exhibits, or experiences you want them to see. This pre-visit provides the opportunity to visit the different trade shops and sites, or whatever different components a living history site offers. It is also helpful to gain a sense of how long it will take to walk to different parts of the site, where the group entrance is, and what other factors you may have to take into account for your visit (e.g. where you can have lunch, what to do if it rains, whether all parts of the site are accessible).

In addition, it is important to talk with museum staff about special or seasonal programs. For example, Mr. Smith tries to time his visit to Jamestown for a time of the year when they are actively digging. Although this will depend in part on the weather, this means he goes relatively early in the fall, as this is also the time he can align it with his curriculum. As a result, his students get to experience seeing the archaeologists at work and often get a chance to ask questions or see artifacts being unearthed, as was the case several years ago when they saw an armor breastplate being uncovered. Similarly, living history sites such as Colonial Williamsburg often have street theatre or other special programming going on during their heavier tourist months. Ms. Sampson experienced the historic area through the Summer Teachers Institute held each year at Colonial Williamsburg, and she tries to bring her students during a time when some of the "Revolutionary City" programming is happening, although this is not always possible as they are not at the relevant point in the curriculum until late fall.

Both Ms. Sampson and Mr. Smith communicate with tour guides in advance to make sure they can fit the tour to the objectives for the class. As they are interested in the work of the historical interpreters and archaeologists, they often request guides who are more knowledgeable on those subjects. Often Ms. Sampson has the same tour guides year after year. Tour guides are usually happy to accommodate specific requests for adapting the tour, if reasonable, and they welcome input from the teachers to help make the trip a success.

Finally, Ms. Sampson in particular talked about carefully selecting chaperones to accompany her groups. She noted,

> Field trips are not about letting the students run freely anymore or the teacher being let off the hook for instruction on a particular day. Getting approval is difficult, and when you do get it teachers want the experience to be worthwhile.

Some parents want to come along more for the social part of the trip or to be with their children rather than to lead the groups through the planned activity. Ms. Sampson often has special education aids and recently retired teachers, as well as parents with whom she is comfortable, to take the role of chaperones. She does not put an open call out for volunteers but sends requests individually. Although some parents have been disgruntled in the past, she noted that this was in the best interest of her students and necessary for the trip to be a success.

There is a Need to Balance Entertainment and Education

A second feature of living history museums, and one that has brought many critiques from museum professionals, is the role of living history as "edutainment", meant to entertain more than to educate. The sites described in this chapter all take their educational work very seriously, but they also know they need to draw visitors. However, a well-structured activity helps students to focus on particular aspects of the museums and opportunities for educational interactions beyond getting a picture in the stocks or buying a three-cornered hat.

It is important that students do enjoy themselves and have some choice during the experience, but Ms. Sampson noted that in her experience they have fun regardless of what they are doing at Colonial Williamsburg. She said that the memories her students often come back and talk to her about are their experiences "standing in a jail that once housed some of Blackbeard's crew," and the experience of learning about how the tradespeople made guns or hats or shoes or newspapers at the time. She also noted, however, that as a result of their research of one particular occupation and discussion of the historical interpretation they experienced, many students began to look more critically at the history they read, in their textbooks in particular. The key to focusing on the education endeavors of a field trip is the combination of structure, choice, and fun, according to Mr. Smith and Ms. Sampson.

Pre-Visit Activities Promote Active Student Engagement Over Potentially Didactic Tours

Both of the teachers in this chapter noted that they have been impressed with the tour guides they have worked with at Colonial Williamsburg and Jamestown in terms of their knowledge, their ability to engage with the students, and their flexibility. They also both explained, however, that the tours are set up to be generally didactic, with the tour guide providing the content and framing the interactions. This is largely by design as the guides cannot assume that the students know anything about the history they describe or that the teacher has any particular structured activity that coincides with the visit. Overall the thoughtfulness and expertise of a good guide is extremely useful, but the teachers in these cases want students to be more actively involved. This is why they have students prepare questions in advance and do so much preparation work before their visits. Prepared students who ask questions get more out of the experience and, in the opinion of both teachers, make for a better tour, as the guides react with energy and information when they work with an active and inquisitive group.

Both teachers also identify the importance of their students being able to compose thoughtful questions about the past and what they are studying, and therefore emphasize this skill development as part of their visit to the museum. They also have students share questions, and if a student's question is not answered during the tour, Ms. Sampson will often send a few of the questions students are most interested in to a staff member at Colonial Williamsburg to get an answer. In some years she has also followed up this activity with a visit from a historical interpreter or military re-enactor, most often during the Civil War unit, to talk about how interpreters prepare for their roles and to talk about the daily lives or work of soldiers, or whatever the historical character may be. This again emphasizes the interpretive nature of this kind of historical representation, as well as good content she wants her students to think about. Similarly, Mr. Smith often brings up the topic of archaeology later in the year during a unit on the environment when he asks students to think about what future archaeologists may think of some of the items they find in landfills. He says this is particularly poignant as many of the key finds at Jamestown were from an old well that was then used as a trash dump.

NOTE

1   Special thanks to Colonial Williamsburg staff Jae Ann White and Menzie Overton for their help in providing information on educational tour group programs, and to Tom Patton from Preservation Virginia for providing information on Historic Jamestowne's program.

RESOURCES

Colonial Williamsburg: www.history.org

Colonial Williamsburg School Tour Group Information (includes pre- and post-visit lessons plans, links to information on Colonial Williamsburg activities, and group reservation contact information): www.history.org/history/teaching/groupTours/index.cfm

Historical character interpretation from Colonial Williamsburg: www.history.org/history/teaching/enewsletter/volume7/dec08/teachstrategy.cfm

Historic Jamestowne—Preservation Virginia: www.historicjamestowne.org/

Historic Jamestowne archaeological dig information: www.historicjamestowne.org/the_dig/

Historic Jamestown National Park Service: www.nps.gov/jame/index.htm

Jamestown Settlement and Victory at Yorktown: www.historyisfun.org/jamestown-settlement.htm

Jamestown Settlement and Victory at Yorktown educational page: www.historyisfun.org/educational-adventures.htm

Kelso, B. (2006). *Jamestown, The Buried Truth*. Charlottesville, VA: University of Virginia Press.

Yorktown Battlefield National Park Service: www.nps.gov/yonb/index.htm

CHAPTER 8

Memorials and Monuments

The Memorials and Monuments of 9/11

Figure 8.1 State of Connecticut 9/11 memorial in Westport, CT.

INTRODUCTION

In 1994 artist Gunter Demnig began a memorial project to remember and honor victims of the Holocaust including Jews, homosexuals, mentally disabled, and others targeted by the Nazis. Demnig designed and installed stumbling blocks, *stolpersteine*, outside the homes or offices where the victims lived or worked. The blocks look like small brass plaques that are placed into the brick or stone sidewalk (see Figures 8.2 and 8.3). There are now over 13,000 stumbling blocks across Germany, Austria, Hungary, and the Netherlands. Each stone lists the person's name, date of birth, when they were deported, and where and when they died.

Figure 8.2 Stolpersteine memorials in Amsterdam, the Netherlands.

The Stolpersteine project is a microcosm of monuments and memorials covering many events and people all over the world. The stumbling blocks remember and honor those who prematurely lost their lives, promote individual reflection, and echo values and norms from the time period in which they were created. They serve as a European collective memory of the Holocaust. In addition, like many monuments, the Stolpersteine project generated controversy. Some people believe it is demeaning to the victims to walk on stones with victims' names. Others say that those who stop and look and have to stoop low to read the names are helping to remember the victims in a positive manner. While most German towns and cities are receptive to the stones, the mayor of Munich rejected the project, saying the city already had many memorials. Numerous monuments and memorials face similar controversy over their location, physical appearance, purpose, and meaning.

Monuments and memorials provide valuable opportunities for students to study the past because they can be found in most towns and cities, reflect the time period in which they were created, influence and echo society's collective memory, and often present national historical narratives through a local or regional lens. As a result students can study historical events/time periods through monuments as well as consider broader issues of how the past is constructed and remembered.

This chapter explores the potential of monuments[1] as a teaching tool. The chapter portrays monuments as opportunities for students to analyze historical perspectives, evaluate historical significance, and connect the past with the present. The chapter begins with an overview of the role of monuments in remembering the past and monuments' unique features. The chapter then presents two cases centered on monuments erected

Figure 8.3 House and sidewalk where the stones in Figure 8.2 are located.

to remember and commemorate the terrorist attacks of September 11, 2001, and concludes with suggestions for effective activities with monuments.

IMPORTANT CHARACTERISTICS OF MONUMENTS AND MEMORIALS

Monuments and memorials are among the most common ways our society remembers the past. There are thousands of monuments across the United States, with most cities and towns adorned by their presence. Monuments honor the dead, commemorate victory in war, celebrate milestones in politics, science, education, industry, and social history, and can promote healing and reflection.

Monuments are unique in their purpose, function, format, and location. In planning for learning experiences with monuments there are several important characteristics of monuments to take into account. These characteristics include that monuments serve a variety of purposes, usually contain a narrow perspective, often situate local history within a national historical narrative, possess a unique format, and exist in most towns and cities. Each of these features is discussed below.

Monuments Serve a Variety of Purposes While Influencing Collective Memory

First, monuments serve a variety of purposes such as to remember victims, create heroes, promote patriotism, and celebrate victories, but ultimately these purposes all function to perpetuate and influence collective memory. Monuments allow groups in society to create and maintain collective memory, thus contributing to the collective memory of the nation (along with other forms of narrative, such as popular culture). Collective memory can also be defined by what is not chosen to be represented with monuments. Collective memory is a shared set of thoughts and beliefs about the past that is constructed by society. As time passes there is a distance placed between individuals and specific events. Details are often forgotten or distorted, and the meaning of an event supersedes the exact details. This meaning becomes part of the collective memory. Monuments become a mechanism through which societies and cultures pass on the meaning of an event to those who did not experience it, and thus help to perpetuate memory of the event, a memory that may be broad and inclusive or distorted and narrow. Monuments work together with popular culture, saved artifacts, and oral history to represent collective memory. That is not to say that monuments are always inclusive of all perspectives or that a nation's collective memory is representative of all views, but monuments still contribute, most often, to the dominant collective memory narrative.

The other types of museums discussed in this book may also operate as a form of collective memory, but museums such as living history museums, and artifact and display museums, change their narratives over time, use primary source documents and artifacts, provide additional resources, and often provide multiple narratives. Monuments, however, usually present a static representation of the past, do not have supporting documents, and usually present a narrow perspective.

Monuments Represent Narrow Perspectives

Monuments are more narrow in the perspectives included and much less likely to be critical; rather, they promote a past that the people who created the monument—though not necessarily everyone who lived at the time—can be proud of, celebrate, and feel good about (at least at the time of the monument's creation). Also, monuments serve social, political, economic, cultural, and educational purposes (Loewen, 1999), all of which promote the collective memory of society.

Monuments Often Present Local History Within a National Context

Another important characteristic of monuments is the interplay between national history and local history. The majority of monuments are created and funded locally or regionally. They often celebrate local heroes or mourn local victims, often within a national context. For example, many WWII monuments honor local heroes and mourn local soldiers who died. These monuments function to localize and personalize a national event. Another example is Gettysburg Battlefield from the Civil War, where there are numerous monuments that commemorate various local, state, and ethnic military units, among others. There is still often a national collective memory or common thread connecting the monuments (mourning the dead and celebrating the war), but it is done through a local lens. As this chapter explores later, the same applies to many 9/11 monuments, particularly monuments in the northeast of the country, which primarily mourn local victims of the attacks. This interaction between local and national history is particularly prominent with monuments.

The Format of Monuments is Unique

Monuments have a distinctive format. They typically have a written component and an artistic or aesthetic element. The text often provides historical context and other information. Most monuments contain the date when they were dedicated and the person or organization doing the dedication; thus, monuments capture two moments in their conception. The first is the actions of people at the time of creation—the way the monument reflects the time period in which it is created. The second is the collective memory of people at a later time. The most traditional type of monument is stone and/or metal because of the material's durability, though certainly there are many non-traditional monuments. For the vast majority of monuments, the written and aesthetic elements are static. They are rarely changed or updated. While they may be renovated or maintained, typically monuments are not redesigned when new historical information becomes available or as societal attitudes change. At face value, monuments may come across as dated and inert to students, while also being misinterpreted through a lack of background information or educational support. They may appear to be authoritative, but they may be misunderstood more than museums that have supporting documentation and staff to assist in interpretation. However, the advantage to this lack of fluidity is that monuments become great resources to study how history, and the collective memory of the past, is reflected by the time period of their creation.

In addition, most monuments purport to be self-explanatory. They come with no education director, no historian, and no set of lesson plans. There are a handful of monuments with online resources, particularly national monuments, but these resources are still not nearly universal. And for the most part monuments are not particularly interactive. Most are available to touch, but they do not have video, photographs, interactive computer screens, re-enactments, or manipulative artifacts that might exist at other types of museums. Most monuments command a particular kind of receptive stance from those who come into contact with them. They invite attention and reverence, not interaction. Monuments direct a message at the viewer, rather than inviting inquiry from or interaction with the viewer. This is an intentional expression of the authority of the message.

Monuments Are Widely Available and Accessible

Monuments, like historic houses, are among the most common and available forms of public history. Artifact and display museums, historic sites, etc., are certainly plentiful, but monuments exist in most towns and cities, and even at many schools. Numerous monuments are also available to view on the internet. There is an almost endless supply of monuments at teachers' and students' disposal (see resources on page 154 and in Appendices B and C).

Other Features of Monuments and Memorials

There are two additional features of monuments that are important to consider when developing activities with students.

First, monuments, and the past that they represent, cannot be properly understood outside of the political, social, and economic context in which they were created. Their purposes tend to favor unidimensional patriotic narratives about the past—they "don't just tell stories about the past; they also tell visitors what to think about the stories they tell" (Loewen, 1999, p. 22). The ability to maintain collective memory is contingent "on the socioeconomic power of the groups who produce and maintain them" (Mitchell, 2003, p. 443). Collective memory is strongly connected to social identity, nation building, and ideology (Santos, 2001), and reflects national myths that "reinforce collective identities, social values, and moral orientations" (Seixas, 2002, p. 1).

Second, monuments can reignite animosities and generate controversy. There is often significant debate regarding what story about the past a monument should tell or even whether a monument should exist at all. For example, it took fifty years before there was agreement on creating the FDR Memorial in Washington, D.C. Even the final monument sparked controversy for its historical accuracy because, among other things, it does not show FDR smoking, a politically correct modification reflective of the late 1990s when the memorial was built. Other monuments become controversial long after they are unveiled due to changes in society. Nathan Bedford Forrest has more monuments in Tennessee than any single individual in any state (Loewen, 1999). Forrest was a Confederate general during the Civil War and the first leader of the Ku Klux Klan. Through changing societal beliefs in more recent times his monuments generate debate about the appropriateness of glorifying his memory. In a related case, Richmond, Virginia is well known for its controversial Monument Avenue. Not only is the avenue home to monuments for such Civil War Confederates as Jefferson Davis and Robert E. Lee, but more recently, native son and African American tennis star Arthur Ashe was honored with a monument, spawning significant debate and disagreement.

Monuments present teachers with unique opportunities and challenges to study the past. Monuments are important sources of historical evidence that can complement the written records that students often study, while at the same time characterizing the glaring gaps in historical memory based on race, ethnicity, condition of servitude, sex or gender, or disability (Loewen, 1999). Monuments should be an integral part of K-12 history education because they are widely viewed in public and are often perceived as objective or truthful, and therefore they influence collective memory and the national historical narrative. In order to use monuments effectively, they need to be analyzed and visited, keeping in mind their unique features.

THE MEMORIALS AND MONUMENTS OF 9/11

The events of September 11, 2001 united Americans behind ideas of freedom and democracy in a way rarely exhibited elsewhere in the post-Cold War era. That unity quickly gave way to disagreement and discord, not just about our military engagements abroad, but about how we should collectively remember 9/11. Among the many perspectives is the view that 9/11 be told as a national narrative about attacks on freedom. Another views 9/11 as a local story of grieving families. Yet another asks if 9/11 memorials should focus exclusively on patriotism or also allow U.S. citizens to look inward, seeing much to praise and much to criticize. What is the message society wants to send to future generations about what happened that day? While 9/11 is certainly the "ultimate teachable moment" (Hess and Stoddard, 2007, p. 231), as the event becomes further removed in time and our students no longer draw on lived memory (Wineburg, 2001), there is a remarkable teachable moment in exploring how we remember 9/11 through our monuments.

The events of 9/11 occurred within the context of a widely (but not universally) held belief in American physical and moral superiority, and 9/11 challenged this ethos. Memorials of 9/11 may serve to reassure the American public in their belief that the United States is a great country and promote a positive American collective memory. Initially, the creation of some 9/11 memorials, particularly at the site of the World Trade Center buildings, generated conflict over their messages and "memory" (Marcus, 2007). Families of firefighters and other first responders clashed with families of other victims and with government officials over the design of the Ground Zero memorial, as well as its message. Students can examine multiple sites of memory to determine whether the collective memory of 9/11 is one of consensus, and thus an authoritative collective memory (Goldberg, Schwartz, & Porat, 2008), or if there is in fact no single 9/11 narrative that we can collectively remember (and what the multiple narratives are).

Students need to advance their historical consciousness by, among other things, understanding the interpretive choices and constraints used to construct historical accounts, understanding the challenges in representing the past in the present, and acknowledging historical actors' differing perspectives (Seixas, 2002). Monuments themselves can promote the intensification of historical consciousness by examining the monument's story of creation, the perspectives included and omitted, and the reception by the public.

Since the events of 9/11, towns, cities, and states have erected hundreds of monuments across the country. Many are designed and created by local towns or private organizations to remember specific victims or to commemorate the events more broadly. Several state governments also sponsored monuments. The largest and most nationally representative monument is at Ground Zero in New York City (see the resources on p. 154 for websites that provide comprehensive lists of 9/11 monuments/memorials).

In Connecticut there are more than thirty monuments, mostly located in the southwest portion of the state near New York City.[2] They range from small plaques to large sculptures, and also include the official State of Connecticut memorial on Sherwood Island in Westport, which has a stone structure but is also a "living history" site. Living history memorials—not to be confused with living history museums, which we discuss in Chapter 7—are designed in partnership with the National Park Service and focus on designing 9/11 memorials that include trees, flowers, or other living, green spaces in the form of a forest, town center park, or community garden. In addition, the Connecticut Historical Society created a traveling monument/exhibit, which toured the state. The Connecticut monuments focus primarily on remembering the 153 victims of the 9/11 attacks who were from Connecticut, and many of the monuments were created at the instigation of relatives of the victims.[3]

Just as the Ground Zero site in New York has generated controversy, Connecticut 9/11 monuments are not immune to disagreement about their appearance, location, and/or message. For example, in Easton, Connecticut a 9/11 monument honoring town citizens killed in the attacks was stalled numerous times. The quest for the monument began in 2003. It took until 2008 for a town council vote, at which time they rejected the location (and did so again in 2009). In addition, some town residents said the monument would bring back painful memories, while other residents believed the monument would help the healing process. The monument was eventually approved. In Greenwich, Connecticut there was significant debate about whether a 9/11 monument should contain the names of the twelve official town residents killed or also include the additional fourteen people killed who had some affiliation with the town. The monument constructed contained all twenty-six names, but the compromise is that a second monument will most likely be developed and erected (Loh, 2010). And, in perhaps the most controversial case, in Kent, Connecticut the father of a victim asked that the words "Murdered by Muslim terrorists" be included on the monument, creating disagreement about the purpose and message of the monument, and making national news. The town council rejected the proposed wording, believing it inappropriate for a public monument using public money and placed on public land.

The case for this chapter presents activities for using the 9/11 monuments in Connecticut as part of a lesson on monuments, memorials, and history.

ACTIVITIES FOR A VISIT TO 9/11 MEMORIALS AND MONUMENTS

For this case we present two activities that utilize 9/11 monuments, one developed by Mrs. Reddell, who teaches in Connecticut, and a second enacted by Mr. Strickland, who teaches in North Carolina. These two activities are appropriate for a current events class, a United States history class, or a government/civics class. Both activities encourage students to critically evaluate the purpose and message of monuments.

Activity #1

Overview

Mrs. Reddell believes in incorporating current events into her history class and, whenever possible, making explicit connections between the past and the contemporary world. She is always seeking new and unique resources to enhance her instruction and requires students to actively participate in classroom endeavors. For Mrs. Reddell, history is about doing, not about passively listening. She brings her students on several museum visits a year, including a four-day trip to Washington, D.C., several visits to regional museums, and multiple walking tours in the local community. Her inspiration for working with museums began during a field experience at a state historical society as part of her pre-service teacher education program.

Mrs. Reddell's monument activity described here requires students to create their own monuments, as well as visit monuments in the community, and is implemented near the end of the year in her college prep U.S. history class of mostly high school juniors when they study the 1990s through today.

Mrs. Reddell's activity helps students think about how and why monuments can reflect different perspectives on the same past events. She asks students to examine two monuments created to commemorate Shays' Rebellion, to visit 9/11 monuments, and then to create their own monuments for 9/11 from a variety of different perspectives.

Objectives

The objectives of this assignment are for students to:

- Understand the subjective nature of monuments and markers.
- Evaluate the impact of 9/11 on various groups from the group's perspective, and thus develop historical empathy.
- Recognize how monuments reflect and shape society's collective memory.

Essential Question

How do we remember 9/11 and subsequent events?

Pre-Visit Activities

Prior to the class field trip Mrs. Reddell's students participate in an activity that demonstrates the subjectivity of monuments, particularly the way they focus on a narrow perspective about the past. The activity includes the following:

- Mrs. Reddell asks the students what they know about Shays' Rebellion[4] and facilitates a discussion around their knowledge (they have studied the rebellion earlier in the year). Students usually respond with comments such as, "farmers in Massachusetts were upset . . . the banks were taking farms . . . farmers closed the courts . . . farmers fought the army . . . it showed the Articles of Confederation were too weak."
- Next, she provides a brief overview of Shays' Rebellion, building on students' knowledge and covering enough background and context to understand two monuments about the rebellion.

Table 8.1 Text of monuments for Shays' Rebellion.

First Monument (Dedicated in 1927)

In this town on Sunday morning, February fourth, 1787, Daniel Shays and 150 of his followers, in rebellion against the commonwealth, were surprised and routed by GENERAL BENJAMIN LINCOLN in command of the Army of Massachusetts, after a night march from Hadley of thirty miles through snow in cold below zero. This victory for the forces of government influenced the Philadelphia Convention which three months later met and formed the Constitution of the United States. Obedience to law is true liberty.

Second Monument (Erected in 1987)

In this town on Sunday morning, February fourth, 1787, CAPTAIN DANIEL SHAYS and 150 of his followers who fought for the common people against the established powers and who tried to make real the vision of justice and equality embodied in our revolutionary declaration of independence, was surprised and routed, while enjoying the hospitality of Petersham, by General Benjamin Lincoln and an army financed by the wealthy merchants of Boston. True Liberty and Justice may require resistance to law.

- Third, Mrs. Reddell displays and reads the inscriptions from two monuments[5] (see Table 8.1) commemorating Shays' Rebellion. These monuments present very different views of Shays and his role in history. The original monument criticizes his actions while the more modern one celebrates what he did and what he stands for.

Many students are surprised at the difference in the messages about Shays and usually have several questions. The most typical are, "Who created these monuments, and when?", "Was Shays a good guy or a bad guy?", and "How much of an influence did this really have on the creation and ratification of the Constitution?" After answering student questions about the monuments Mrs. Reddell facilitates a class discussion about how each monument "remembers" Shays' Rebellion. For each one, students discuss:

- What is the message about Shays? What are the perspectives?
- When do you think it was dedicated? What are the possible purposes of each monument?

Only after the discussion does she inform them of the date each monument was completed. This exercise allows students to see how the same event and the same person can be viewed through two very different perspectives as presented by monuments. Students begin to see how monuments are subjective, how they reflect the time period in which they were created, and how they could shape society's collective memory.

The final component for the pre-visit activity is a homework reading. Mrs. Reddell asks students to read an article from *The New York Times* that provides a straightforward and comprehensive overview of key events on 9/11 (Schmemann, 2001), and to answer several questions based on the reading. Each year she finds that students, even those growing up in the greater New York area, know fewer and fewer details about the events of 9/11. For Mrs. Reddell, this content background is critical. "Without knowledge of the content," she says, "students cannot possibly understand the monuments or place them within any kind of historical context." With this set-up students are ready to examine 9/11 monuments.

During-Visit Activities

For this segment Mrs. Reddell accompanies students on an all-day visit to local 9/11 monuments. They visit the official State of Connecticut monument in Westport, as well as monuments in Danbury and Ridgefield, and also three in Milford, all locations situated in the southwest portion of the state, close to New York. Table 8.2 provides an overview of the monuments; for images of some of the 9/11 monuments visited by Mrs. Reddell's class, see Figures 8.4, 8.5 and 8.6.

During the visit to each site students are given enough time to explore the monument, take notes, and reflect on the monument and the events of 9/11. Mrs. Reddell provides questions to guide the notes. These include the following. (1) What is the monument's primary message about 9/11? (2) How does the monument make you feel? (3) How does the monument make use of words, light, architecture, materials, sound, symbols, and other aesthetics to convey its message, establish a mood, impact a visitor, etc.? (4) Which perspectives are included, and which are left out? (5) How does this monument compare with the others visited? Mrs. Reddell reports that these questions are particularly effective for recognizing how the monuments both reflect and potentially shape society's collective memory of 9/11. Mrs. Reddell does not discuss the monuments while on site, believing it is more important to spend the day visiting as many sites as possible and to debrief after students have had a chance to reflect.

In recalling the first time she took students to visit 9/11 monuments, Mrs. Reddell reflected, "I was unprepared to answer questions about the monuments' creation and I was not ready for some of the students' emotional reactions." In subsequent years she added more time for students to reflect and process their emotions, as well as to answer the question about how the monuments made them feel. Mrs. Reddell also completed extensive research on the monuments' backgrounds. For each monument she explored online resources about 9/11 monuments (see the resources listed on p. 154), called the town offices where each monument is located and spoke with town employees who could provide background information, and read archived newspaper articles that reported on the monument's creation and dedication, including any controversies and the public reaction. She says the research is invaluable for enhancing the field trip experience and for expanding her own understanding of monuments more broadly.

Post-Visit Activities

After the visit to the 9/11 monuments Mrs. Reddell guides students through five steps over one-and-a-half class periods.

Day One

First, Mrs. Reddell moderates a discussion of the 9/11 monuments visited based on the five guiding questions from the field trip. Students use their notes as a reference and Mrs. Reddell displays multiple photographs of each monument to help trigger

Table 8.2 Monuments visited by Mrs. Reddell's Class.

Location of Monument	Year of Creation	Format/Structure	Description and Other Details	Created/Erected by
Sherwood Island State Park, Westport, CT	2002	Living history and granite monument	The official State of Connecticut 9/11 memorial. Granite monument and granite bricks with names of victims. Lots of trees and shrubs. Next to Long Island Sound (see Figures 8.1, 8.5 and 8.6).	State of Connecticut
Milford, CT	2002	"Flight 93 Heroes Park"—living history, 37 acres of open space	Open space owned by the town that resembles the PA field where United Flight 93 crashed.	Town of Milford
Milford, CT	2006	"Milford Remembers" monument and flowers	The official Town of Milford memorial. Located behind Town Hall next to a river and waterfall. Three-sided granite monument with plaques. One side each for NY, D.C. and PA.	Town of Milford
Milford, CT	2002	September 11 memorial garden and monument	Originally a garden and small park, it was updated to be a memorial for 9/11. Concrete from Ground Zero in NY is buried at the site. There is a stone monument with a plaque and benches.	Live Oaks School Community
Danbury, CT	2004	Plaque/marker, glass column, and park area	Located within a park, the memorial includes a 12-foot-tall column of starfire glass and a plaque (see Figure 8.4). The sculpture and plaque are connected by a gray brick walkway and surrounded by shrubs, trees, and flowers. The interior of the glass column is empty, representing the twin towers, and the names of all CT victims are etched on the glass.	City of Danbury
Ridgefield, CT	2011	Sculpture with three benches and trees	There are three benches representing the three town residents killed in the 9/11 attacks. The sculpture includes a beam from the destroyed twin towers at Ground Zero in New York. On public land but privately funded.	Town of Ridgefield

IMAGES OF SOME OF THE 9/11 MONUMENTS VISITED BY MRS. REDDELL'S CLASS

Figure 8.4 Plaque at 9/11 memorial in Danbury, CT.

Figure 8.5 Names in granite at 9/11 memorial in Westport, CT.

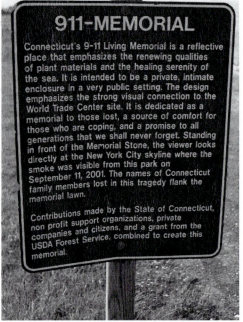

Figure 8.6 Sign at 9/11 memorial in Westport, CT.

conversation. "At first," Mrs. Reddell explains, "students are reluctant to participate either because they are not confident about their answers or perhaps because of the emotional nature of the content." However, based on several years of leading this discussion, she finds that students are quite adept at understanding and explaining the primary messages of the monuments and at processing their emotions. Where she says they struggle is in thinking about the aesthetic components of the monuments and at teasing out the perspectives included and left out. Students are not accustomed to thinking about monuments in this way. Her use of photographs during this activity is particularly helpful in prompting discussion of the aesthetics. For example, a photo of the official state monument in Westport helps students to remember the views of the granite etched with victims' names, with Long Island Sound in the background, a beautiful and peaceful setting. Students are able to be much more specific when reflecting on the site with these visual references.

Next, students are placed into small groups. Each group creates the text and aesthetic features for a new 9/11 monument. They must also choose a location for the monument. Each group is assigned a unique perspective and is required to create their monument from that perspective. Assigned perspectives include: women, firefighters/police officers, officials from the Saudi Arabian Embassy in New York, Wall Street bankers, and U.S. government officials. Students are provided with one-page descriptions of their perspective, with contextual information. To guide the students Mrs. Reddell urges them to consider what they want the message of their monument to be, and what they want society to know, understand, and feel fifty or a hundred years from now. The students need to consider the text as well as what colors, materials, textures, and shapes they will use.

Third, Mrs. Reddell instructs students to work in their groups to create the text and aesthetics for their monument on large poster paper. At first, students struggle with an instinct to only tell a patriotic story. As she walks around to confer with each group, Mrs. Reddell pushes the students to think carefully about how their perspective would want to remember 9/11.

Day 2

Fourth, the students post their monument texts and aesthetic descriptions on the walls of the classroom and then complete a museum gallery walk. During the walk Mrs. Reddell asks the students to take notes regarding how the monuments depict the same event from the various perspectives. Students are provided with guiding questions to answer during the gallery walk, including: (1) what are the similarities and differences between your 9/11 monument and others in terms of the message, aesthetics, and perspective? (2) Not including your own, which monument do you feel is the most historically accurate? Which one did you like the best? (3) How are these monuments similar to and different from the monuments we visited around Connecticut? Mrs. Reddell smiles when discussing this segment of the lesson. She explains:

> This is a key "Aha!" moment . . . students really begin to see how 9/11 can be viewed from different perspectives and that they had the power—the agency—to shape the message of their monument. In our later discussions students get very excited and want to race out to research monuments in our own community—Civil War monuments, WWII monuments, and one in our town dedicated to Ella Grasso[6] . . . "Who created them?" they

want to know, and "How are they subjective?" I always feel like I created junior historian monsters.

Finally, Mrs. Reddell facilitates a whole class discussion of the student-created monuments and their perspectives to assess students' content knowledge and their understanding of the way monuments are created with subjectivities and agendas. By creating their own monuments from different perspectives, students build on the Shays activity and are able to grasp the way in which monuments are subjective, while considering the importance of recognizing historical perspectives.

Activity #2

Overview

Mr. Strickland's monument activity has many of the same goals as Mrs. Reddell's lesson, but takes a different approach. Mr. Strickland is a technology wiz and loves to use online resources whenever possible. He believes working online provides students with valuable skills for later in life. Mr. Strickland is also a great student of Civil War history. He visits battleground sites each summer and participates in re-enactments as a Confederate soldier. The more he learned about the Civil War and the more he visited historic sites, the more he realized the importance of monuments as a way to remember and study the Civil War. He merges his interests in technology, the Civil War, and monuments in this activity, which takes place during the Civil War unit of his United States history course. Over 90 percent of Mr. Strickland's students are African American.

Mr. Strickland's activities require students to apply and expand their knowledge of the Civil War while simultaneously considering the role of monuments in remembering the past and contributing to collective memory. First, he leads a set of classroom activities that examine monuments in the U.S., including 9/11 memorials, as an opportunity to practice analyzing and evaluating monuments. Next, students are required to visit three local monuments in their community. Finally, students conduct online research on Civil War monuments.

Objectives

The assignment objectives include:

- Students will understand how monuments and markers reflect the time period in which they are constructed.
- Students will analyze events of the Civil War through monuments.
- Students will evaluate how U.S. society remembers the Civil War through monuments.

Essential Question

How do we remember the Civil War through monuments and memorials?

Pre-Visit Activities

Prior to the monument visit, Mr. Strickland uses two class periods to introduce the topic of monuments as representations of the past. Mr. Strickland starts class with a grabber. One at a time he displays images of historical markers on his interactive whiteboard. One marker reads: "On this site stood Robert Oknos, who thought that global warming would not affect him in his lifetime.—United States, Department of Education, 2006." Another reads: "On this site stood a local market bankrupted by the monopolistic, make-it-cheaper-in-China, anti-union big box store where you shop.—United States, Department of Education, 2007." And a third states: "On this site stood Karen DeWitt, who could not afford the prescription drugs that would have saved her life.—United States, Department of Education, 2007." Physically, the markers appear to be authentic historical markers created and maintained by the United States government. In fact, they are the project of artist Norm Magnusson, who is placing the "markers" along the I-75 corridor to be thought-provoking (I-75 Project, 2011). Mr. Strickland's students immediately want to know if they are "real." The discussion about the markers both hooks the students into the topic and effectively forces them to consider the subjectivity of how the past is told to the public.

Next, he provides students with the activity's guiding questions and asks students to discuss monuments they have seen around town and when traveling. "Where have you seen monuments?" he asks, and "What is the topic of the monuments? What are they about? What do they look like?" Typically, students remember one of several Civil War or WWII monuments in local town parks, and someone always mentions the Martin Luther King monument in the school courtyard, donated by the graduating class of 1986. "The monuments always seem to be statues of people," is a typical student answer, or, "They are always about things that happened a long time ago." Occasionally students recall monuments they saw on a trip to Washington, D.C. (the Vietnam Memorial, the Washington Monument), a common destination for Mr. Strickland's students. Many students comment that most people they observe don't seem to notice the monuments: "people walk by or even sit near them [the monuments], without really looking at them." Through this discussion of monuments Mr. Strickland hopes to get students to think about the purpose and nature of monuments. At this point in the lesson he does not expect students to be able to critically analyze monuments, but to realize they are all around them, serve a public function, cover many time periods, and are not as uniformly aesthetic as the students might think.

After that, Mr. Strickland lectures about 9/11 memorials, reviewing key events from 9/11 and then showing images of over thirty 9/11 monuments. Some of the monuments he discusses include over a dozen international and national monuments (such as ones in Fort Carson, Colorado; San Antonio, Texas; Rome, Italy; Centralia, Washington; and Prague, Czech Republic), as well as numerous monuments in New Jersey, New York, and Connecticut. Mr. Strickland then chooses several of the monuments from Connecticut to discuss in more depth. His parents, sister, and other family members live in Connecticut; therefore, he has personally visited many of the Connecticut 9/11 monuments, leading to his focus in that state. He also chose Connecticut monuments as a focus because there are a significant number of victims from Connecticut and there are interesting cases to discuss. The case studies include the monuments in Easton, Greenwich, and Kent discussed earlier in the chapter, as well as the state monument in Westport and two monuments in Windsor (see Figures 8.7–8.11 of Windsor monuments).

For each of these monuments Mr. Strickland provides background on the history of the monument (e.g. the design and building, the funding, any controversies) and shows

9/11 MONUMENTS IN WINDSOR, CONNECTICUT

Figure 8.7 9/11 sculpture and garden at Windsor High School, Windsor, CT.

Figure 8.8 Plaque in the 9/11 garden at Windsor High School, Windsor, CT.

Figure 8.9 Sculpture in 9/11 memorial in Settlement Hill neighborhood, Windsor, CT.

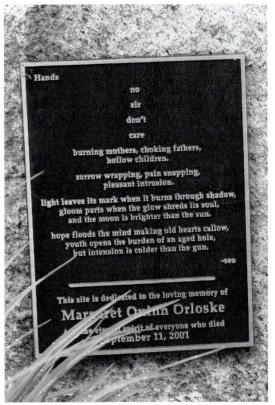

Figure 8.11 Plaque in 9/11 memorial in Settlement Hill neighborhood, Windsor, CT.

Figure 8.10 Plaque, bench, and garden in 9/11 memorial in Settlement Hill neighborhood, Windsor, CT.

multiple photos of the monument, including any text and all other features. While viewing the photos students are required to answer several questions and participate in a discussion of the monument. The questions include: (1) what is your first impression of this monument? (2) What is the message about 9/11? (3) What needs of any specific groups of people were met when it was created? What evidence supports your answer? (4) What symbols, words, shapes, colors, materials, etc., does the monument use to convey its message? (5) Whose values and perspectives are best represented, and whose values/perspectives are left out? (6) What does the monument portray in a positive way? What does it portray in a negative way?

During the discussion of these questions Mr. Strickland observes a noteworthy shift in students' ability to consider how monuments reflect the time period in which they are created and in judging the way monuments help society remember the past.

In preparation, Mr. Strickland spent significant time researching and visiting the monuments. Each year he visits additional monuments. Like Mrs. Reddell, he is able to find considerable background information and images via the internet and newspaper articles. In a few cases he even contacted the artist(s) for information—a luxury available to him given the young age of the monuments. In addition Mr. Strickland speaks with family and friends at social gatherings to ask their thoughts on 9/11 monuments. Finally, he periodically spends several hours at a monument observing visitors and occasionally engaging visitors in conversation. Although this is not formal research, it provides an illuminating perspective, particularly about public perception. Mr. Strickland says more than 90 percent of visitors did not come specifically to see the monument, but happened to be walking by and became interested. He describes the most common reactions he finds among visitors as "sadness, sympathy, and, once in a while, anger." All of Mr. Strickland's efforts provide him with the expertise to fully engage his students in an exploration of 9/11 monuments.

During-Visit Activities

Mr. Strickland does not visit local monuments as a class but instead assigns students to find three local monuments to visit on their own and report back to the class. Students are given two weeks to complete their visits. He provides the students with a list of regional monuments as well as online sources to search for monuments. Students are required to visit at least one Civil War monument (there are numerous monuments available in the area) but can choose topics and/or monuments of interest for the other two visits. Mr. Strickland encourages students to look for monuments that reflect their own interests (e.g. women's history, African American history, civil rights, sports). Prior to visiting, students must research the history of the site through online resources and/or calling the town or other agency that is responsible for the monument. During the visit students must take at least three photographs of the monument to share in class and answer the same questions used to discuss the 9/11 monuments in class: (1) what is your first impression of this monument? (2) What is the message about the event depicted? (3) What needs of any specific groups of people were met when it was created? What evidence supports your answer? (4) What symbols, words, shapes, colors, materials, etc., does the monument use to convey its message? (5) Whose values and perspectives are best represented, and whose values/perspectives are left out? (6) What does the monument portray in a positive way? What does it portray in a negative way?

In order to facilitate student visits and analysis of monuments Mr. Strickland sends a letter home to parents describing the project and encouraging participation/support. He also begins each class during the two-week monument visit period with a check-in about the visits. This allows students to ask questions and troubleshoot any difficulties, and also acts as a reminder to complete the assignment. Mr. Strickland says that some students are shy about calling a town to ask about a monument and are initially hesitant about their ability to analyze a monument. However, after the first visit, he says students get into a comfort zone and build confidence in their ability.

Post-Visit Activities

After all the monument visits are completed students meet in groups of three. Within the groups each student presents his or her monuments by showing images (either printed or via computer), providing a brief history of the monument, and sharing answers to the questions. Following the small group presentations Mr. Strickland leads a whole class discussion about the monuments. His goal for the small group work and class discussion is to build the students' abilities to see how monuments reflect the time period in which they were created and to transition from monuments more broadly to a focus on the Civil War. He continues the discussion, and will ask questions if necessary, until he gauges that the students are ready to independently complete a thorough monument evaluation.

Next, students work in pairs to research Civil War monuments online—usually for one or one-and-a-half class periods, depending on the group. Mr. Strickland asks each pair to research two monuments, one located in a Confederate state outside of North Carolina and one located in a Union state. Students must use monuments that have photos available online. For each monument students answer the same questions used for their monument visits, along with four additional questions: (1) how does the monument portray events of the Civil War? (2) How does the monument's message and presentation of the Civil War reinforce or contradict what we have learned about the Civil War? (3) How does the monument reflect the time period in which it was created? (4) How might the monument be used by, or affect, its community today? Mr. Strickland provides an extensive list of websites where students can begin their research (see page 154 and in the appendices). He continually monitors the students, offering suggestions for finding monuments and discussing the monuments they have found. After twenty minutes of research Mr. Strickland leads a short debrief as a way to check that students are successfully finding monuments and accurately evaluating monuments. The debriefing helps him to assess students' progress, but also acts as a reinforcing mechanism for groups that may be struggling by providing modeling from peers. Students then continue to research.

Upon completion of the research each group is matched with another group. All groups present their Civil War monuments from the South. Then all groups present their Civil War monuments from the North. After each presentation there is a period of question and answer for the students to interrogate each other. The critical feature of this discourse is thinking about the similarities and differences between Civil War monuments in the South and the North. To facilitate this discussion Mr. Strickland provides a guide that students fill out during the presentations and question and answer session. The guide contains a T-chart that asks students to compare Southern and Northern monuments in terms of the messages portrayed, the aesthetics, and the potential reception of, and impact on, society. He finds that students are surprised at both the number of common features and some of the stark differences. For example, for commonalities, most of the monuments they find are celebrating specific war heroes (e.g. military leaders) or broadly praising the soldiers who fought, and the monuments use stone and metal as their primary materials. On the other hand, a big difference is that Northern monuments are viewed through the eyes of the victors, while many Southern monuments remain defiant. Mr. Strickland notes that his students are also very aware of how issues of race, particularly slavery, are included or left out of the monuments' narratives. His mostly African American students complain that too many of the Southern monuments glorify Confederate viewpoints, often aligned with the racist and pro-slavery sentiment of the Civil War period. Meanwhile, Northern monuments frequently cite saving the Union as an important outcome of the Civil War, but less frequently mention slavery.

Mr. Strickland reports that students,

> take a giant leap in their understanding of historical thinking when comparing the [Southern and Northern] monuments . . . while their textbook presents one narrative of the Civil War, the monuments they find invariably tell multiple narratives. This is a shock to their system, and you can see a change in how they approach historical sources for the rest of the year.

Following the presentations Mr. Strickland leads a wrap-up discussion centered on his second objective of analyzing events of the Civil War through monuments. This serves to round off the monument activities and transition to the culmination of the Civil War unit. Specifically, he asks students to compare the people, events, and message of the monuments with the people, events, and messages of all other sources used during the Civil War unit. He modifies this activity each year depending on time and student interest, but the other sources he uses include some combination of the textbook, Matthew Brady photographs, clips from the feature films *Glory*, *Andersonville*, *Gettysburg*, and *Ride with the Devil*, excerpts from the Ken Burns Civil War documentary film, and letters from Civil War soldiers. While he does not have students formally complete the monument creation activity that Mrs. Reddell uses, he concludes by asking the students what they would include—text and aesthetics—if creating a new Civil War monument in their town.

REFLECTIONS ON THE CASE

The activities enacted by Mrs. Reddell and Mr. Strickland enable students to better understand monuments and the history they traverse. Students learn to critically analyze and evaluate monuments, examining: (1) the perspectives included in (and omitted from) their narratives; (2) the purposes and media of monuments; (3) the manner in which monuments represent the time period in which they were created; and (4) the idea that monuments contribute to and are reflective of collective memory. Students are thus better able to develop historical empathy, evaluate historical evidence, connect the past and the present, and consider issues of historical significance. The activities presented here focus on 9/11 memorials and the Civil War, but each could be implemented for any time period in U.S. or world history, especially given the available online resources.

Suggestions for Activities with Monuments

From these activities we can derive numerous criteria for using monuments effectively with students. These include the following.

Utilize Local Monuments and Memorials

Take advantage of monuments in your school, town, and region to evaluate how the past is remembered in your town or state, to explore local connections to national narratives, and to help students make personal connections to the past. Mrs. Reddell's students analyzed how 9/11 is remembered and memorialized in Connecticut, and how 9/11 is as much a local/regional and personal story as a national one, while Mr. Strickland's students compared how the Civil War is memorialized in the South vs. in the North.

Draw on the Internet to Find Monuments Worldwide

In addition to local monuments, there are rich online resources to find monuments that can be used in class. Both Mrs. Reddell and Mr. Strickland used online monument resources as an important element of their lesson.

Research is an Essential Component to Classroom Instruction

Visiting and analyzing monuments is not enough. Monument visits, in person or virtually, require extensive research. Monuments are most often not accompanied by tour guides or brochures. Background research about the history of the monument's creation, purpose, funding, etc., is critical to understanding the monument and evaluating the monument's present-day message and contribution to collective memory. Mrs. Reddell and Mr. Strickland conducted research online, called town officials who have knowledge of monuments, read newspaper articles about the monuments, contacted monuments' artistic creators, and spoke with other visitors. Mr. Strickland also guided students to carry out research, allowing more freedom to choose monuments and developing important skills.

Use Monuments to Teach About History as a Discipline

Monuments are a unique and powerful way not only to teach content, but to think about history as a discipline and the ways in which we remember the past and study what society values and how those values change. Mrs. Reddell asks students to evaluate 9/11 monuments and to create their own monuments, providing students with first-hand experience and insight at designing the message and purpose for a monument. Mr. Strickland expects students to think about how Civil War monuments reflect the time period in which they were created and to compare monuments with other sources of knowledge about the past, such as the textbook and film.

Connect Monument Visits and Activities to the Curriculum

The activities presented here are in part successful because they connect to the course curriculum. Monuments are not visited for the sake of visiting, but because they enrich the content of the course. The monument activities enable students to create more multifaceted and nuanced meaning about the events of 9/11 and/or the Civil War, and about society today.

Focus on Issues of Referent, Aesthetics, and Reception

Uhrmacher and Tinkler (2008) posit a three-step approach to analyzing monuments: an analysis of referent (who or what is being memorialized); an analysis of design (the aesthetic and representational decisions made in creating a monument); and an analysis of reception (how the audience makes meaning from a monument). Mrs. Reddell and Mr. Strickland required students to do all three steps. For example, for 9/11 monuments students considered the subject of the monuments, the perspectives represented or left out, and the monuments' messages. They also examined what materials were used, the color and texture, how the monument made them feel, and other aesthetic considerations. Finally, students appraised how the 9/11 monuments were received, including some of the controversies surrounding the monuments' creation.

Students Require Thorough Background Knowledge to Evaluate Monuments

Without sufficient prior knowledge students would find these assignments very difficult because they would not understand the historical context of 9/11 or the Civil War. For Mrs. Reddell's activity the students had to draw on background knowledge to successfully create a monument from a particular perspective. They also needed to understand the political, economic, and social ramifications of 9/11, and how those are reflected in the monuments. In Mr. Strickland's class, adequate knowledge of the Civil War, including events, people, and perspectives, is critical to evaluating Civil War monuments.

The activities described hint at potential obstacles for monument visits. It can be difficult to take a large group (e.g. an entire tenth grade from a high school) to visit monuments. Unlike many larger museums, historic sites, and living history museums, monuments are limited in scope, and only so many visitors can cluster around a monument at any one time. Teachers are also at the mercy of weather conditions, and may face a shortage of bathrooms and other facilities. These are important issues to consider and research ahead of time. For those fortunate enough to visit multiple sites within walking distance, students can travel in small chaperoned groups and rotate among monuments. In Mrs. Reddell's case, she built in scheduled stops at rest areas and eateries so students could attend to their personal needs.

Monuments present us with messages about our heritage for our benefit and enjoyment, for their own political, ideological, and/or social agendas, and to help society collectively remember the past. Monuments create opportunities for students to analyze historical perspectives, evaluate historical significance, and connect the past and the present. Not only can students reflect on the message of the monument, but they can examine a monument's narrative of creation, including funding, choice of location, choice of text, choice of aesthetics, etc. And monuments allow students to better understand that the construction of history is a powerful, fascinating, and human activity. But the advantages to monuments can only be utilized through thoughtful lessons informed by extensive research.

NOTES

1   For the purposes of this chapter the term "monument" will be used to include monuments, memorials, and historic markers.

2   There is no one definitive list of 9/11 monuments in Connecticut.

3   A special thanks to Kailee Donovan for assistance with the research on 9/11 monuments and to staff at Ridgefield, Connecticut and Milford, Connecticut town halls, and Raymond Vitali of Milford, Connecticut for providing information and images for 9/11 monuments.

4   Shays' Rebellion was the armed uprising of mostly farmers in central and western Massachusetts from 1786 to 1787.

5   The activity for Shays' Rebellion monuments is adapted from http://shaysrebellion.stcc.edu. Text of the monuments was retrieved from http://shaysrebellion.stcc.edu/shaysapp/artifactPage. do?shortName=barregazette_19feb1987&page=.

6   Ella Grasso was the first woman elected in her own right as governor of a state in the U.S. See http://www.cslib.org/gov/grassoe.htm.

RESOURCES

Resources for 9/11 Memorials

Resources and images: www.911-remember.com

List of many 9/11 memorials: http://911memorials.org

Official site for the national memorial in New York: www.national911memorial.org

Information and resources for the 9/11 Community: www.voicesofseptember11.org

Resources about preserving and interpreting the physical evidence of the September 11 attacks on the Pentagon and the World Trade Center: www.911history.net

List of 9/11 living memorial projects (forest, town center, park, community garden, found space): www.livingmemorialsproject.net

General Resources for Memorials and Monuments

Database of historical markers in the U.S.: www.hmdb.org

Field guide to U.S. monuments and memorials: www.monumentsandmemorials.com

Teaching with historic places—lessons using properties listed in the National Park Service's National Register of Historic Places: www.cr.nps.gov/nr/twhp

Books

Loewen, J. (1999). *Lies Across America: What Our Historic Sites Get Wrong*. New York: Touchstone.

CHAPTER 9

Bringing the Museum to the Classroom

Outreach Programs, Museum Kits, and Virtual Resources

Figure 9.1 Civil War traveling trunk.

Source: Courtesy of the American Civil War Center, photo by Sean Kane.

INTRODUCTION

Museums offer a literal and virtual bounty of resources for teachers who desire additional collaboration with museums in addition to a visit, or who cannot visit because of logistical or other barriers. Specifically, many museums support outreach programs and staff who can visit the classroom, send museum artifact kits and "museums in a box" to classrooms, and provide web-based resources and virtual galleries or field trips. These three resources—outreach programs, museum artifact kits, and virtual resources—cannot replace an on-site visit, but offer complementary and supplementary artifacts, staff, narratives, secondary sources, lesson plans, and more. They help teachers bring the disciplinary lenses used in museums, from historians and archaeologists to curators and historical interpreters, into the classroom. In this chapter we discuss each of the three museum resources, provide several exemplary models, and consider how these resources can be used to enhance student learning of history.

OUTREACH PROGRAMS

Museums provide a number of outreach programs where staff from the museum visit classrooms. Visits take many forms, ranging from costumed role-playing or bringing artifacts to analyze, to more traditional classroom lessons. Museum staff visits can serve as important pre-field trip preparation, can be a rigorous way to follow up a field trip, or, in many cases, will allow students to experience an aspect of the museum when a field trip is not possible. In the cases where it is difficult for students to visit a museum and/or too far for museum staff to visit a school, some museums are also providing opportunities for a form of personalized virtual field trip. These field trips provide an opportunity for students to interact with staff and "visit" a museum through the use of streaming two-way video.

Two museums that operate excellent outreach programs are Plimoth Plantation in Massachusetts and the Minnesota History Center discussed in Chapter 4. Plimoth Plantation's outreach programs provide two unique classroom experiences: (1) a visit by a costumed interpreter who uses language, diction, knowledge, and cultural disposition to portray a resident of the "Pilgrim" settlement of Plymouth, Massachusetts, in 1627; and (2) a visit by a contemporary member of the Wampanoag tribe of eastern Massachusetts who, speaking as a tribal member, describes the lifestyle and customs of the Wampanoag people at the time of their contact with European settlers in the seventeenth century. Plimoth Plantation's outreach programs have a national following, and museum educators may be found in schools across the nation, especially during the months when the outdoor museum is closed for the winter.

Serving primarily schools in Minnesota, the History Center provides costumed interpreters who portray individuals in Minnesota history through their "History Players" program. These individuals include Harriet Bishop, the first public school teacher in St. Paul, and Thomas Lyles, an early African American community activist, among others. They also connect with schools at the far corners of the state through video-conferencing virtual field trips and through programs related to National History Day, where the Minnesota History Center or Minnesota Historical Society staff help to train students to do original historical inquiry.

Plimoth Plantation

Plimoth Plantation is a living history museum with two distinct yet inter-related components. The first is a Wampanoag homesite that focuses on the traditions and culture of the indigenous people of what is now southeastern New England. The second is a seventeenth-century palisaded English village that was home to the Pilgrim colonists associated with the Thanksgiving story. The average annual visitation to Plimoth Plantation is over 350,000, 75,000 of whom are students on field trips or participating in other educational programs (Plimoth, 2011). Not all teachers are able to bring their students to the museum. As an alternative, Plimoth Plantation staff can visit classrooms and present "People of the East" and/or "Life in 1627 Plymouth Colony." Both programs are available for grades 1–12, and individually tailored to the particular grade levels.

Plimoth Plantation built its reputation for living history on the fidelity with which its educators portrayed the residents of the 1627 English colonial village. Through intensive training in genealogy, history, early modern culture, linguistics, and dialect, characters who assume the identities of English settlers are trained to look, act, and sound like seventeenth-century colonists, even down to the regional dialect a particular colonist would have had. However, when developing the museum's Wampanoag interpretation programs—developed many years after the original village—the tribal members elected to take a different approach. Because they want their educational programs to reflect both Wampanoag lifestyles and customs of the seventeenth century and their contemporary tribal culture, the Wampanoag interpreters speak from a twenty-first-century perspective, as a museum educator and as a Wampanoag.

The "People of the East" program is a one-hour program through which students learn about the Wampanoag culture, customs, and lifestyles of the seventeenth century and in the twenty-first century. False stereotypes about Wampanoag and other indigenous people are often addressed, as are issues of contemporary cultural respect. The highly sought-after program is taught by Native American staff, who demonstrate Wampanoag cultural practices with tools, skins, and artifacts made or processed by Wampanoag craftspeople. One of the reasons for the popularity of the program is the clarity with which it addresses issues of multiculturalism and tolerance, and the alternative perspective it provides on the iconic and mythic American historical tradition of Thanksgiving.

The "Life in 1627 Plymouth Colony" program involves the role-play by staff of a resident of the 1627 Plimoth Colony and is noted not just for the depth of knowledge of the character interpreters, but for its ability to create historical empathy, the understanding that the past really was "a foreign country," and that we must be cautious in applying contemporary perspectives to other times (Lowenthal, 1999). In this program the character portrayed comes into the classroom and talks about his or her life in the village, and in some cases about his or her experience aboard the *Mayflower* when coming to America.

An enjoyable part of the program for students comes from the fact that interpreters do not "know" or understand any terms about things that did not exist in 1627. If a teacher or student points a camera at an interpreter to take his or her picture, the interpreter may react in alarm and confusion. Similarly, if a student talks about television or a movie scene, the interpreter professes total ignorance and may respond to an explanation of what a movie is with an expression that it must be a "diabolical" creation. Students quickly learn, that the past was very much a different world, and it is with this understanding that their interaction with the 1627 character proceeds. For most of the visit the interpreter describes his or her own life and the life and customs of the seventeenth-century villagers. Students are often surprised at many aspects of colonial life, including attitudes held toward Indians and views about children, and find the classroom visit an

Figure 9.2 Traveling trunk: "Understanding Women's Suffrage: Tennessee's Perfect 36."
Source: Photo courtesy of the Tennessee State Museum.

illuminating exchange with the past. They may be asked to try on colonial clothing or headgear, or identify reproduction artifacts. Near the end of the visit, the interpreter removes a part of his costume and enters the twenty-first century, becoming a modern museum educator, at which time he answers students' questions about his role-playing, and clarifies for them any lingering misconceptions about seventeenth-century life. The "1627 Life" program and the Wampanoag interpretive program are powerful educational tools for bringing the seventeenth-century experience of colonial settlement alive for students, from the perspective of both the colonists and those who made them welcome.

Minnesota History Center

The Minnesota History Center, as described in Chapter 4, offers visiting programs geared for elementary and middle-school students, called "History Player in the Classroom." Teachers can choose from one (or more) of eight historical figures who then visit the students in their classroom. These visits with costumed interpreters last forty-five minutes and are considered interactive lessons. Teachers receive a lesson packet with activities to prepare students for the visit and materials for a post-visit activity. These lessons help the students to start to think about the lives of the historical characters that will be visiting and help to provide some historical context to develop empathy for their experiences. The characters available for a visit include:

- Harriet Bishop (1817–1883), St. Paul's first public school teacher.
- Frederick McKinley Jones (1892–1961), African American inventor and self-taught engineer.
- Maud Hart Lovelace (1892–1980), author of the Betsy-Tacy series of children's books.
- George Nelson (1786–1859), fur trade clerk for the North West and Hudson's Bay companies.
- Virginia Mae Hope (1921–1944), World War II Women Airforce Service Pilot.
- Thomas Lyles (1843–1920), African American community activist and entrepreneur.
- Mary Dodge Woodward (1826–1890), domestic manager of a bonanza farm.
- William de la Barre (1849–1936), chief water engineer for Minneapolis.

Similar to Plimoth Plantation, the Minnesota History Center players attempt to engage students in thinking critically about important events from the period they are portraying, as well as the differences in daily life between the past and present. This task is well suited to the History Center as their main focus is social and cultural history, which we described in Chapter 4. In addition to these two cases, similar outreach programs are offered by many of the major living history sites, forts, and house museums, such as Colonial Williamsburg. Many museums are now offering streaming video programs as well as site visits, which provide less interaction but still allow students access to museums and museum experts that they would not otherwise be able to interact with as part of their history class.

The Benefits and Challenges of Museum Outreach Programs

Outreach programs that bring museum staff into the classroom provide both advantages and disadvantages compared with student field trips. One advantage is that unlike a museum exhibit, which must appeal to a variety of audiences, a museum outreach program is specifically classroom-oriented. The material presented has usually been selected to provide information matched to state curriculum standards at a grade-appropriate level of detail, and formatted to work in a classroom rather than a museum setting. They also often promote more educator–student interaction and dialogue than is possible at the museum. Additionally, in-class education programs can be scheduled to coincide with the time in the school year when a museum's content is actually being covered in the class, a real advantage over some seasonal sites that may be closed when their content material is covered in the classroom. It can cost significantly less, too, to bring a museum educator into a class than to bring the class to the museum. Museums often charge both a fee for the school program and travel expenses for the museum educator, but the savings over a full class field trip are often substantial. This is especially true for streaming video programs, although some sort of minimal technological capacity often needs to exist at a school to enable participation.

In-school museum programs can sometimes be tailored to the specific needs of an individual teacher, based on the museum's educational capacity and program policies. Some museums encourage teacher involvement in school program planning, while others have a what-we-have-is-what-you-get approach to outreach. For this reason, active engagement by the teacher with the museum's education department in planning the in-school visit is absolutely essential.

The potential advantages of classroom-oriented programs (such as cost savings, greater educator–student interaction, and closer match to the curriculum that may result from an in-school visit) must be weighed against the liability of not giving students exposure to the range of materials and experiences available at the museum itself. A museum lends itself to the kind of curiosity-based free-choice learning that lies at the heart of education, and even a terrific in-class museum program does not lend itself to that kind of exploration. There is also no way that a traveling program can even come close to emulating a museum's content or programming. Teachers inviting museum educators into their classrooms should also be aware of the differences in practice between museum educators and teachers. Many museum staff do not have formal teacher training, and while they are often quite adept at presenting to students in a classroom setting, they may be more or less familiar with classroom management strategies, understanding goals, issues of assessment, and the learning needs of a specific, unfamiliar group of students.

Finally, it is important and motivating for students to have the opportunity to leave the school building and experience the world outside—to examine issues of place and space in their understanding of the past and the world in general (Nespor, 2000). However, for schools that face logistical or economic constraints, museum outreach programs provide a wonderful opportunity to engage students in an exploration of the past in a way that is likely different from their everyday routine. Similarly, teachers could identify a historic landmark, monument, or building in the neighborhood of their school for a field trip close to home (see Chapter 8 for an example). A local historical society member or long-time neighborhood resident could be identified to help students understand the history of the area or particular building. Students could investigate the history of a particular building using archives to see who owned it over time, or which stores or businesses occupied a storefront. If in a rural area, students could examine the records of the original homesteader as well as subsequent owners and then tie this information back into the historical and social context they are learning about in class. While not substitutes for the programming museums offer, these types of activities can help students to think more critically about the construction of history and their own role in inquiring into the past.

MUSEUM ARTIFACT KITS/MUSEUM IN A BOX

Museum artifact kits serve many of the same purposes as outreach programs. They can be used effectively as part of a museum pre-visit preparation or post-visit follow-up, or in place of a visit. The kits are assembled by museum staff and include artifacts or reproduction artifacts, lesson plans, and secondary sources. Many museums have multiple kits covering a variety of topics and are targeted for different age groups. These kits often present a highlight of the types of artifacts and programming offered at the actual museum. For example, one highly developed program is the American Civil War Center at Historic Tredegar's "Civil War Trunk" program. Their trunks include replica Civil War uniforms and women's clothing, equipment such as camp dishes, period music and document sources, and background information and lesson plans for teachers to use the trunk materials. These trunks are checked out to teachers for up to a two-week period.

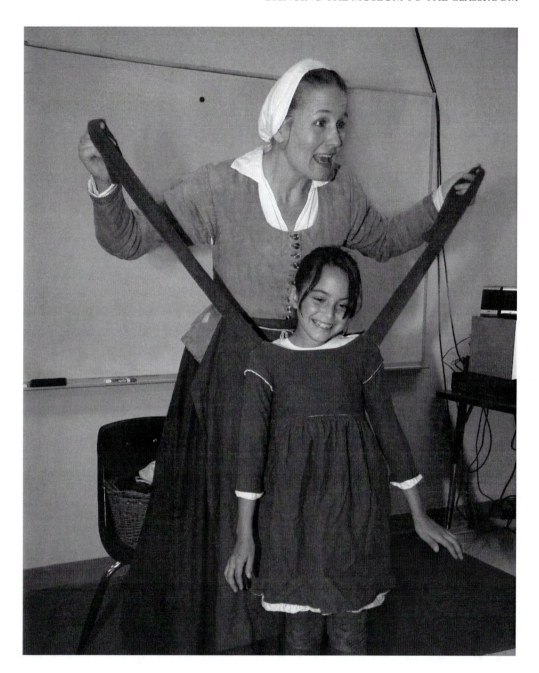

Figure 9.3 A Plimoth Plantation staff member visits a classroom.

Source: Photo courtesy of Plimoth Plantation.

The key difference between the outreach programs described above and kits such as the Civil War Trunk is that it is up to the teacher to implement the artifact kit without museum staff. Two other content-rich and pedagogically valuable approaches to providing museum kits come from the Tennessee State Museum in Nashville and the Autry National Center in Los Angeles, California.

The Tennessee State Museum

The Tennessee State Museum, with support from the National Endowment for the Humanities, has developed a comprehensive traveling trunk program to assist in the teaching of state history. The trunks, which can be reserved individually for up to a three-week period, are available for free, though teachers must pay shipping costs back to the museum. There are ten trunks, each covering a theme of central importance in American history, as experienced in Tennessee. Trunk topics include:

- The Life and Times of the First Tennesseans.
- Daily Life on the Tennessee Frontier.
- Cherokees in Tennessee: Their Life, Customs, and Removal.
- The Age of Jackson and Tennessee's Legendary Leaders.
- The Life of a Civil War Soldier.
- The Lives of Three Tennessee Slaves and Their Journey Toward Freedom.
- Understanding Women's Suffrage: Tennessee's Perfect 36.
- Transforming America: Tennessee on the World War II Home Front.
- The Modern Movement for Civil Rights in Tennessee.
- Tennessee: The Land and Its Peoples.

Each of the Tennessee traveling trunks is filled with real and/or reproduction artifacts, paintings, portraits, music CDs, books, and DVDs. Each is also accompanied by step-by-step lesson plans enabling the teachers to use the trunks as part of a comprehensive investigation of the topic covered. For example, the "Daily Life on the Tennessee Frontier" trunk, which helps teachers to highlight and explore life on the Tennessee frontier with students, includes the following items:

- raw cotton, flax, and wool;
- chamber pot;
- animal skins;
- moccasins;
- frontier-styled clothes for boys and girls; and
- frontier games.

The overall purpose of the trunk is to help students recognize the hardships and challenges of frontier life, along with the reasons why so many chose to risk those hardships to make a future for themselves and their families. These artifacts present the opportunity for students to develop empathy with frontier life and the economic, political, and social issues the settlers faced.

The trunk titled "Understanding Women's Suffrage: Tennessee's Perfect 36" highlights women's fight for the vote in Tennessee and the fact that on August 24, 1920,

Tennessee became the 36th and final state needed to ratify the 19th amendment to the United States Constitution, giving women the right to vote. The suffrage trunk includes:

- A replica of a pro-suffrage banner made in Tennessee.
- Primary source photographs and political cartoons related to Tennessee's suffrage movement.
- A copy of the letter Febb Burn sent to her son Harry urging him to vote yes on suffrage.
- A reproduction pro-suffrage sash.
- Twenty yellow and twenty red roses for students to wear in support of or in opposition to women's suffrage.

The accompanying lesson plans provide primary sources and procedures for recreating the debates over suffrage that occupied Tennesseans during the summer of 1920. Students create pro- and anti-suffrage banners, posters, and buttons, wear roses showing their position on the suffrage question, and finally conduct a classroom debate on suffrage, mirroring the 1920 debates. In the culminating activity, the classroom votes, as the Tennessee General Assembly did, to approve or reject suffrage.

While the "Understanding Women's Suffrage: Tennessee's Perfect 36" trunk clearly works best when used with the accompanying lesson plans (or modifications thereof), the "Tennessee Frontier" trunk seems much more flexible, capable of being integrated in some form or other into any unit on western expansion, the frontier, or the development of the state. This is one of the attributes common to traveling trunks. While many of them come with more or less specific instructions on how to use them, all are capable of adaptation to a pre-existing curriculum or a creative impulse of the teacher.

The Autry National Center

Staff at the Autry National Center supply teachers with Community Stories Outreach Kits. Using a variety of materials, each kit profiles one of seven communities (e.g. Chinese, African Americans, cowboys) through the narrative of a real person. These kits provide some of the opportunities for students to explore oral history or social history, as described in the activities in Chapter 4. They also go beyond oral history or secondary accounts to provide material culture artifacts that provide an additional layer to the stories being told. These kits, and even the trunks that hold them, are specially designed to fit the historic "owner." The kits and the accompanying lessons provide opportunities for historical interpretation or role-play in addition to historical analysis. The people and communities include:

- Ellen Cook: African Americans in the West.
- Tom Shee Bin: Chinese Americans in the West.
- Matthew Wheelwright: Overland Migration.
- Isabel Esparza Huizar: Ranching and Cowboys.
- The Siva Family: Cahuilla Indians.
- Dame Shirley: The Gold Rush.
- Kelly Roth: Immigration and Community.

The lesson plan accompanying the trunk for Ellen Cook, a newly freed African American who had moved west to Los Angeles, is a good example of the Autry Center's resources. The materials describe the Autry Center's goals for teachers who use the trunk with students:

> Using the life of Ellen Cook as a framework, this lesson looks at the choices freed slaves needed to make at the end of the Civil War. The lesson asks students to reflect upon the new circumstances African Americans faced after gaining freedom in a role-playing exercise. Working in small groups, students will be given a fictional nineteenth century identity and will use problem-solving skills in order to make decisions about a fictional situation . . . What does it mean to be a good citizen? What qualities and values are important in the United States? Are these values important in all democracies? This lesson introduces the concepts of civic values, rights, and responsibilities. Students will discuss and compare the requirements for citizenship in 1896 and today. In small groups students will create their own countries and use written and artistic representations to depict the qualities of a good citizen.
>
> (Autry National Center, no date, p. 2)

The lesson engages students in developing empathetic understandings for newly freed slaves with a focus on the cultural, social, economic, and political issues that newly freed African Americans faced, and on African American decision-making and experiences. Similar to the living history experiences, however, the teacher's role with these kits is to engage students deeply in attempting to understand the experiences of Ellen Cook and her family while also helping them to recognize their distance from these experiences.

The Benefits and Challenges of Museum Artifact Kits/Museum in a Box

Traveling trunks occupy a middle ground in the area of classroom/museum educational partnerships. They are certainly not the equivalent of a museum field trip. Nor do they have the inherent interest or engagement of a school outreach program presented by a living museum educator. They fall into a specialized category all their own: supplemental educational materials produced by a museum. As such, they can help a committed teacher add some of the excitement and hands-on engagement of a museum visit to classroom lessons. But to do so requires a teacher to achieve a high degree of knowledge about the trunk materials themselves.

As with any supplementary educational materials, teachers will use the contents of traveling trunks in the ways best suited to their own pedagogy. But to do so, the teacher needs to become familiar with the entire contents of the trunk (and any accompanying lesson plans.) Sometimes, a trunk may in fact be so well aligned with a teacher's curriculum that the materials can be used right out of the box. Often, a teacher will make selective use of the contents or lessons, and incorporate them into his or her pre-existing lesson plans. Trunks usually remain in a teacher's possession for a limited amount of time (two or three weeks), so teachers electing to use them must be prepared to study and incorporate the trunk materials in a timely manner. The advantages of using trunk materials, however, are significant. Adding tactile engagement with artifacts to an in-class lesson adds an important additional dimension to the learning process. In addition, the reproduction primary sources included in trunk kits are often much more "realistic" and accessible to students than similar sources copied from a textbook or downloaded from the internet. Like visiting staff, traveling trunks cannot replace a museum field trip, but they are unique in their ability to add exciting supporting materials to class lessons.

VIRTUAL GALLERIES AND VIRTUAL FIELD TRIPS

Over the past twenty years we have seen a renaissance in the amount of access and the nature of educational interactions provided by the emergence and development of the World Wide Web. This renaissance has impacted history educators as much as anyone, as these teachers can now have their students access historical archives and experts from all over the world. For museums and museum educators, the web (and now web 2.0) platforms enable opportunities to both provide access to collections digitally and even create engaging opportunities for a new generation of virtual field trips and experiences that cross time and space. In particular, they allow students to engage in the exploration of museums and museum collections from around the United States and different corners of the globe. In this section we highlight two typical models for online museum resources, virtual galleries and virtual field trips, and provide some insights into the value and challenges these models present.

Virtual Galleries

The first emergence of museums on the web, beyond providing information for visitors to the actual museum, was in the creation of online galleries of selected exhibits or artifacts. These static web pages presented a combination of images and text that allowed visitors to the site to distill information from their collection even if they were not able to visit. As the capacity of the web and the technological savvy of museum staff increased, these virtual galleries developed to also include audio or video "podcasts" of experts or curators describing the exhibits, and now even three-dimensional virtual exhibits that allow online visitors to explore the museum's exhibits in more depth. For example, the Smithsonian's National Museum of Natural History is home to a prominent and sophisticated virtual gallery that allows visitors to look at every nook of the museum's main exhibit space. Visitors can pan and zoom around exhibits and move effortlessly from room to room to explore the different exhibit themes. The interface for the virtual gallery takes a little time to master, and it is difficult to read some of the artifact placards, but this exhibit allows young people who may never be able to visit Washington, D.C. access to the amazing collection of early history that the museum houses.

Similarly, the Roman Bath Museum in Bath, England, has a panoramic gallery that allows visitors to explore the ancient Roman bath culture and the period of Roman rule over large parts of the present-day United Kingdom. It is one of the only surviving Roman baths in the world. The quality of the panoramics at the Roman Bath Museum, similar to those at the Smithsonian, are not powerful enough to clearly read the placards. The Roman Bath Museum site does provide some insights, however, in the level of interpretation and digital reconstruction undertaken at their exhibit, which even includes holographic images of Romans exiting one of the baths. A separate section on their website also allows visitors to search their collections for more in-depth information and images of specific artifacts.

The general pedagogical application for these sites is similar to a museum field trip. Teachers engage students in exploring the site with guiding questions or another activity that requires students to find information throughout a museum's online gallery. These sites provide great potential, but also present some instructional challenges. They provide opportunities for historical inquiry or developing historical empathy, as described above, and require the same type of preparation and structure as a museum visit. For example, a teacher may want students to explore the Roman Bath Museum site to examine the lifestyle of the upper-class Romans as well the servants, some of whom had to crawl under the floor of the heated changing rooms to small coal fires that were still burning, and to clear out the ashes. Students could be asked to chart out the roles of the various groups of people who would congregate at the baths and compare and contrast their roles and experiences there. This activity would engage students in exploring the archaeological and artifact-rich Bath site, as well as provide some structure to study Roman society and the experiences of different groups in Roman-ruled territories.

Even less sophisticated and static virtual galleries can be extremely useful for the classroom. For example, the California State Railroad Museum provides access to a vast amount of information and images of their collection of historic trains and train cars, archives related to the development of the railroads in the West of the United States, and the stories of the many who emigrated to California and other western destinations via the railroad. In addition to images of the various steam, internal combustion and compressed air locomotives, the site provides rich contextual and technical information about the trains. The site also includes the stories of the Pullman Porters and various immigrant groups who rode the rails to California to try to strike it rich in the gold rush or to work in the vast agricultural industry. Teachers could also use the sites to help students develop visual literacy skills in analyzing the different images. This site provides great opportunities for doing web-based historical inquiry into westward migration, technology and industry, and the social histories of immigrants and migrants who went west.

Similar static virtual galleries provide access to the stories of peoples from around the world. In particular, virtual galleries provide access to the histories and stories of people who may be marginalized in a history textbook or state curriculum. For example, the Australian History Museum, located at Macquarie University in Sydney, Australia, includes a virtual gallery titled "Indigenous Australia" that tells the story of the Aboriginal "Day of Mourning" through pictures and a rich narrative. The Day of Mourning was declared by Aborigine leaders and coincided in 1938 with the celebration of the 150th anniversary of British occupation of Australia. This virtual gallery is a great example of a topic not often included in world history textbooks. It is a powerful story of resistance and empowerment on the part of Aborigines and presents opportunities for teachers to challenge students' understanding of Aboriginal history and culture or to get students to compare the histories of indigenous people in different parts of the world, including the history of indigenous peoples in the United States.

Virtual Field Trips

In contrast to the virtual galleries described above, virtual field trips are designed more coherently to emulate on-site museum education programs. They are designed to actively engage students and work toward particular goals. One of the earliest was

Figure 9.4 Homepage for "Raid on Deerfield: The Many Stories of 1704" website.

Source: Image courtesy of the Pocumtuck Valley Memorial Association (PVMA) and Memorial Hall Museum.

Colonial Williamsburg's "Electronic Field Trip" program, which originally included live video feed from the historic living history village, and question and answer sessions with historical interpreters and historians. Although engaging, this type of virtual field trip was limiting for teachers as it was played once or twice in a day and did not necessarily align with teachers' schedules or the curriculum (Stoddard, 2009). This program has evolved to being primarily web-based and resource-rich, similar to other more recently developed virtual field trip programs, and also more flexible and useful for teachers. One of the richest virtual field trips, which also provides the flexibility needed for teachers who may have up to five sections of a particular class in a day, is the "Raid on Deerfield: The Many Stories of 1704" virtual field trip developed by the Memorial Hall Museum in partnership with the Pocumtuck Valley Memorial Association.

The "Raid on Deerfield" site is illustrative of the advancements being made in museum websites over the static virtual galleries and the first generation of virtual field trips. The Deerfield virtual field trip combines museum artifacts and exhibits with multimedia and a display of competing perspectives centered primarily on one particular event and its surrounding history. In this case the event is the 1704 raid by the French and allied Kanienkehaka (Mohawk), Wendat (Huron), and Wôbanaki forces on the English settlement of Deerfield, Massachusetts. One hundred and ten English settlers were kidnapped and taken by the raiders. Many of these captives were eventually returned, but up to one-third chose to stay in the French or native settlements. The site of the Deerfield settlement was the historic homeland of the Wôbanaki, who were displaced by the English. The virtual field trip leads you through the perspectives and histories of the five groups that were involved and also a timeline of historic moments leading up to the 1704 raid.

The key to this virtual field trip is that it engages students in authentic questions of the past, in this case posing the questions: "Was this dramatic pre-dawn assault in contested lands an unprovoked, brutal attack on an innocent village of English settlers? Was it a justified military action against a stockaded settlement in a Native homeland? Or was it something else?" (Pocumtuck Valley Memorial Association, 2011). Students are then engaged in the histories of the groups, the timeline of events leading up to the raid, and some possible explanations of what happened. These explanations make it clear, however, that they are only interpretations, and students are invited to construct their own interpretations. These aspects of the virtual field trip, including a large number of museum artifacts, provide an authentic historical inquiry for students that challenges them to consider competing perspectives and interpretations of the event.

The Benefits and Challenges of Virtual Galleries and Virtual Field Trips

Virtual galleries provide access to museum collections from around the world. They include rich visual and textual archives of artifacts and information that can provide depth to any history curriculum. They also, however, present challenges of how to actively involve students in analyzing this information and engaging with the sites, similar to the challenges of a museum visit. Teachers need to provide a structure for doing historical inquiry with the resources of these sites, and many virtual galleries provide resources such as lesson plans to help them. Also, many web inquiry projects or other online history lessons have been developed to use online archives and museum sites. For example, the Historical Scene Investigation project (see the resources opposite) provides a structure for doing historical inquiry using resources pulled from the Library of Congress archives.

Many of the virtual field trips provide more structure for educational activities and student "visits," and are often based on models of historical inquiry. These resources also provide access to materials at no cost and can be fitted to almost any school schedule or course curriculum. However, they still present some logistical and technological challenges. Depending on how a teacher utilizes the virtual resources, computer lab time or a laptop cart will need to be reserved. In some schools it is difficult to reserve computer time for multiple days in a row, thus limiting the amount of time students can participate in the virtual field trip. Some of the newer and higher-bandwidth sites, such as the Smithsonian and Roman Bath examples described earlier in this chapter, also require relatively new computers and a powerful network in order to run smoothly, especially if twenty-plus computers are using the same site at once. These sites provide great opportunities to explore museum resources that would otherwise be difficult or impossible to experience, but still require technological and pedagogical efforts to be successful.

Similar to physical museums, these virtual galleries and field trips also construct particular narratives about the past and are told from specific perspectives. For example, the CIA's virtual tour includes several fascinating artifacts that help to tell the story of the history of the U.S. intelligence service, including a robotic fish named Charlie, designed to do wireless underwater reconnaissance. These artifacts, when combined with the narrative of the history of the CIA, build to tell a particular story about the agency's role and history. As with the activities described in previous chapters, teachers need to help students recognize these narratives and the perspectives they reflect. The "Raid on Deerfield" example consciously avoids one overarching narrative of the event, but is still guided by curatorial decisions and the availability of information and evidence from the various perspectives. Overall, these virtual resources provide the raw materials for rich and engaging historical inquiry and empathy development, but do require work on the part of the teacher to develop or adapt activities to take advantage of the resources museums provide.

Museum outreach programs, traveling museum kits, and virtual resources give teachers and students the opportunity to engage with museum resources when it is not possible to visit the museum itself or as a precursor or follow-up to a museum visit. None of these programs can replace a visit to the museum, but they can provide a unique experience that teachers may not be able to otherwise recreate in their classrooms. These resources all also present challenges, many reflecting similar challenges to those of the museums described in previous chapters. More importantly, they provide many of the benefits of engaging students in the study of historical artifacts, interacting with historical interpreters, or interacting with ever more sophisticated virtual resources. They also present fewer logistical challenges, as students do not need to leave school grounds, and you can often use these resources without changing or disrupting the school schedule. Finally, they are easily adaptable to the objectives of the course curriculum, present opportunities for use in a wide array of activities, and can be used across multiple grade levels.

RESOURCES

American Civil War Center: www.tredegar.org

Australian History Museum virtual gallery—Indigenous Australia: www.austhistmuseum.mq.edu.au/galleries/indigenous/index.htm

Autry Center: http://theautry.org

California State Railroad Museum: www.csrmf.org

California State Railroad Museum Online Collection Archive: http://csrrm.crewnoble.com

Central Intelligence Agency virtual tour: https://www.cia.gov/about-cia/cia-museum/cia-museum-tour/index.html

Historical Scene Investigation: www.wm.edu/hsi

Minnesota History Center: http://minnesotahistorycenter.org

National Museum of Natural History virtual tour: www.mnh.si.edu/panoramas

Plimoth Plantation: www.plimoth.org

"Raid on Deerfield: The Many Stories of 1704": www.1704.deerfield.history.museum

Roman Bath Museum: www.romanbaths.co.uk

Roman Baths Walkthrough: www.romanbaths.co.uk/walkthrough.aspx

Smithsonian National Museum of Natural History: www.mnh.si.edu

Tennessee State Museum: www.tnmuseum.org/Teachers/Traveling_Trunks

Ten Strategies for Effective Museum Visits

Here are our key recommendations for strategies that support effective museum visits:

VISIT THE MUSEUM PRIOR TO BRINGING STUDENTS

If at all possible, visit a museum before planning activities and taking students. Visiting the museum allows you to experience what the students will experience, meet with museum staff, research the history of the museum, plan logistics, and understand what content background to provide students with. Just as you would not show a film without watching it first, visiting a museum prior to a visit with students is essential when logistically possible.

Key Questions

How much time do students need at any particular exhibit? How structured do the student activities need to be at this museum? What is unique to this museum in terms of content, the physical structure, biases, preparation needed, resources available, etc.? Is the museum accessible for all of my students?

COLLABORATE WITH MUSEUM STAFF TO PLAN ACTIVITIES FOR STUDENTS

Collaboration means teachers provide museum staff with the objectives for the visit, students' specific learning needs, and how the visit fits within the larger curricular goals. Meanwhile museum staff provide expertise in the specific exhibits, the content covered in the exhibits, the history of the museum, activities for students, and more. Staff are often willing to modify or create programs tailored for teachers' specific students. Museum staff and teachers can work together to plan visits, but can also both take active roles during the visit. Finally, teachers can follow up with staff to debrief the visit. Follow-up promotes an ongoing dialogue and provides museum staff with information they can use to modify activities for students.

Key Questions

What do I need to ask the museum staff? What do the museum staff need to know about my students' learning and logistical needs? What resources, knowledge, and experiences do museum staff have that can support the goals for the museum visit? What assistance do they have for students with disabilities?

TAKE STUDENTS TO MUSEUMS TO BOTH LEARN CONTENT AND DEVELOP AN ANALYTICAL AND CRITICAL STANCE TOWARD HISTORY

Learning specific content is an important part of a museum visit. However, the full potential of museum visits includes the opportunity to develop a more critical stance toward the discipline of history. Museums can be approached as valuable, but also as human-created, and thus subjective. Explicitly critiquing a museum's presentation of the past—perspectives included and left out, written information that accompanies artifacts, docent narratives, etc.—provides students with a richer understanding of how the history we study is a biased construct of past people and events.

Key Questions

What can my students learn about history as a discipline and/or about the role of museums in presenting the past? What skills do my students need to acquire as part of our visit? How do students view the nature of history presented in museums?

BUILD VISIT ACTIVITIES AROUND CURRICULAR GOALS AND EXPLICITLY CONNECT THE VISIT TO CLASS WORK

Rather than stand-alone activities, visits to museums are more effective when incorporated within the existing curriculum and connected to class work prior to and after the visit. Students will get more out of the visit and be more likely to take field trip activities as serious academic work if explicit goals for the trip are identified by the teacher and students are assessed in some way on what they learn. The visit will be easier to plan because it fits within an existing structure. Connecting to the curriculum is also one of the criteria to use in deciding whether a visit to a particular museum is appropriate.

Key Questions

How does the visit meet my curricular objectives as well as district or state standards? What added value does the museum contribute to student learning?

PLAN BOTH PRE-TRIP AND POST-TRIP ACTIVITIES

Personal experience and research tell us that a visit to a museum without prior preparation or without adequate follow-up is a missed opportunity. Students can only fully take advantage of all a museum has to offer if their preparation includes content background, expectations for the museum experience, and an ability to critically think about how museums present the past. Similarly, the potential of museum visits is only fully realized with follow-up activities that allow students to reflect on the content and larger issues of historical representation, hold students accountable, and build on the museum activities.

Key Questions

What preparation do my students need in order to utilize museum resources and complete required activities? What follow-up activities can best build on the museum visit and push students' knowledge and skills?

CONDUCT EXTENSIVE RESEARCH

Research about the museum and on the content presented at the museum provides important contextual and background information. Research could be conducted on site at the museum, via online resources, and through written materials. It can explore the museum's history, purpose, and unique features, as well as available educational resources, exhibit information, and the overall mission of the museum and the resulting stories it constructs.

Key Questions

What are the unique features of this museum? What might my students learn about the content covered at the museum? What is the history and background of the museum? Who funds and runs the museum? What types of exhibits are housed there? What types of artifacts? What are the overall stories or historical narratives the museum's exhibits tell? How does the content in the museum meet curricular goals? Does it challenge or expand what my students have already learned about the content topics?

PROVIDE A BALANCE OF STRUCTURED ACTIVITIES AND FREEDOM OF CHOICE DURING THE VISIT

Elements of an effective museum visit provide students with guidance through questions, activities, or other structures. This guidance keeps the students focused and on task. At the same time, effective visits allow students some freedom to choose where to go and where to spend time based on their interests and needs.

Key Questions

What guidance do students need to focus their learning? Are there specific exhibits, artifacts, etc., that are critical for students to see/explore/understand? Where and when is it appropriate for students to explore on their own? What level of structure or scaffolding is needed? What scaffolding needs to be done in person versus through the structure of the activity?

ESTABLISH A NORM OF MUSEUM VISITS AS A SCHOLARLY ENDEAVOR, NOT A DAY OFF

Too often visits to museums are perceived as a day off by students, more about social activity than scholarly pursuits. Provide students with specific goals, hold them accountable for pre-, during-, and post-visit assignments, and communicate reasonable but high expectations for the learning component of a museum visit.

Key Questions

What are my students' previous experiences with museums? What are my students' attitudes and beliefs about museum visits? How am I setting students up for our visit? How can I make goals and expectations explicit?

PROVIDE ADMINISTRATORS WITH A STRONG RATIONALE FOR YOUR VISITS TO HISTORY MUSEUMS

Administrative support for museum visits goes a long way to dealing with the red tape, overcoming colleagues' concerns, acquiring funding and buses, and promoting social studies education more broadly. Prepare a rationale for administrators about why a visit to a museum is important to your students' learning, how it connects to district and state standards, and how the experience at the museum is not only valuable but can't be duplicated. Invite administrators to join you on the trip so they can experience the power of a well-executed museum visit.

Key Questions

How does this museum visit support student learning in ways that are unavailable in the classroom? What are my administrator's concerns and how can I alleviate them?

SELECT CHAPERONES CAREFULLY AND PROVIDE THEM WITH SUPPORT AND EXPECTATIONS

When selecting chaperones to accompany a field trip to a museum, think carefully about who will work best toward the goals of the museum visit and who students will enjoy engaging with. It is ideal to have additional school personnel along on field trips, including assistant principals or other administrators, special education or Title 1 aides, or other teachers or regular school volunteers. Parents are also great, but may need more help in understanding what their role should be and in ensuring trip goals are being met.

Key Questions

Which school personnel can accompany the group? Which parents or other volunteers will be the most responsible and receptive to helping students work toward the goals for the museum visit? How many chaperones are needed and what should their role be?

Complete List of Museums Discussed in the Book

Alphabetical by Category

ARTIFACT AND DISPLAY MUSEUMS

American Civil War Center: www.tredegar.org

Atomic Testing Museum: www.atomictestingmuseum.org

Australian History Museum Virtual Gallery: Indigenous Australia: www.austhistmuseum.mq.edu.au/galleries/indigenous/index.htm

Autry National Center: http://theautry.org

British Museum: www.britishmuseum.org

California State Railroad Museum: www.csrmf.org

California State Railroad Museum Online Collection Archive: http://csrrm.crewnoble.com

Central Intelligence Agency Virtual Tour: www.cia.gov/about-cia/cia-museum/cia-museum-tour/index.html

Charles H. Wright Museum of African American History: www.chwmuseum.org

Ellis Island: www.ellisisland.org

Historical Scene Investigation: www.wm.edu/hsi

History Miami: www.historymiami.org

Jewish History Museum: http://nmajh.org/about_the_museum/index.htm

Mashantucket Pequot Museum and Research Center: www.pequotmuseum.org

Minnesota History Center: http://minnesotahistorycenter.org

Museum of History and Industry: www.seattlehistory.org

National Civil Rights Museum in Memphis: www.civilrightsmuseum.org

National Museum of African American History and Culture: http://nmaahc.si.edu/section/programs/view/38

National Museum of the American Indian: www.nmai.si.edu

National Portrait Gallery in London: www.npg.org.uk

Newseum: www.newseum.org

New York City Tenement Museum: www.tenement.org

Ohio Historical Society, Ohio Case Histories (traveling trunk program): http://ohsweb.ohiohistory.org/portal/oht-p.shtml

Roman Bath Museum: www.romanbaths.co.uk

Smithsonian Institution: www.si.edu

Smithsonian National Museum of American History: www.americanhistory.si.edu

Smithsonian National Museum of Natural History: www.mnh.si.edu

Smithsonian National Museum of Natural History virtual tour: www.mnh.si.edu/panoramas

Spy Museum: www.spymuseum.org

Tennessee State Museum Traveling Trunks: www.tnmuseum.org/Teachers/Traveling_Trunks

Truman Presidential Library: www.trumanlibrary.org

United States Memorial Holocaust Museum: www.ushmm.org

HISTORIC SITES/FORTS

Architect of the Capitol, Washington, D.C.: www.aoc.gov

Bents Old Fort National Historic Site, CO: www.nps.gov/beol/index.htm

Cahokia Mounds: http://cahokiamounds.org

Castillo de San Marcos National Monument, St. Augustine, FL: www.nps.gov/casa/index.htm

Colonial National Historic Park, VA: www.nps.gov/colo/index.htm

The Fort at No. 4, Charlestown, NH: www.fortat4.com

Fort Bowie National Historic Site, AZ: www.nps.gov/fobo

Fort Caroline National Memorial, FL: www.nps.gov/timu/historyculture/foca.htm

Fort Donelson National Battlefield, TN: www.nps.gov/fodo/index.htm

Fort Larned National Historic Site, KS: www.nps.gov/fols

Fort Machilimackinac, MI: www.mackinacparks.com/fort-mackinac

Fort McHenry National Monument and Historic Shrine, MD: www.nps.gov/fomc/index.htm

Fort Sumter National Monument, SC: www.nps.gov/fosu/index.htm

Fort Ticonderoga, Ticonderoga, NY: www.fortticonderoga.org

Fort Vancouver National Historic Site, OR: www.nps.gov/fova/index.htm

Historic Fort Snelling, MN: www.historicfortsnelling.org

Historic Forts of Maine: www.travel-maine.info/historic_forts.htm

Minuteman Missile National Historic Site, Rapid City, SD: www.nps.gov/mimi/index.htm

Morristown National Historic Park, Morristown, NJ: www.nps.gov/morr/index.htm

National Register of Historic Places, "Teaching with Historic Places": www.nps.gov/nr/twhp/descrip.htm

North American Forts 1526–1956: www.northamericanforts.com

"Raid on Deerfield: The Many Stories of 1704": www.1704.deerfield.history.museum/home.do

Springfield Armory National Historic Site, MA: www.nps.gov/spar/index.htm

Thomas Jefferson's Monticello, Charlottesville, VA: www.monticello.org

Valley Forge National Historic Park, PA, " History and Culture": www.nps.gov/vafo/historyculture/index.htm

HISTORIC HOUSES/PROPERTIES

Bacon's Castle, Surrey, VA: http://preservationvirginia.org/BaconsCastle

Carpenters Hall, Philadelphia, PA: www.ushistory.org/carpentershall

Hasbrouck House, Newburgh, NY: http://nysparks.state.ny.us/historic-sites/17/details.aspx

The Hermitage, Nashville, TN: www.thehermitage.com/mansion-grounds/mansion/preservation

Johnson County Historical Society: www.jchsiowa.org

Louis Armstrong House, Corona, NY: www.louisarmstronghouse.org/visiting/overview.htm

Mark Twain House, Hartford, CT: www.marktwainhouse.org

Middleton Place, Charleston, SC: www.middletonplace.org/house-museum.html

Mount Vernon, Mount Vernon, VA: www.mountvernon.org/index.cfm?

Pappy Thornton Farm Museum, Clovis, NM: www.discoverourtown.com/NM/Clovis/Attractions/old-homestead-museum-pappy-thornton-farm-museum/54183.html

Plum Grove, Iowa City, IA: www.uiowa.edu/~plumgrov

Sod House Museum, Aline, OK: www.okhistory.org/outreach/homes/sodhousemuseum.html

LIVING HISTORY MUSEUMS

Colonial Williamsburg: www.colonialwilliamsburg.com

Historic Jamestowne, Preservation Virginia: www.historicjamestowne.org

Historic Jamestowne, The Archaearium Museum: www.historicjamestowne.org/visit/archaearium.php

Jamestown Settlement/Yorktown Victory Center: http://historyisfun.org

Old Sturbridge Village: www.osv.org

Pioneer Farms: www.pioneerfarms.org

Plimoth Plantation: www.plimoth.org

MONUMENTS AND MEMORIALS

9/11 Monument, Danbury, CT: www.hmdb.org/marker.asp?marker=22833 and http://ctmonuments.net/2009/04/911-memorial-danbury

9/11 Monument, Ridgefield, CT: www.ridgefield911memorial.com

9/11 Monument, Westport, CT: www.friendsofsherwoodisland.org/Pages/Park/P-911-Memorial.htm

9/11 Monuments, Windsor, CT: www.voicesofseptember11.org/dev/memorials.php?mem_id=397 and www.voicesofseptember11.org/dev/memorials.php?mem_id=90

Shays' Rebellion Monuments: http://shaysrebellion.stcc.edu/shaysapp/artifactPage.do?shortName=barregazette_19feb1987&page=

Stumbling Blocks (Stolpersteine) Memorials in Europe: www.stolpersteine.com (official site but you will need to translate into English) and www.stolpersteine.cz

Resources

BOOKS/ARTICLES

Builder, P.H. III. (2002). "Past, present and future: The place of the house museum in the museum community." In J.F. Donnelly (ed.) *Interpreting Historic House Museums* (pp. 18–41). Walnut Creek, CA: AltaMira Press.

Donnelly, J.F. (ed.) (2002). *Interpreting Historic House Museums*. Walnut Creek, CA: AltaMira Press.

Falk, J. & Dierking, L. (2000). *Learning from Museums: Visitor Experiences and the Making of Meaning*. Walnut Creek, CA: AltaMira Press.

Hammond, J.M. (1915). *Quaint and Historic Forts of North America*. London: Davies Press.

Handler, R. & Gable, E. (1997). *The New History in an Old Museum: Creating the Past at Colonial Williamsburg*. Durham, NC: Duke University Press.

Hooper-Greenhill, E. (2000). *Museums and the Interpretation of Visual Culture*. New York: Routledge.

Kirshenblatt-Gimblett, B. (1998). *Destination Culture: Tourism, Museums, and Heritage*. Berkeley, CA: University of California Press.

Langford, T. (2010). "Review of Fort Vancouver National Historic Site." *The Public Historian*, 32 (4), 144–149.

Levy, A.B. (2002). "Historic house tours that succeed: Choosing the best tour approach." In J.F. Donnelly (ed.) *Interpreting Historic House Museums* (pp. 192–209). Walnut Creek, CA: AltaMira Press.

Loewen, J. (1999). *Lies Across America: What Our Historic Sites Get Wrong*. New York: Touchstone.

Mackintosh, B. (1985). *The Historic Survey and National Historic Landmarks Program: A History*. Washington, D.C.: National Park Service.

Mackintosh, B. (1987). "The National Park Service moves into historical interpretation." *The Public Historian*, 9 (2), 50–63.

Manucy, A. (1997). *Sixteenth-Century St. Augustine: The People and Their Homes*. Gainesville, FL: University Press of Florida.

Marcus, A.S. (2007). "Representing the past, reflecting the present: Museums, memorials, and the secondary history classroom." *The Social Studies*, 98 (3), 105–110.

Marcus, A.S. & Levine, T.H. (2010). "Remember the Alamo? Learning history with monuments and memorials." *Social Education*, 74 (3), 131–134.

Marcus, A.S. & Levine, T.H. (2011). "Knight at the museum: Learning history with museums." *The Social Studies*, 102 (3), 104–109.

Organization of American Historians. (2002). *Magazine of History*, 16 (2), winter (entire issue devoted to issues of public history).

Parkman, E.B. (1996–1997). "Fort and settlement: Interpreting the past at Fort Ross State Historic Park." *California History*, 75 (4), 354–369.

Rosenzweig, R. & Thelen, D. (1998). *The Presence of the Past: Popular Uses of History in American Life*. New York: Columbia University Press.

Stoddard, J. (2009). "Toward a virtual field trip model for the social studies." *Contemporary Issues in Technology and Teacher Education*, 9 (4), December, 412–438.

Walker, P.C. & Graham, T. (2000). *Directory of Historic House Museums in the United States*. Walnut Creek, CA: AltaMira Press.

Young, L. (2002). "Is there a museum in the house? Historic houses as a species of museum." *Museum Management and Curatorship*, 22 (1), March, 59–77.

WEBSITES

American Association of Museums: www.aam-us.org

American Association of Museums list of accredited museums by state: www.aam-us.org/museum resources/accred/list.cfm?mode=state

The Association for Living History, Farm and Agricultural Museums (listings of living history sites): www.alhfam.org

Database of Historical Markers in the U.S.: www.hmdb.org

Field Guide to U.S. Monuments and Memorials: www.monumentsandmemorials.com

Museum Link (list of museums by state): www.museumlink.com/states.htm

Museum Stuff (worldwide guide to museums by location or topic): www.museumstuff.com

Step Into History (state by state list of many history museums): www.stepintohistory.com/index.htm

Teaching with Historic Places—lessons using properties listed in the National Park Service's National Register of Historic Places: www.cr.nps.gov/nr/twhp

References

American Association of Museums. (1965). *A Statistical Survey of Museums in the United States and Canada.* Washington, D.C.: American Association of Museums.

Autry National Center. (no date). *Freedom's Opportunity: Pre-Visit Lesson Plan.* Los Angeles, CA: Autry National Center.

Bamberger, Y. & Tal, T. (2006). "Learning in a personal context: Levels of choice in a free environment in science and natural history museums." *Science Education*, 91, 75–95.

Barton, K.C., & Levstik, L.S. (2004). *Teaching History for the Common Good.* Mahwah, NJ: Lawrence Erlbaum Associates.

Boyd, W.L. (1999). "Museums as centers of controversy." *Daedalus*, 128 (3), 185–228.

Builder, P.H. III (2002). "Past, present and future: The place of the house museum in the museum community." In J.F. Donnelly (ed.) *Interpreting Historic House Museums* (pp. 18–41). Walnut Creek, CA: AltaMira Press.

Chhabra, D. (2008). "Positioning museums on an authenticity continuum." *Annals of Tourism Research*, 35 (2), 427–447.

Chicago History Museum (2011). Retrieved June 7, 2011, from http://chicagohistory.org

Crang, M. (1996). "Magic kingdom or a quixotic quest for authenticity?" *Annals of Tourism Research*, 23, 415–431.

Davison, H. (2010, Fall). "Review of Fort Vancouver National Historic Site." *The Public Historian*, 32 (4), 144–149.

Donnelly, J.F. (ed.). (2002). *Interpreting Historic House Museums.* Walnut Creek, CA: AltaMira Press.

Falk, J. (ed.). (2001). *Free-Choice Science Education: How We Learn Science Outside of School.* New York: Teachers College Press.

Falk, J. & Dierking, L. (1997). *The Museum Experience.* Washington, D.C.: Whalesback Books.

Falk, J. & Dierking, L. (2000). *Learning from Museums: Visitor Experiences and the Making of Meaning.* Walnut Creek, CA: AltaMira Press.

Gardner, H. (1993). *Multiple Intelligences: The Theory in Practice.* New York: Basic Books.

Goldberg, T., Schwarz, B.B., & Porat, D. (2008). "Living and dormant collective memories as contexts of history learning." *Learning and Instruction*, 18, 223–237.

Griffin, J. (2004). "Research on students and museums: Looking more closely at the students in school groups." *Science Education*, 88 (1), 59–70.

Griffin, J. & Symington, D. (1997). "Moving from task-oriented to learning-oriented strategies on school excursions to museums." *Science Education*, 81, 763–779.

Griffiths, J. & King, D. (2008). *Interconnections: A National Study of Users and Potential Users of Online Information*. Washington, D.C.: Institute for Museum and Library Services.

Handler, R. & Gable, E. (1997). *The New History in an Old Museum: Creating the Past at Colonial Williamsburg*. Durham, NC: Duke University Press.

Hess, D. (2009). *Controversy in the Classroom: The Democratic Power of Discussion*. New York: Routledge.

Hess, D. & Stoddard, J. (2007). "9/11 and terrorism: 'The ultimate teachable moment' in textbooks and supplemental curricula." *Social Education*, 71 (5), September, 231–236.

History Miami (2011). Retrieved June 10, 2011, from www.historymiami.org

Hooper-Greenhill, E. (2000). *Museums and the Interpretation of Visual Culture*. New York: Routledge.

I-75 Project (2011). Retrieved June 20, 2011, from www.thei75project.com

Janofsky, M. (1994). "Mock auction of slaves: Education or outrage?" *New York Times*, October 8. Retrieved June 12, 2011, from www.nytimes.com/1994/10/08/us/mock-auction-of-slaves-education-or-outrage.html

Kirshenblatt-Gimblett, B. (1998). *Destination Culture: Tourism, Museums, and Heritage*. Berkeley, CA: University of California Press.

Kisiel, J.F. (2003). "Teachers, museums, and worksheets: A closer look at a learning experience." *Journal of Science Teacher Education*, 14 (1), 3–21.

Ladson-Billings, G. (2003). "Lies my teacher still tells: Developing a critical race perspective toward the social studies." In G. Ladson-Billings (ed.) *Critical Race Theory Perspectives on the Social Studies* (pp. 1–11). Greenwich, CT: Information Age Publishing.

Leftwich, M. (2006). "Bringing the world's museums into the classroom." Paper presented at the annual conference of the National Council for the Social Studies, Washington, D.C.

Leinhardt, G., Crowley, K., & Knutson, K. (2002). *Learning Conversations in Museums*. Mahwah, NJ: Lawrence Erlbaum Associates.

Lenoir, Y. & Laforest, M. (1986). "Le musée, un apport didactique au milieu scolaire ... s'il facilite les apprentissages prescrits!" In G. Racette (ed.) *Musée et éducation: modèles didactiques d'utilisation des musées* (pp. 20–23). Montréal: Société des Musées Québécois.

Levy, A.B. (2002). "Historic house tours that succeed: Choosing the best tour approach." In J.F. Donnelly (ed.) *Interpreting Historic House Museums* (pp. 192–209). Walnut Creek, CA: AltaMira Press.

Loewen, J. (1999). *Lies Across America: What Our Historic Sites Get Wrong*. New York: Touchstone.

Loh, Tim. (2010). "Honoring victims of 9/11 proves to be divisive subject." *Connecticut Post*, September 13. Retrieved June 1, 2011, from www.ctpost.com

Lowenthal, D. (1999). *The Past is a Foreign Country*. Cambridge, UK: Cambridge University Press.

Mackintosh, B. (1985). *The Historic Survey and National Historic Landmarks Program: A History*. Washington, D.C.: National Park Service.

Manucy, A. (1997). *Sixteenth-Century St. Augustine: The People and Their Homes*. Gainesville, FL: University Press of Florida.

Marcus, A.S. (2007). "Representing the past, reflecting the present: Museums, memorials, and the secondary history classroom." *The Social Studies*, 98 (3), 105–110.

Marcus, A.S. (2008). "Rethinking museums' adult education for K-12 teachers." *Journal of Museum Education*, 33 (1), 55–78.

Marcus, A.S., Grenier, R., & Levine, T. (2009). "How secondary history teachers use and think about museums: Current practices and untapped promise for promoting historical understanding." Paper presented at the Annual Conference of the College and Faculty Assembly, National Council for the Social Studies, Atlanta, GA.

Marcus, A.S., Metzger, S.A., Paxton, R.J., & Stoddard, J.D. (2010). *Teaching History with Film: Strategies for Secondary Social Studies*. New York: Routledge.

Marstine, J. (ed.). (2006). *New Museum Theory and Practice*. Malden, MA: Blackwell Publishing.

Mitchell, K. (2003). "Monuments, memorials, and the politics of memory." *Urban Geography*, 24 (5), 442–459.

National Park Service (2011) "History and culture." Retrieved June 30, 2011, from www.nps.gov/vafo/historyculture/index.htm

Nespor, J. (2000). "School field trips and the curriculum of public spaces." *Journal of Curriculum Studies*, 32 (1), 25–43.

Plimoth (2011). Retrieved June 28, 2011, from www.plimoth.org

Pocumtuck Valley Memorial Association. (2011). "Raid on Deerfield: The Many Stories of 1704." Retrieved June 18, 2011, from www.1704.deerfield.history.museum

Rosenzweig, R. (2000). "How Americans use and think about the past." In P. Stearns, P. Seixas, & S.S. Wineburg (eds) *Knowing, Teaching, and Learning History* (pp. 262–283). New York: New York University Press.

Ross, E.W. (1997). "The struggle for the social studies curriculum." In E.W. Ross (ed.) *The Social Studies Curriculum* (pp. 19–42). Albany, NY: State University of New York Press.

Santos, M.S. (2001). "Memory and narrative in social theory: The contributions of Jacques Derrida and Walter Benjamin." *Time and Society*, 10, 163–189.

Schmemann, S. (2001). "Hijacked jets destroy twin towers and hit Pentagon." *New York Times*, September 12, p. A1.

Seixas, P. (1996). "Conceptualizing the growth of historical understanding." In D. Olson & N. Torrance (eds) *Handbook of Education and Human Development* (pp. 765–784). Cambridge, MA: Blackwell Publishers.

Seixas, P. (2000). "Schweigen! Die Kinder! or Does postmodern history have a place in the schools?" In P. Stearns, P. Seixas, & S.S. Wineburg (eds) *Knowing, Teaching and Learning History: National and International Perspectives* (pp. 19–37). New York: New York University Press.

Seixas, P. (2002). "The purposes of teaching Canadian history." *Canadian Social Studies*, 36 (2), winter.

Shaffer, D. & Resnick, M. (1999). "'Thick' authenticity: New media and authentic learning." *Journal of Interactive Learning Research*, 10 (2), 195–215.

Sheppard, B. (2007). "Meaningful collaboration." In J. Falk, L. Dierking, & S. Foutz (eds) *In Principle, in Practice: Museums as Learning Institutions* (pp. 181–194). New York: AltaMira Press.

Skramstad, H. (1999). "An agenda for American museums in the twenty-first century." *Daedalus*, 128 (3), 109.

Smithsonian Institution (2011). Retrieved May 15, 2011, from www.si.edu/about/history.htm

Stoddard, J. (2009). "Toward a virtual field trip model for the social studies." *Contemporary Issues in Technology and Teacher Education*, 9 (4), 412–438.

Stoddard, J. & Marcus, A. (2006). "The burden of historical representation: Race, freedom and 'educational' Hollywood film." *Film and History*, 36 (1), spring, 26–35.

Stover, K. (1989). "Is it *real* history yet? An update on living history museums." *Journal of American Culture*, 12 (2), 13–17.

Trofanenko, B. (2006). "Interrupting the gaze: On reconsidering authority in the museum." *Journal of Curriculum Studies*, 38 (1), 49–65.

Uhrmacher, P.B. & Tinkler, B. (2008). "Engaging learners and the community through the study of monuments." *International Journal of Leadership in Education*, 11 (3), July–September, 225–238.

USHMM (United States Holocaust Memorial Museum) (2011). Retrieved March 3, 2011, from www.ushmm.org

VanSledright, B.A. (2002). "Confronting history's interpretive paradox while teaching fifth graders to investigate the past." *American Educational Research Journal*, 39, 1089–1115.

Walker, P.C. & Graham, T. (2000). *Directory of Historic House Museums in the United States*. Walnut Creek, CA: AltaMira Press.

Wineburg, S.S. (2001). *Historical Thinking and Other Unnatural Acts: Charting the Future of Teaching the Past*. Philadelphia, PA: Temple University Press.

Young, L. (2002). "Is there a museum in the house: Historic houses as a species of museum." *Museum Management and Curatorship*, 22 (1), March, 59–77.

Notes on Contributors

Alan S. Marcus is an Associate Professor in the Department of Curriculum and Instruction in the Neag School of Education at the University of Connecticut.

Jeremy D. Stoddard is an Associate Professor in the School of Education at the College of William and Mary.

Walter W. Woodward is an Associate Professor of History at the University of Connecticut and is the Connecticut State Historian.

Figure Permissions and Credits

Figure 8.6   Photo by Alan S. Marcus.

Figure 8.7   Photo by Alan S. Marcus.

Figure 8.8   Photo by Alan S. Marcus.

Figure 8.9   Photo by Alan S. Marcus.

Figure 8.10   Photo by Alan S. Marcus.

Figure 8.11   Photo by Alan S. Marcus.

Figure 9.1   Courtesy of the American Civil War Center, photo by Sean Kane.

Figure 9.2   Photo courtesy of the Tennessee State Museum.

Figure 9.3   Photo courtesy of Plimoth Plantation.

Figure 9.4   Image courtesy of the Pocumtuck Valley Memorial Association (PVMA) and
                 Memorial Hall Museum.

Index